Culture, Class, and Critical Theory

ie thi

Routledge Studies in Social and Political Thought

For a full list of titles in this series, please visit www.routledge.com

Culture, Class, and Critical Theory

Between Bourdieu and the Frankfurt School

David Gartman

Routledge
Taylor & Francis Group

NEW YORK   LONDON

First published 2013
by Routledge
711 Third Avenue, New York, NY 10017

Simultaneously published in the UK
by Routledge
2 Park Square, Milton Park, Abingdon, Oxfordshire OX14 4RN

First issued in paperback 2014

*Routledge is an imprint of the Taylor and Francis Group,
an informa business*

Library of Congress Cataloging-in-Publication Data
Gartman, David, 1950–
    Culture, class, and critical theory : between Bourdieu and the Frankfurt
school / by David Gartman.
        p. cm. — (Routledge studies in social and political thought ; 78)
    Includes bibliographical references and index.
    1. Critical theory. 2. Culture. 3. Bourdieu, Pierre, 1930–2002.
    4. Frankfurt school of sociology. 5. Sociology. I. Title.
    HM480.G36 2012
    306dc23
    2012020063

ISBN 978-0-415-52420-9 (hbk)
ISBN 978-1-138-92058-3 (pbk)
ISBN 978-0-203-08081-8 (ebk)

Typeset in Sabon
by IBT Global.

To my teachers
Randall Collins and Joseph Gusfield
who provided not only an excellent education but also an
exemplar of intellectual commitment and integrity

Contents

Preface

The essays collected in this book were written over the course of twenty-five years of empirical research in the sociology of culture. They were forged by the practical problems of making sense of two artifacts of material culture—the automobile and architecture. This does not mean, however, that these theoretical ideas emerged wholly out of the empirical data, as the advocates of grounded theory suggest. I began my cultural studies with preconceived theoretical notions of how culture legitimates social inequality, drawn largely from the Frankfurt School of critical theory. However, the discrepancies and inconsistencies of my specific cases, as well as general trends in sociology as a whole, eventually led me to the powerful cultural theory of Pierre Bourdieu. I was initially critical of his theory of culture as class distinction, because it did not seem to be a good fit for the empirical case that occupied my attention at the time—the history of American automobile design. The aesthetics of cars seemed to legitimate social inequality by *obscuring* class differences, not by *symbolizing* these differences and making some classes seem superior to others, as Bourdieu claims. But my research in the history of modern architecture soon led me to recognize the validity of Bourdieu's approach, and forced me to think about how the validity of the two theories vary by both historical period and type of culture, i.e., material and nonmaterial.

Out of these empirical problems and specifications, I struggled to develop a unified critical theory of culture, one that took into account the insights of both Bourdieu and the Frankfurt School. This task was facilitated by the vicissitudes of Bourdieu's theory over the course of some forty years. Although he never explicitly acknowledged revising his theory, it is clear that in the late 1980s he reversed himself on such importance issues as the validity of Kant's theory of aesthetics. It seems that his increasing political involvement in the European movement against neoliberal economic policies led him to embrace Kant's standard of disinterestedness as a bulwark against the subordination of culture to the market's standard of profitability. This politically motivated shift in his cultural theory brought him in line with the Frankfurt School, which also argued that critical culture must be autonomous from the market. So the integration of these two theories was implicitly initiated by Bourdieu himself. My task then became to make this explicit.

For assistance and encouragement over the course of the evolution of my thinking I acknowledge the editors and referees of the journals in which these essays first appeared: *The American Journal of Sociology, Theory and Society, Theory, Culture and Society,* and *Sociological Theory.* They pushed me in the right direction, even though I did not initially realize it. My colleague Douglas Marshall often served as my primary interlocutor about these issues. Even when we disagreed, his comments were insightful. David Swartz has also been central in molding and correcting my ideas on Bourdieu, as well as offering advice on the structure of the book.

Finally, I feel compelled to acknowledge an intellectual and personal debt long in arrears to the teachers most influential on my development as a sociologist. I abjure use of the more popular term, "mentor," not merely because of its clichéd overuse but also because of its paternalistic implications. Randall Collins and Joseph Gusfield did not "take me under their wings," nor protect this fledgling intellectual from the slings and arrows of academic contention. They *educated* me, giving me the knowledge to hold my own in the academic arena. Joseph Gusfield taught me to see beneath the superficial issues of social contention to the symbolic dimension, where people express, often unconsciously, the aspirations and fears behind their actions. That I have become a *cultural* sociologist is largely attributable to him. Randall Collins taught me to see society as an arena of complex and imbricated contests, in which even seemingly innocent actions have implications for who gets what. If recently his conflict sociology has become less cynical by discovering the inherent potential for human solidarity in all interactions, this only serves for me to highlight by contrast the injustice of many existing arrangements. In addition to the specific insights that my teachers transmitted, they also provided me with an exemplar of committed intellectual effort. Watching them go about their work of educating students, conducting research, and contributing to a university and a discipline with a serious and committed, yet joyful attitude inspired me to follow in their footsteps. It is to you, Randy and Joe, whom I dedicate my efforts here, in the hope that I have not fallen too far short of your example.

Acknowledgments

I thank the following copyright holders for permission to republish essays that originally appeared in their pages. The essays have been revised for this book.

American Sociological Association:

> Chapter 2. "Reification of Consumer Products: A General History Illustrated by the Case of American Automobile," *Sociological Theory* 4 (Fall 1986): 167–85.

> Chapter 6. "Bourdieu's Theory of Cultural Change: Explication, Application, Critique," *Sociological Theory* 20 (July 2002): 255–77.

Sage Publications:

> Chapter 4. "Three Ages of the Automobile: The Cultural Logics of the Car." The final, definitive version of this paper has been published in *Theory, Culture & Society* 21 (Aug.–Oct. 2004): 169–95, by Sage Publications Ltd. All rights reserved. © Theory, Culture & Society Ltd.

> Chapter 5. "Why Modern Architecture Emerged in Europe, Not America: The New Class and the Aesthetics of Technocracy." The final, definitive version of this paper has been published in *Theory, Culture & Society* 17 (Oct. 2000): 75–96, by Sage Publications Ltd. All rights reserved. © Theory, Culture & Society Ltd.

University of Chicago Press:

> Chapter 3. "Culture as Class Symbolization or Mass Reification? A Critique of Bourdieu's *Distinction*," *American Journal of Sociology* 97 (Sept. 1991): 421–47. © 1991 by The University of Chicago. All rights reserved.

Springer:

> Chapter 7. "Bourdieu and Adorno: Converging Theories of Culture and Inequality," *Theory and Society* 41 (Oct. 2011): 41–72.

1 Modern Culture as Mass Unity or Ranked Diversity

For critical sociologists, two of the foremost theories informing the debate on how culture legitimates inequality in modern society are those of Pierre Bourdieu and the Frankfurt School. Each theory has its separate advocates, but seldom do they address one another, preferring instead to ignore the challenge posed by the other theoretical tradition. This is also true of the founders of these theories. Of course, by 1979, when Bourdieu's *Distinction* was published, all of the founding members of the Frankfurt School were dead, depriving them of the opportunity to respond to this major work on culture. Bourdieu, on the other hand, had ample opportunity in his lifetime to address the work of the Frankfurt School, but generally chose to ignore it, beyond some cheeky dismissals such as characterizing Theodor Adorno as "an arrogant theoretician who refuses to sully his hands with empirical trivia and who remains too viscerally attached to the values and profits of Culture to be able to make it an object of science" (Bourdieu 1984: 511).

The mutual and willful ignorance of these important theoretical traditions is unfortunate, for it has prevented them from clearly formulating and researching the issues that both unite and divide them. Both Bourdieu and the Frankfurt School share a critical perspective on modern culture, arguing that ideas, beliefs, art, and artifacts reproduce and legitimate the inequalities of wealth and power in capitalist society. But what divides them is not, as some have suggested, Bourdieu's empirical research versus the Frankfurt School's theoretical focus, or even Bourdieu's structuralism versus the Frankfurt School's Marxism. The real division between these similarly critical sociological theories is not on research methods or theoretical foundations, but on the concrete issue of diversity in the culture of modern society. Bourdieu argues that modern society is characterized by a ranked diversity of cultural objects, which distinguishes different classes and simultaneously makes some seem superior to others. This hierarchical culture legitimates the unequal distribution of power and wealth by making the dominant class seem more deserving because it consumes the "right" culture, and the dominated class less deserving because it consumes the "wrong" one. The Frankfurt School, by contrast, argues that modern society is characterized by a leveled unity or similarity of cultural objects, which hides the real class divisions of capitalist society. This mass culture, consumed by all, legitimates inequality by creating the illusion that all members of society are basically equal, with some just having more of what all desire because they work harder in the market and receive more income. Ultimately, then, the difference between these two great theories of modern culture is reduced to this question: Does modern society possess a mass culture shared by all, or a ranked diversity of class cultures?

MARX: CULTURE AS MASS UNITY

These two theories of culture ultimately owe their origins to two great founders of sociology—Karl Marx and Max Weber. To understand these contemporary theories and their differences, it is first necessary to review their classical origins. The Frankfurt School derives its theory of a mass culture as obscuring the class differences of capitalist society from Marx's concept of commodity fetishism, which he develops in the first volume of *Capital*. Marx derives this concept of fetishism from the general theory of ideology developed in his earlier work. In *The German Ideology* Marx and Engels argue that most societies are unified by a common set of beliefs and values that originate in the economy. Even though the material interests of the ruling or owning class, and the laboring class of each society are opposed, "the ideas of the ruling class are in every epoch the ruling ideas" and are widely shared by all (Marx and Engels 1976a: 59). Why? Marx and Engels give two answers.

Their simplistic and instrumental answer holds that the class that owns the means of material production also controls the means of cultural production—e.g. newspapers, publishing houses, television networks—and consciously uses them to disseminate ideas that serve its material interests. Directly following this, however, Marx and Engels offer an alternative answer that is more complex and structuralist. "The ruling ideas are nothing more than the ideal expression of the dominant material relations, the dominant material relations grasped as ideas; hence of the relations which make the one class the ruling one, therefore, the ideas of its dominance" (Marx and Engels 1976a: 59). This version implies that class position does not directly determine ideas, but that both the dominant class and the dominant ideas are determined by the overall structure of production relations in a society. This social structure determines ideas largely through molding the cognitive limits of human consciousness. For example, in capitalism the division of society into different occupations and different classes prevents people from consciously coordinating their own economic activity, and turns the allocation of labor over to the chance workings of the market. Consequently, these relations of production make people's own labor *appear* in their consciousness as an alien or estranged entity, governed by laws of nature they cannot control. "The social power . . . which arises through the cooperation of different individuals as it is caused by the division of labor appears to these individuals, since their cooperation is not voluntary but has come about naturally, not as their own united power, but as an alien force existing outside them, of the origin and goal of which they are ignorant, which they thus are no longer able to control" (Marx and Engels 1976a: 48).

In *Capital*, Marx (1967a: 71–83) calls this fallacious consciousness "commodity fetishism" and sees it as an ideology that unites all classes and obscures the inequalities between them. Because all commodities, including labor power, sell for a value equal to the labor time expended in their production, the exploitative wage relation between labor and capital appears to be a fair exchange between equal parties. The relations between conscious humans hence take on the appearance of relations between things, which are governed by objective laws of the market beyond human control. Capitalism thus creates in the consciousness of people a world turned upside down, a fantasy world in which humans are reduced to mere things, and things (commodities) are endowed with the human traits of consciousness and will. But Marx argues that the rise of new forces of production breaks the spell of commodity fetishism. Competition forces capitalists to replace small workshops with a few workers by giant factories, in which the efforts of thousands are coordinated and commanded like an army. Modern industry thus impresses on the consciousness of everyone the social character of labor, and the possibility that the conscious, collective allocation of society's labor can replace the market's unplanned chaos of individual exchanges (Marx 1967b: 262–66; Marx and Engels 1976b: 489–93).

MARX'S LEGACY: LUKÁCS, THE FRANKFURT SCHOOL, AND REIFIED CULTURE

Half a century after Marx introduced his concept of commodity fetishism the Marxist philosopher and literary critic Georg Lukács renames it "reification," and argues that this fallacy of seeing human relations as things is the unifying structure of all capitalist culture. In his 1923 *History and Class Consciousness*, however, Lukács argues that the industrial proletariat is in a structural position to break the spell of reification. Members of the bourgeoisie are structurally incapable of penetrating the ideology of reification, for they experience themselves as both subjects and objects. They make subjective decisions about their businesses, but in doing so simultaneously experience the objective limits of the laws of the market. Proletarians, on the other hand, experience themselves only as objects, for the capitalist labor process strips from them all subjective actions and turns them into the commodity of labor power dominated by the market. Consequently, these workers are able to see the human, subjective core behind the reified façade of the commodity, for they *are* that core. They are the physical, mental, and moral beings behind the false "thingness" of the commodity of labor power, and are thus able see that all commodities are products of human creation (Lukács 1971a: 159–81).

Lukács's work on reification sets the agenda for the subsequent analysis of culture by the Frankfurt School. When he was writing in the early 1920s, his notion of a revolutionary proletariat that could penetrate the myth of reification to become class conscious seemed to be validated by historical events—the Russian revolution of 1917 and the German revolution of 1918. But throughout the later 1920s and early 1930s, both the Soviet Union and the Weimar Republic increasingly replaced the goal of revolutionary social change with that of rapid industrialization, and relied on authoritarian rule to accomplish this. Support for these reactionary policies by substantial fractions of the working class seemed to contradict Lukács's idea of the structural capacity of the proletariat to cut through reified consciousness. But a group of Marxist intellectuals at the University of Frankfurt's Institute for Social Research inventively use Lukács's concept of reification to explain these developments.

Max Horkheimer, Theodor Adorno, Erich Fromm, Herbert Marcuse, and others, who collectively became known as the Frankfurt School, develop an argument that the consciousness and personality of all classes living under capitalism, including workers, are distorted by the structure of this system. The new structure of monopoly capitalism, which is dominated by large-scale, mass-production corporations, generates authoritarian personalities that crave domineering leaders and tolerate no dissent. And the cultural products of this economy are necessarily homogenized and uncritical commodities, offering to all people the same superficial escape from alienated reality that make them content with the system. In other words, culture also becomes a reified commodity, which obscures the oppressive production relations between people behind a façade of things that seem inevitable (Horkheimer and Adorno 1972).

The Frankfurt School retains Marx's notion that culture is produced by the general form of social relations, and thus, unlike Lukács, does not believe that any particular class has privileged access to true consciousness. But they reject Marx's assertion that reified consciousness can be broken by the increasingly socialized means of production. Although they recognize that capitalism creates giant bureaucratic organizations that consciously coordinate the labor of thousands, they argue that this socialized mechanism of production does not break but reinforces the aura of reification. The bureaucracies of monopoly capitalism themselves become seen not as *human* creations but as the inevitable technical means for producing more commodities, more things for all.

The Frankfurt thinkers argue that these reified production organizations also leave their marks on cultural products, helping to produce reified consciousness. To cheaply mass produce culture for large markets, these bureaucracies rigidly standardize not merely work tasks but also the products themselves. Diversity and innovation are eliminated from products in order to achieve the efficiencies required for profitable production. So, for example, to allow mass production of autos, the Ford Motor Company not only eliminated all models but the Model T, but also eliminated from it all beauty and embellishment that was superfluous to the efficient production of basic transportation. However, these cultural products molded by cost-cutting efficiencies create an unanticipated consequence—they expose to consumers the oppressive social relations under which they are produced. The standardized, unchanging Model T, for example, testified to a labor process that treats workers not as individuals but as standardized, unthinking things, rigidly controlled for the production of value for others.

This exposure by cultural products of the oppressive relations of monopoly capitalism is dangerous in a society in which workers are themselves consumers, and demand that their products provide an escape from the alienated conditions of their work. Under market pressure to meet this demand, capitalists are forced to offer consumers products with the diversity and change that are denied them at work. They do so not by changing production but merely by hiding the telltale signs of standardization and dehumanization in their products under diverse, changing, humanized surfaces. Consequently, the Frankfurt School argues, the culture industry's products themselves become reified—their appearance as individuated, ever-changing, exciting things disguise the reality of the unchanging, alienated relations under which they are produced. Further, because consumers of all classes are offered the same standardized products, which are differentiated only superficially, the real class divisions of capitalism are obscured. The differences between high and low culture that previously symbolized class inequality are thus eradicated, and this rigidly stratified society takes on the appearance of a leveled democracy in which all are equally served by mass-produced abundance (Adorno 1993; Horkheimer and Adorno 1972).

WEBER: CULTURE AS RANKED DIVERSITY

This analysis of culture originated by Marx and developed by the Frankfurt School continues to be influential in sociology, especially in the 1960s and 1970s. But for many sociologists its assertions of direct causal connections between the structure of the economy and a pervasive, unified consciousness that legitimates inequality are too simplistic to account for the variety of cultural struggles in modern society. Many skeptics look to the work of Max Weber for a more convincing conception of culture. Although Weber shares Marx's view of ideas and beliefs as a legitimation of social inequality, he differs on how this is accomplished. While Marx sees culture as a direct reflection of economic organization, Weber recognizes culture as comprising a potentially independent status order, in which people with different beliefs and values struggle for honor or prestige. And while Marx sees culture as maintaining inequality by imposing on all a false unity of similar beliefs that hides real class differences, Weber believes that culture legitimates inequality by establishing a ranking of different beliefs, which makes the holders of some seem superior to others.

Weber makes a general argument for the analytic independence of culture from the economy in *Economy and Society* (1968: 926–40). He defines classes as constituted by a common position in the economic market, where goods are *produced*. Classes are distinguished largely by the property possessed and services offered in the market. By contrast, status (cultural) groups are constituted by a common style of life, determined by how goods are *consumed* (937). But Weber argues that while analytically the two types of groups are defined by different resources, empirically and historically they are intertwined in complex ways. And nowhere does he better reveal the complex relation between economic class and cultural status group than in his sociology of religion.

Weber does not conceive religion as a cultural reflex of the economy, as does Marx in his infamous analysis of religion as the opium of the masses (Marx 1975: 175). Rather, he sees it as a realm of struggle in itself, with its own particular kind of status goods and organizations that dispense them. While Weber admits that the most primitive religions promise to magically influence economic outcomes, he argues that as religion develops the rewards offered individuals shift from economic to spiritual ones, like redemption or salvation. Religions of salvation generally develop among the economically repressed strata, for they need deliverance from suffering in another world more than privileged strata, which are favored in this one (Weber 1946b: 272–77). The price the repressed pay for this salvation increasingly becomes not economic, but cultural—i.e. adherence to a set of ethical norms, enforced by religious officials in separate organizations. Thus, religion produces a cultural economy, so to speak. Religious producers, such as churches, sects, and virtuosos, compete with one another to deliver spiritual goods to consumers, who must pay in ethical conformity. But religious organizations offer to adherents not merely the promise of salvation in another world but also the distinction in *this* world of being considered worthy of salvation, that is, charisma or personal giftedness. Thus, Weber (1946b: 287) argues, religion creates a cultural inequality, and becomes part of the status stratification of society.

Having established religion as a separate realm of status conflict, however, Weber shows that this realm is intertwined with class conflict. He argues that different classes have different religious preferences, determined not directly by economic interest, but indirectly by the practical conduct demanded by economic position. Thus, members of different classes have an "elective affinity" to ideas that validate or glorify their way of being in the world, which is heavily influenced by their economic conduct (Weber 1946b: 284). For example, Weber argues that ethical salvation religions are usually created by privileged groups like intellectuals. But once in existence, petite bourgeois and artisans have an elective affinity to these religions, because they validate the rational, self-denying practices required by their occupations (Weber 1968: 486–87).

If religious beliefs do not originate directly from the economic interests of the followers, what ensures the production of beliefs that have an affinity to their practical conduct? Weber finds the answer to this question not on the demand side of the cultural economy, but on the supply side. It is the competition among religious entrepreneurs for followers that forces them to create religious goods that match the latter's status demands (Weber 1968: 456, 466). So, for example, Weber states that salvation religions are usually produced by intellectuals, who are motivated by their own metaphysical need to understand the world as a meaningful cosmos (1968: 499). But to attract a broader range of adherents, these religions are forced to alter their beliefs to accommodate the demand of the lower classes for compensation for suffering. So just like producers in the economic marketplace, the competition of producers in the cultural marketplace drives them to offer new and different status goods to maintain old consumers and attract new ones. This creates a dynamic of product differentiation similar to that which drives the economic market (Weber 1968:452–67).

For Weber, like Marx, the ideas and beliefs of culture often serve to legitimate inequalities of power and wealth. For example, he argues that the primary function of religion for the privileged classes is "legitimating their own life pattern and situation in the world" (1968: 491). By contrast, the economically unprivileged seek in religion not legitimation of their position in this world, but compensation for their suffering in another one. So for Weber, unlike Marx, culture is diverse, not unified. The cultural beliefs and practices of the privileged group are not *shared* by all, but they are somehow *recognized* by all to be superior. And he argues that the main determinant of the status ranking or relative recognition of different cultures is sheer power. "The development of status is essentially a question of stratification resting upon usurpation. Such usurpation is the normal origin of almost all status honor" (Weber 1946a: 188). Weber recognizes that the source of this power is sometimes economic wealth, but he also shows that political power may also influence cultural dominance, especially in religion (1968: 411–20).

WEBER'S LEGACY: BOURDIEU AND CULTURE AS CLASS-RANKED DIVERSITY

In modern sociology no one owes more to Weber's analysis of culture than Pierre Bourdieu, who explicitly acknowledges this debt (Bourdieu 1998c: 57–58). He argues, like Weber, that cultures generally contain a diversity of ideas and beliefs, which are influenced not directly by economic interests but indirectly by practical preferences molded by class position. For Bourdieu, the ideas of an economic class are shaped by its habitus, a set of unconscious dispositions that are in turn conditioned by class position. This seems compatible with Weber's concept of elective affinity between ideas and a group's "way of being in the world," although there is a difference. While Weber focuses on a group's characteristic economic *actions* as conditioning its cultural preferences, Bourdieu focuses on a group's economic *resources*, which are said to condition the actions of individuals from an early age, even before they enter the work force.

Bourdieu asserts, for example, that because the dominant class or bourgeoisie has an abundance of economic capital, its members are conditioned early on to be unconcerned with the functions of things to meet their material needs. They are thus instilled with a habitus that privileges the aesthetic forms of things—e.g. clothing and food—over their material functions. By contrast, the dominated or working class has a scarcity of economic capital, which dictates that its members must always be concerned with meeting their material needs. This concern instills a habitus that privileges material function over aesthetic form in all their cultural preferences (Bourdieu 1984: 169–225). For Bourdieu then, as for Weber, economic positions indirectly influence cultural preferences through conditioning affinities to objects and ideas, which ultimately produces cultures of diversity, not unity.

Bourdieu's assertion of a diversity of beliefs then raises the questions of which among these becomes dominant? And how? On the question of how, Bourdieu agrees with Weber—one set of ideas become dominant because its advocates have the power to impose it on all. While Weber calls this usurpation, Bourdieu calls it symbolic power or symbolic violence, and argues that in modern societies it is the state that monopolizes this power to define the legitimate ideas and tastes (Bourdieu 2000: 164–205). He has focused much of his research on the main function through which the state imposes this symbolic monopoly—education. Schools impose the cultural standards of the dominant class on all by determining the curriculum and evaluating student performance. Students from the lower classes cannot possibly meet these standards, since their economic positions instill dispositions favoring the practical functions of things over their forms. But schools force them to recognize the superiority of the standards of the dominant class, thus legitimating their failure to succeed as a personal failure, not a social injustice (Bourdieu and Passeron 1977; Bourdieu 1996b).

Bourdieu's analysis also converges with Weber's in recognizing that ideas and beliefs are shaped not only by the interests of cultural consumers, but also by the interests of cultural producers. Specifically acknowledging Weber's insight (Bourdieu 1998c: 57), he develops a theory of the internal dynamics of the field of cultural production. Bourdieu argues that cultural producers serve the interests of classes external to the field not by consciously adjusting their products to these interests, but by pursuing their own interests in competition with other producers. By seeking to advance their internal interests, cultural producers create products that serve the interests of those external classes which stand in the same position in the social field (of classes) as they do in the cultural field.

Bourdieu states that the cultural field in modern societies is divided into two subfields. One is the subfield of large-scale or mass production, in which producers are driven by the practical interests of making money by satisfying the needs of the largest market. This subfield generally draws producers from the middle and lower classes, whose habitus privilege practical function over form. The other subfield is that of restricted or small-scale production, in which producers are driven not to make money but to receive recognition (cultural capital) from other producers. This subfield generally draws producers from the high bourgeoisie, whose habitus privilege form over function. So cultural producers in each subfield are motivated by both external habitus and internal competition to produce cultural goods that meet the needs of the different classes. In doing so, they also legitimate the overall system of economic inequality by elevating the tastes of the dominant class over those of the dominated class (Bourdieu 1993c: 112–41.

Bourdieu's analysis of modern culture as a diversity of beliefs ranked by power corresponds to Weber's analysis in most respects save one—the determinant of the power to impose ideas. Bourdieu holds that cultural power is always determined by economic power, while Weber argues that the connection between economic class and cultural status varies between societies.

TOWARD A CRITICAL THEORY OF CULTURE BETWEEN BOURDIEU AND THE FRANKFURT SCHOOL

In modern sociology we thus have two critical theories of culture that explain the way in which cultural ideas and practices are associated with and ultimately legitimate social inequality. But their explanations are diametrically opposed. Drawing on the Marxist tradition, the Frankfurt School argues the culture of modern society is a unity, with people from across the class spectrum adopting the same ideas and practices shaped by the structure of the capitalist economy. This creates a reified culture, one that hides the real class differences in power and wealth behind a façade of standardized, mass-produced things consumed by all. Drawing on the Weberian tradition, Bourdieu, by contrast, argues that the culture of modern society is characterized by difference, with classes consuming qualitatively different types of cultural products. This differentiated and hierarchical culture legitimates inequality by making members of the dominant class seem individually superior to others, as a consequence of their distinct tastes.

I do not believe that progress will be made in developing a critical theory of culture by asking which of these theories is more empirically valid than the other. There is ample empirical evidence to reveal that both contain elements of validity. The most fruitful research questions are those that seek to *specify* the validity of each theory. Under what conditions is modern culture more likely to be configured as a leveled unity than a ranked diversity? In which type of society? In which historical period? In which cultural field within a given society? Research on such comparative questions promises to further progress toward a critical theory of modern culture.

The following chapters seek to advance this end. Written over the last twenty-five years, they explicate the concepts and propositions of one or both of the cultural theories of Bourdieu and the Frankfurt School. But these essays also attempt to evaluate the theories against the empirical evidence drawn from case studies of two important cultural artifacts—the automobile and architecture. Several characteristics of these cases make them important for assessing the validity of the two theories. First, both are historical, examining the subject not merely in the present but over the course of an extensive historical development. This longer temporal view captures the vicissitudes of cultures, and avoids the fallacy of generalizing from data derived solely from the present. Second, these artifacts occupy different positions in modern culture, to which both Bourdieu and the Frankfurt School have attributed important differences in development. The automobile is a part of mass culture, or in Bourdieu's particular terminology, the cultural subfield of large-scale production. Architecture, by contrast, is part of legitimate or high culture, which Bourdieu calls the cultural subfield of small-scale production. Examining these two cases historically allows us to determine whether differences between mass culture and high culture are being leveled, as postulated by the Frankfurt School's theory of reification, or maintaining their differences, as postulated by Bourdieu's theory of class distinction.

Third and finally, these two artifacts also differ on another variable which may affect their development—the materiality of culture. The automobile is an artifact of material culture, requiring mainly economic capital or money to consume. Although architecture also requires substantial economic capital to build, it differs from autos in also requiring cultural capital to consume—that is, its proper appreciation requires knowledge of aesthetic styles and periods. The leveling or cross-class sharing of an artifact may vary by the distribution of the type of resource it requires for consumption. If the distribution of economic capital becomes more equitable, then more consumers are able to purchase artifacts of material culture, thus leveling the differences in this type of consumption. If the distribution of cultural capital becomes more equitable, then more consumers are able to appreciate artifacts of nonmaterial culture, thus leveling the differences in this type of consumption.

A final issue that must be addressed before proceeding to the essays is the changes in the theories themselves. Although I have so far assumed that the two theories of modern culture are complete and unchanging wholes, this assumption is unwarranted, especially with respect to Bourdieu. There are also changes in the cultural theory of the Frankfurt School and its separate thinkers, but these merely elaborate and specify the basic premises laid down in the 1930s and 1940s. The matter is entirely different with Bourdieu's theory, however. In his scholarship and political interventions after about 1988, he reverses some of his most important positions. He begins to defend high culture, which he previously criticized as legitimating class privilege, against the encroachment of mass culture, which he defended as the authentic expression of the working class. In the process, he abandons his concept of culture as relative to class position and develops a theory of cultural universalism, arguing that all culture must be measured against certain universal standards inherent in human potentialities. This latter position bears a remarkable resemblance to the theory of the Frankfurt School, although important differences remain. Unfortunately, Bourdieu's death prevented him from systematically presenting and elaborating his changing ideas on culture.

Despite the beginnings of a convergence of these two powerful theories, important work remains to be done in developing a critical theory of culture. Much of this concerns the variation in the structure of culture, both within and between national societies. Drawing on my case studies, I suggest some generalizations that may explain some of this variation. But these suggestions are tentative and underdeveloped. I hope that the following essays help to clarify some of the dimensions and issues of a critical theory of culture, and in so doing make a small contribution to this ongoing enterprise, which is important not merely for scholars but also for all people with an interest in an authentically open and egalitarian culture.

2   Reification of Consumer Products
A General History Illustrated by the American Automobile

It is common knowledge in advanced capitalist society that consumer products are not shaped by utility alone. There is widespread awareness that we live in a consumer *culture*, if we follow Lukács (1973c: 4) in defining culture as the valuable products and abilities that are dispensable to the immediate maintenance of life. The majority of goods are not related to vital material needs but pander instead to consumers' fantasies and self-images.

Before the 1980s, however, the social and cultural disciplines gave little theoretical attention to the material products of consumer culture, preferring instead to focus on nonmaterial manifestations of mass culture, like music, literature, and film. Two exceptions to this dearth of attention are the traditions of the Frankfurt School and semiology, both of which have used the concept of reification to analyze the material products of capitalism. Frankfurt thinkers and radical semiologists have borrowed this concept from Marx's analysis of capitalist production and extended it to capitalist consumption as well. But despite their theoretical power, these analyses have failed to specify the concrete historical mechanisms by which reification is extended from capitalist production to consumption, and have relied instead on abstract, formal mechanisms like analogy and homology.

I attempt to build on their analysis of reified consumer products by explaining how historically situated human activity, in the forms of class conflict and capitalist competition, is responsible for transferring the reality of reification from economic production to cultural consumption. I develop a general history of the emergence of reified consumption through these practical activities, and then illustrate it with the quintessential consumer product of the twentieth century—the automobile. This examination of the design and styling of the American automobile reveals that the "thingification" of the social relations of production is the result of capitalist attempts to overcome both the class conflict of workers and the competition of rival firms.

MARX'S THEORY OF REIFIED PRODUCTION

The concept of reification was developed by the young Marx to analyze the social relations of production within capitalism, but it underlies the entire corpus of his work. It describes a process whereby the social relations of capitalist labor grow out of human control and appear as things, governed by natural laws. Marx (1964) conceptualizes this reification as the negation of the essential form of human labor, in which people interact with nature to create an objective world that not only satisfies their material needs but also realizes their nature. Through labor humans realize their potential for free and conscious action, and also express their social nature by producing for others as well as themselves. This essential form of labor is repressed and distorted, however, by historical forms of production like capitalism. In this mode of production, Marx argues, private ownership expropriates from laborers the means of production they need to realize their life activity. In order to live they are thus forced to transform their human abilities into a commodity and sell it for a wage to a capitalist, who puts it to work producing other commodities for a profit. Thus, the labor through which humans should express their nature becomes an alien thing beyond their control, used for purposes other than their own.

Marx reveals two interrelated moments of the reification of labor in capitalism—one originating in the marketplace, the other in the workplace. In the marketplace, the products of labor meet and exchange according to laws beyond human control. The actual interdependencies between people are obscured behind the relations between the things they produce, which are apparently autonomous. To producers, "their own social action takes the form of the action of objects, which rule the producers instead of being ruled by them" (Marx 1967a: 75). The market also obscures the class inequality of capitalism. Because all commodities, including labor power, receive in exchange a value equivalent to the labor time expended on them, the exploitative relation between labor and capital appears as a fair deal between equal parties.

In the workplace, human labor is also transformed into an alien thing, governed by laws beyond human control. To maximize surplus value, capitalists strip labor of all of its conscious characteristics by dividing and mechanizing it, thus centralizing all discretion into their hands. Labor is thus reduced to the simple expenditure of energy, and then measured and manipulated by capital. The human relations of cooperation between workers appear not as the expression of their social nature, but as relations between abstract things governed by quantitative laws. The exploitative relations between classes are thus obscured behind the seemingly natural rule of science (Marx 1967a: 322–507).

LUKÁCS' THEORY OF CULTURAL REIFICATION

Although Marx develops the concept of reification to understand the capitalist economy, it carries cultural connotations as well. After all, it describes the *appearance*, or representation in consciousness, of social relations *as if* they were things. But these cultural connotations remained largely undeveloped until the Hungarian Marxist, Georg Lukács, published his pathbreaking *History and Class Consciousness*, which treats reification as a form that permeates the totality of capitalist society. Rejecting the simplistic conception of culture as a mere superstructure reflecting the content of the economy, Lukács holds that it is the social *form* of capitalism that is reproduced in culture (1971a: 83–92). The reification of labor in economic production provides to actors in the cultural realm the basic problems of human experience with which they must grapple, as well as the limits of their grappling. The cultural works of capitalism are thus the voluntary attempts of individuals and institutions to deal with the determinate social conflicts and contradictions defined by reified production. In the process of offering conceptual solutions to these problems, the works reproduce their forms.

Lukács argues (1971a: 104–49), for example, that modern philosophy is an attempt to resolve ideally the problem of reification created materially by capitalism. Reified production separates human subjects from the commodified objects they produce, subjecting the former to the economic laws of the latter. Modern philosophy is a series of unsuccessful attempts to overcome this separation conceptually. Kant, for example, tries to conceive the object of knowledge as the mental creation of the knowing subject. But he ultimately fails when confronted with the separateness of the objective content of knowledge. Lukács (1971b, 1973a) finds modern literature similarly haunted by this separation of subject and object. Novelists thus constitute heroes as solitary subjects standing in opposition to a hostile and alien environment. The plot is the story of a reconciliation of hero and world—a discovery of meaning, a proving of soul, a homecoming. But usually the reconciliation stresses the dominance of one side of the opposition and ends up, like Kant's philosophy, merely reproducing the split.

Lukács sees these attempts by cultural producers to overcome reification conceptually as ideological, for they obscure the source of the problem in capitalist production. But this ideology is the result of the limits placed on thought by the social and historical position of these bourgeois writers. Because all writers living after 1848 have no personal experience of the human struggles that created capitalism from feudalism, they experience this mode of production as an objective, inevitable system, a fact of nature (Lukács 1973a). But bourgeois writers are especially incapable of conceptually transcending the reified separation of subject and object because as member of this class, they live the separation daily. The bourgeois experience themselves as both subjects and objects—they simultaneously make conscious decisions affecting their businesses, but in doing so also experience the objective laws of the marketplace. Only the position of the proletariat provides the possibility of cutting through the duality of reification to conceive reality as the creation of humans. Proletarians perceive themselves only as objects, since the capitalist labor process removes from them all subjective action and turns them into the commodity of labor power. And only when humans themselves become totally reified is the veil of objectivity over capitalism lifted to reveal the subjective core of the commodity, which is human effort itself. With this unreified consciousness, proletarians struggle to bring human relations under conscious, collective control for the first time (Lukács 1971a: 159–81).

Lukács reveals how reification infiltrates capitalism's nonmaterial culture, as bourgeois writers and artists grapple with the problems and struggles it produces from their own position. But he does not deal systematically with the reification of material culture, which would seem to have a greater impact on the proletariat than the nonmaterial high culture of literature and philosophy. This task is left to a later generation of Marxist analysts of culture, who extend Lukács' analysis of reified culture to the growing consumer culture of material commodities.

THEORIES OF REIFIED CONSUMER CULTURE: THE FRANKFURT SCHOOL AND SEMIOLOGY

Two schools of Marxist-influenced social theory make insightful use of the concept of reification to analyze contemporary capitalism's culture of mass consumption. The social philosophers associated with the Frankfurt Institute for Social Research—especially Max Horkheimer, Theodor Adorno, and Herbert Marcuse—draw directly on the analysis of reification in Marx and Lukács. The radical semiologists like Roland Barthes and Jean Baudrillard, by contrast, are influenced only indirectly by this analysis. But both types of theory agree that the extension of the logic of reification into the realm of material consumption constitutes a new stage of capitalism, in which the hopes of Lukács and others for a class-conscious, revolutionary working class are dashed.

The foundation text of the Frankfurt School's critique of contemporary capitalist culture is "The Culture Industry: Enlightenment as Mass Deception," a chapter in Horkheimer and Adorno's *Dialectic of Enlightenment* (1972: 120–67). Here the authors argue that culture under monopoly or administered capitalism is transformed into an industry that is governed by the same logic that underlies economic production. They call this logic technological or instrumental rationality, but it shares with Lukács' reification the trait of reducing the concrete, substantive qualities of humans to abstract, formal properties in order to dominate them for external ends. In capitalist production technological rationality takes the form of the mechanization and rationalization of work, reducing human workers to abstract labor power dominated by the capitalist purpose of profit-making. In capitalist consumption, technological rationality results in the monopolies abstracting from the real qualitative needs of people and classifying them into "markets segments," whose needs may be artificially manipulated. Products are then manufactured in superficially distinguished hierarchies, like automobile models, in order to appeal to the different market segments.

Consumers' human needs, like freedom and individuality, thus appear as commodified things that are alien to them and must be reappropriatied through stultifying labor. These things, however, are the mere illusions of real needs, which disguise and justify the reality of the unfree, alienated work process.

> Amusement under late capitalism is the prolongation of work. It is sought after as an escape from the mechanized work process, and to recruit strength in order to be able to cope with it again. But at the same time mechanization has such power over a man's leisure and happiness, and so profoundly determines the manufacture of amusement goods, that his experiences are inevitably after-images of the work process itself. The ostensible content is merely a faded foreground; what sinks in is the automatic succession of standardized operations. What happens at work, in the factory, or in the office can only be escaped from by approximation to it in one's leisure time (Horkheimer and Adorno 1972: 137).

Just as the rationalization of labor in the factory obscures the human relations of production behind a facade of seemingly natural laws—e.g. "scientific management"—so too does the rationalization of consumption obscure the manipulation of products and needs behind a screen of naturalism. The sterile uniformity of capitalist culture is said to be required by the technology of mass production in order to produce goods for the many. Besides, claim the system's apologists, product standards are based on consumer needs anyway, as determined by scientific surveys, so people really want what the culture industry gives them. There is no recognition that the system itself produces the type of alienated needs that its reproduction requires.

> The result is the circle of manipulation and retroactive need in which the unity of the system grows ever stronger. No mention is made of the fact that the basis on which technology acquires power over society is the power of those whose economic hold over society is greatest. A technological rationale is the rationale of domination itself. It is the coercive nature of society alienated from itself. (Horkheimer and Adorno 1972: 121)

Developing these themes for the even more commodified capitalism of some twenty years later, Herbert Marcuse argues that advanced industrial society is one-dimensional and noncontradictory, dominated in all its parts by the repressive technological rationality. And this one-dimensionality is largely due to the total subsumption of culture by this repressive logic for the first time in history. In the early stage of capitalism, labor is alienated and human needs denied, but culture is not yet infiltrated by technological rationality. Marcuse (1964: 56–83; 1968) argues that early bourgeois high culture is independent from the capitalist infrastructure and remains a world apart, where the needs suppressed by the world of business can be expressed. This culture thus serves a critical function by preserving the denied needs in sublimated artistic forms, which constitute a protest against the society responsible for their denial.

In advanced capitalist society, however, this critical function is destroyed by the integration of culture into the repressive universe of technological rationality. The tremendous productive potential of this society accomplishes the "materialization of ideals," the desublimation of needs from the realm of the spirit into the material realm of commodities. But because this desublimation of needs is accomplished within the bounds of the repressive system of production, it is ultimately repressive. These commodities turn the need for transformed human relations into things—consumer goods—which not only produce a profit but also give people superficial satisfactions that prevent them from acting to achieve their real needs. Freedom and self-determination are narrowed into leisure pursuits, then sold to consumers as products like automobiles, boats, and sporting goods. The integration of the working class into this system of ersatz consumer satisfactions represses its need for revolutionary change and transforms it into another support for the system.

Despite these crucial insights into the reification of material culture under contemporary capitalism, the analysis of the Frankfurt School suffers a crucial weakness—the inability to specify the historical mechanisms by which this comes about. These thinkers do not clarify exactly how and why the production logic of abstraction and rationalization is reproduced in cultural consumption. They ultimately seem to resort to rather undialectical, functionalist explanations. Culture becomes instrumentalized and reified, they imply, because the system requires this. As the traditional repository of the negative, culture is a threat to domination, so the system sees that it is eliminated. The Frankfurt School conceives the contemporary society as a system of total domination, whose development is driven not by human actions but system requirements.

A similar weakness troubles the analysis of contemporary capitalist material culture by the Marxist-influenced semiologists like Roland Barthes and Jean Baudrillard, although this does not prevent them from offering enlightening insights. Following the structural linguist Ferdinand Saussure, who postulated this discipline as the general science of signs, semiologists distinguish between two components of the sign. The signified is the content, or intended meaning, of the sign, while the signifier is the material form through this meaningful content is conveyed. It is a general premise of semiology that the signifiers become abstracted from the signifieds, and governed by separate rules of combination and association. Semiologists focus on the analysis of these underlying rules of form, variously labeled as the code, structure, or paradigm (Barthes 1967).

While most semiologists take this abstraction of form from content as a universal trait of human signification, several have drawn on Marx's theory of reification to explain the social origins of such abstracted communication by the structure of capitalist society. Roland Barthes' *Mythologies* (1972) brilliantly extends the analysis of reification to material objects with his concept of myth, which, he argues, is the form of signification characteristic of bourgeois society. In myth, the signs of one semiological system enter into another, divesting their forms of the original meanings, which, Barthes argues following Marx, is constituted by the historical actions of humans. Thus the sign's relation to human labor is displaced by an image of nature. "What the world supplies to myth is an historical reality, defined . . . by the way in which men have produced or used it; and what myth gives in return is a *natural* image of this reality. . . . Myth is constituted by the loss of the historical quality of things: in it, things lose the memory that they once were made" (1972: 142). Barthes argues that myth is depoliticized speech, because it removes the traces of human relations in shaping the world and thus presents it as an unchangeable thing that must be accepted as it is (142–45).

Barthes, like Lukács, depicts capitalist culture as permeated with reification, the appearance of human relations as things that obscure the activity that shapes the world. But Barthes extends the phenomenon of reification to material objects, which, although originally created for utilitarian reasons, also become invested with social meanings. One remarkable analysis of such a mythical or reified object is Barthes' piece on the 1955 Citroën D. S. In this sleek automobile he sees a magical object that bears no marks of human creation, and thus seems to have fallen from the sky. The streamlining and smoothness of the surface obscure the fact that it was assembled from parts by human labor. "There are in the D. S. the beginnings of a new phenomenology of assembling, as if one progressed from a world where elements are welded to a world where they are juxtaposed and hold together by sole virtue of their wondrous shape, which of course is meant to prepare one for the idea of a more benign Nature" (88–89). In short, the Citroën is a totally reified object, which denies its own production by human labor. Consumption of such objects functions to obscure the alienating capitalist labor process so as to offer people ersatz satisfactions for their real needs denied there.

Barthes' analysis of consumption as an extension of the capitalist logic of reification is extensively developed in the works of Jean Baudrillard, another radical French semiologist. He argues (1975: 119–29) that Marx's political economy, which focuses largely on production, is inadequate for contemporary monopoly capitalism, in which the main problem is the realization of surplus value in consumption. Solving the problem of consumer demand requires capitalists to focus on the control and manipulation of the consumption process, which transfers the system's logic of reification to material objects. Baudrillard argues that in consumption, as in production, the connection of products to the exploitative labor process that produces them is obscured, and they seem to take on a life of their own. Products are consumed as signs, in which their signifiers, or forms, become completely abstracted from their signifieds, or contents provided by human relations. A system of arbitrary, quantitative differences in consumption thus displaces the real system of qualitative class differences in production, hiding the human relations under-lying capitalism. The privileged are distinguished not by ownership of capi-tal, but by their ownership of consumer goods; and the unprivileged take on the appearance not of exploited laborers but of simply lesser consumers. The *contradiction* of class is redefined as the *continuum* of consumption, with the implicit promise that upward mobility is possible, if not inevitable. Baudril-lard (1981: 49–62) thus reveals how the illusory democracy of the market has expanded beyond the seemingly equal exchange of labor power for wages in production to the equal chance to buy the same goods in consumption.

In the process of being transformed into signs carrying reified meanings, consumer products necessarily undergo a material change, Baudrillard holds (1981: 185–203). The material structure of the commodity must be reconciled with its reified meaning, and to do so the profession of industrial designer is born. The designer's job is first and foremost to hide the marks of meaninglessness born on the surface of products, for they testify to a labor process which has no inherent meaning for its participants, either labor or capital, beyond the efficient production of surplus value. To induce consumption, these marks of the relations of production must be displaced by arbitrarily imposed meanings, testifying to the products' usefulness to human needs. Baudrillard argues that this is just what the Bauhaus school of functional design seeks to do—to impose an arbitrary language of use-fulness on manufactured objects in order to reconcile the objects of pro-duction to the very people who produced them, because these producers have no conscious control over them. Functional design "proposes a model of reconciliation, of formal surpassing of specialization (division of labor at the level of objects) by a universally enveloping value. Thus it imposes a social scheme of integration by the elimination of real structures" (189).

Like the Frankfurt School, however, Barthes and Baudrillard fail to specify the concrete human agencies by which reification is extended into consumption and material culture. They write as if the obfuscation of the human origins of things in consumption is an inevitable extension of the system's logic. This type of formal, structuralist determinism, which oper-ates behind the backs of human agents, is ultimately unsatisfying, because abstract structures act only through concrete people. And although these people may not intend to produce the results they do, their actions are always motivated by intentions, however misguided, which must be under-stood in order for scholars to offer convincingly explanations.

THE HISTORICAL EMERGENCE OF REIFIED
CONSUMPTION THROUGH HUMAN PRAXIS

I argue that both the emergence of reification in capitalist production and its extension to cultural consumption may be explained by intentional but contradictory human action or praxis in the forms of class conflict and capitalist competition. Driven by competition with other firms to maximize profits, individual capitalists attempted to lower production costs by extracting more labor out of workers. But they encountered an obstacle to these attempts in the resistance of workers to working longer and harder. To overcome this resistance, capitalists progressively removed all discretion and control from workers, turning their concrete labor into abstract labor that could be quantitatively calculated and controlled. But as both Marx and Lukács recognize, this reification of labor had the ironic result of transforming individual craftworkers into a homogeneous and interdependent collective worker, characterized by heightened class consciousness and conflict. To overcome this renewed conflict, capitalists discovered the strategy of offering workers increased consumption to compensate for the heightened deprivations of production. But to create products that satisfied these displaced needs, capitalists found they had to hide their connections to the reified labor process, where genuine needs were denied. Thus, the reification of products—that is, the obfuscation of the oppressive relations of labor behind the appearance of objective necessity—was the consequence of capitalist attempts to overcome class conflict and sell products to provide substitute satisfactions.

In the remainder of this chapter I offer a general history of the emergence of reified consumer products as a consequence of concrete conflict between the groups involved. This general history will be illustrated, however, by a detailed empirical account of what is arguably the most important consumer product of the twentieth century, the automobile.

PRECAPITALIST SOCIETY: ORGANIC PRODUCTION, SYMBOLIC CONSUMPTION

Reified capitalist production and culture emerged from the nonreified relations of precapitalist modes of production, such as feudalism and slavery. Although these modes were based on the exploitation of labor by an owning class, relations of dominance were not reified but direct and personal. Labor was not an abstract commodity purchased on the market but a concrete use value producing goods and services directly appropriated by owners through political coercion. Consequently, class relations were transparent and did not appear as relations between things alien to humans. The ideologies that legitimated class relations were *social* ideologies, which clearly displayed the relations between classes (Balibar 1970: 218–24).

Due to these concrete relations of production, the products of precapitalist production appeared to people as *human* products. Since the coercive appropriation of surplus labor took place outside of the production process, the direct producers generally organized their own labor as they saw fit. For example, in feudalism the landlords appropriated peasants' surplus labor in kind or in direct services through military coercion, but peasant communities organized agriculture production. Thus, the objects in such societies appeared as products of a cooperative, social process, not as alien things with lives of their own (Jameson 1971: 103–5; Lukács 1971a: 90–91).

Consumption in precapitalist society reproduced this direct, visible form of the relations of production. Here class conflict often took the form of attacks on the person responsible for coercive surplus extraction. In order to fend off such attacks, members of the ruling class had to justify their personal fitness to rule by adorning their bodies with objects that conspicuously displayed their positions in the class hierarchy. Consumption in precapitalist society was thus the display of *symbols*, objects directly connected to the social labor that produced them, as opposed to signs, which abstract from this basis (Baudrillard 1981: 63–68). For example, clothing in feudalism symbolically attested to an individual's position in a class hierarchy marked by the juxtaposition of leisure and toil. Peasant clothes testified to a simple, sparse life of labor close to the soil with their sparingly cut, coarse cloth. By contrast, the fashions of landowning nobles symbolized a leisurely, abundant life based on appropriating others' labor. Since labor power in precapitalist society was a use value, not an exchange value to be conserved, one's class position was attested to by lavish use of it. The amount of labor required to produce the surfeits of cloth and intricate needlework of noble clothing was testimony to their social power to command vast numbers of workers. And since such fashions were wholly unsuited to work, they also bore witness to the intrinsic idleness of this class. These symbolic clothing conventions were formalized in sumptuary laws in late feudal society in an effort to preserve the class order against bourgeois assaults (Ewen and Ewen 1982: 117–28).

EARLY CAPITALISM: CONTINUITIES WITH PRECAPITALIST PRODUCTION AND CONSUMPTION

The rise of capitalism replaced the direct, personal relations of production of precapitalism with indirect, impersonal market relations. No longer a use value, labor power became a commodity purchased on the market, where surplus value was appropriated indirectly and legitimated by seemingly objective laws. From the outset, then, capitalist relations of production were formally reified—they appeared not as human relations but as relations between things (commodities) governed by economic laws beyond conscious control. But in early capitalism this reification was confined largely to the market exchange of goods and did not penetrate their production, since it took over the feudal labor process largely unchanged. Initially the capitalist labor process was just large-scale handicraft production, in which skilled workers remained in control of the details of work. The products of this work thus remained visibly linked to the conscious community of workers producing them.

In the early automobile industry (Gartman 1994: 15–38), for example, the various parts were produced by skilled workers in separate firms, then assembled into vehicles by skilled mechanics in assembly plants. The separate parts were often the highest expression of their respective handicrafts, but these early autos generally failed to achieve a cohesive look because the workers could not coordinate their efforts between firms. The fragmented appearance of these early cars testified to the irrational market mechanism, which brought together a mélange of separately produced parts that were fitted together with little concern for appearance. But under competitive pressure to offer cheaper and more reliable products, manufacturers vertically integrated, bringing together under one roof the diverse craft-workers, who could now consciously coordinate their efforts to produce a cohesive design. From this coordinated craft labor process came the beautiful luxury automobiles consumed by the wealthy as a conspicuous display of their leisure and wealth. Just like the clothes of feudal nobles, these cars testified to the appropriation of the labor of a conscious community of craft-workers which unified work.

The dynamics of capitalism ensured, however, that capitalists would not remain content with the craft process and products, for these high-priced handicrafts had limited markets that restricted the growth and profits of firms. To overcome this problem, many capitalists turned to the mass production of cheap goods for a wider market. But one substantial obstacle stood in their way—the power of skilled workers, who used their considerable control over production to thwart capitalist efforts to quicken and cheapen their labor. This class conflict motivated capitalists to revolutionize the craft labor process in order to seize control of production. By dividing and mechanizing labor, they wrested the control of the details of the labor process out of the hands of recalcitrant craft-workers. Consequently, the production process became increasingly alienated or reified. The organic community of workers that once consciously unified planning and execution was fragmented into a conglomerate of detail jobs planned and unified from the outside by the objective logic of capital (Braverman 1974; Montgomery 1979; Clawson 1980). This reified labor process also transformed the products produced in it, for they lost their connection to human labor and began to appear as the inevitable results of objective laws of work organization.

The American auto industry, the innovator in mass-production, illustrates the transformation of material products that accompanied this new labor process. In order to eliminate recalcitrant skilled workers, auto capitalists like Henry Ford simplified and standardized designs to allow their production by divided and mechanized labor. Like other mass-produced autos, Ford's sole model, the Model T, replaced the flowing curves of the craft-built cars, which required skilled handwork, with square lines, which allowed body parts to be quickly stamped out on presses and assembled by unskilled workers. The T also replaced the early cars' rainbow of lustrous finishes, requiring days of skilled painting and polishing, with a mono-chrome coating of black enamel, which could be mechanically dipped and dried in a matter of minutes (Gartman 1986: 64–66). But by eliminating the skill from auto work in these and others ways, capitalists sacrificed the unity and integrity of the craft-built vehicles. Because the conception of work was now centralized by capital, workers found it impossible to integrate the separate tasks into a cohesive whole. In these autos and other mass-produced commodities, the imperative to increase exchange value by overcoming the power of craftworkers thus extended the capitalist logic of reification from production to the use value of products themselves. The products, just like the production process, became alien things to humans, for they no longer participated in their design.

At this stage of capitalist development, however, these commodities had not yet developed one crucial aspect of reification. The human relations embodied in products had become alien and inhuman, but these relations had not yet been obscured by their appearance as natural relations between things. These early mass-produced products clearly revealed the human relations of inhuman work, bearing the indelible birthmarks of alien-ated labor on their faces. The fragmented and disjointed appearance of these early mass-produced cars, for example, bore visual testimony to the divided, unskilled, and mechanized labor process that produced them. And their monotonous black color spoke of a rigidly controlled process that pro-hibited human variety and choice. In order for people to see their produc-tion relations as totally reified, as totally natural and inevitable—"that's just the way it is"—their things had to hide any marks of inhuman produc-tion. These things had to reflect, or at least appear to reflect, consumers' unique nature as human beings, their natural attributes as conscious crea-tures who voluntarily control their own actions and relations. At this stage of capitalism, however, commodities did not seem to consumers as natural reflections of their own conscious efforts and abilities. They appeared as denials of their natural traits as free and conscious human beings, and tes-tified to relations of coercion and unthinking obedience. For the products of mass production to appear to humans as reified, as natural, they had to hide these unnatural, alien traits and present themselves as fulfilling human needs and nature. In other words, these mass-produced commodities had to be humanized.

This imperative to erase the marks of divided and coercive labor in mass-produced products was articulated by design critics of the day. For example, William Dyce, a nineteenth-century British critic of industrial design wrote of early mass-produced goods: "We all are sensible, and we cannot help being so, that mechanical contrivances are like skeletons without skin, like birds without feathers—pieces of organization, in short, without the ingredient which renders natural productions objects of pleasure to the senses" (quoted in Heskett 1980: 21–23). These early designs adapted to mass production were not pleasurable to human senses precisely because they were associated with the inhuman work that produced them: "A plain, functional form generally signified the often harsh necessities of work . . ." (Heskett 1980: 49). And these harsh necessities included the class inequalities generated by this work. These early mass-produced goods appeared harsh, naked, and alien *in comparison to* the handicrafted luxury goods still produced by a skilled labor process for the privileged classes. The existence of such distinctly different products side by side served to display rather than conceal the hierarchical relations of production, contributing to and reinforcing the class antagonisms emerging in the workplace.

Early automobiles, for example, aroused class hostilities due to their association with the leisure of the rich. Working-class youth often launched stone-throwing attacks on wealthy motorists in cities (Flink 1970: 65–66). And in 1906 Woodrow Wilson worried that automobiles would stimulate socialism by fueling class envy of their wealthy owners (Gartman 1994: 15). The automobile did not cease to serve as a reminder of class differences when mass production allowed ownership to spread to the lower classes. When compared to the handicrafted luxury cars of the highest class, the fragmented and homogeneous mass-produced cars symbolized their owners' degraded class positions. Testifying to the class envy and anger created by these automotive differences were jokes and songs that either ridiculed the cheapness of mass-produced cars, or asserted their ultimate equality to the craft-built luxury makes (Gartman 1994: 53–61). During this early period, cars thus revealed rather than concealed the exploitative human relations of their production.

CLASS CONFLICT AND THE RISE OF
THE REALM OF CONSUMPTION

The visible link of early mass-produced commodities to the inhuman labor process was not problematic at first, but presented itself as such only with the emergence of renewed class conflict produced by this work process. Workers fought the reduction of their labor to an abstract, unskilled, powerless commodity with turnover, output restriction, and union organization. As both Marx and Lukács anticipated, the socialization of the labor process made workers aware of their own collective power behind the capitalist organization of work, and they began to struggle to assert their control over production (Montgomery 1979; Gartman 1986). Capitalists fought back to contain this struggle, and in the process struck on a strategy that ultimately resulted in the completion of the process of product reification. This strategy entailed the displacement of worker demands for human needs from the production process to the realm of consumption. Capitalists gradually discovered that workers could be persuaded to accept substitute satisfactions for needs denied at work, such as self-determination, individuality, and fellowship, in the products that they consumed at leisure. They began in a gradual, uncoordinated way to create a separate realm of consumption centered on the nuclear family and home, which they sought to insulate from the inhumanity of alienated production (Ewen 1976).

The auto industry, especially the Ford Motor Company, also played a leading role in pioneering this realm of mass consumption to compensate for the deprivations of the realm of mass production it created. In the face of unprecedented revolt against the new production methods, Ford offered concessions in the form of increased wages and consumption. Its Five Dollar Day program of 1914 offered workers an unprecedented standard of living, but also molded a new leisure culture that compensated for continued workplace repression. Ford's Sociological Department dispatched investigators to workers' homes to ensure that they spent their new wage in ways that created a disciplined and responsible world of consumption that supported the disciplined, demanding work of their Fordist jobs. Through a combination of cajoling and coercion, Ford created a realm of worker consumption situated in the privatized nuclear family housed in a single-family home and characterized by individualism, dependability, and subservience (Gartman 1986: 2201–32; Meyer 1981).

The auto industry not only pioneered this separate realm of consumption, but also furnished the product that occupied the central place in this realm. From its inception the automobile was seen as a remedy for the ills of work. As early as 1903 one popular journalist promoted motoring as a panacea for workplace problems, declaring that "it will renew the life and youth of the overworked man or woman" (quoted in Flink 1970: 106). Another presciently anticipated the auto as a means of escape, "bringing with it a relief from city life . . . opening up the country for modest homes, to which city workers may daily escape" (quoted in Flink 1970: 108–9).

The importance of the automobile as a palliative to work grew as mechanization brought workers detailed, deskilled drudgery. Robert and Helen Lynd observed in *Middletown*, their ethnography of Muncie, Indiana, that the centrality of autos in workers' leisure lives was directly correlated to the loss of meaning and satisfaction in their work lives. To the deskilled worker, they wrote, the auto "gives the status which his job increasingly denies, and, more than any other possession or facility to which he has access, it symbolizes living, having a good time, the thing that keeps you working" (Lynd and Lynd 1929: 245). This key consumer product defused worker discontent by channeling it away from collective organization and into individual consumption. One 1924 ad for Chevrolet rejoiced, for example, that the American worker who owned a house and a car had actually changed classes. "The once poor laborer and mechanic now drives to the building operation or construction job in his own car. He is now a capitalist . . . How can Bolshevism flourish in a motorized country having a standard of living, and thinking too high to permit the existence of an ignorant, narrow, peasant majority?" (Stern and Stern 1978: 21).

The creation of a distinct realm of consumption, in which the auto occupied the central position, found favor with capitalists not only because it compensated for worker needs frustrated in the workplace but also because it solved the problem of market demand associated with the new process of mass production. The unprecedented productivity of this labor process quickly ran up against the barrier of market saturation. The unintended consequence of the increased wages that capitalists were forced to concede to workers was the expansion of demand for mass-produced goods. And the attempt to offer ersatz satisfactions for the real needs denied in the alienated labor process created new markets for consumer goods, thus easing capitalist competition for limited markets (O'Connor 1984).

THE REIFICATION OF CONSUMER PRODUCTS: OBSCURING ALIENATED PRODUCTION

The visible marks of the fragmented, alienated production process born by early mass-produced products constituted an obstacle to this strategy to displace worker demands. These products were constant reminders in the realm of consumption of the degradation of work in the realm of production. In order to construct a separate realm of consumption to compensate for alienated work, capitalists had to hide the relations of production visible in consumer products. What were in reality human relations had to appear as natural and inevitable relations, so as to block remembrance of the oppressive production process. Or as the Barthes might state it, these products had to be converted from signs, bearing testimony to the human historical action that made them, into myths, whose natural appearance blocked remembrance that they were human products and thus could be changed.

At first the capitalist offensive to seal over the gap between human needs and their inhuman products took place in the realm of ideas alone. Instead of changing the products, ideologists tried to persuade consumers that their forms were the result of natural aesthetic laws, not human production processes. This was the social purpose behind the attempts of modern artists, such as purists, functionalists, and constructivists, to introduce a machine aesthetic early in the twentieth century. They made aesthetic virtues out of the vices of mass-production, such as rectilinearity, standardization, fragmentation, and frugality, by consciously introducing these characteristics into their art and architecture. They portrayed the dehumanizing *social* imperatives of the work process that dictated these forms as universal, natural laws of economy and function that determined the evolution of products suited to human needs. As the modern architect Le Corbusier (1986: 102) stated: "The creations of mechanical technique are organisms tending to a pure functioning, and obey the same evolutionary laws as those objects in nature which excite our admiration. There is harmony in the performances which come from the workshop or the factory." Writing in the revolutionary period after the First World War, Le Corbusier made it clear that it was social urgency, not just artistic trendiness, that demanded the acceptance of mechanical forms in a new consumer society. He recognized that mass production had in many respects thrown society "out of gear" so "the human animal stands breathless and panting before the tool that he cannot take hold of; progress appears to him as hateful as it is praiseworthy" (1986: 271). Humans needed diversion and relaxation from their demanding labor in a new, home-based mass culture, wrote Le Corbusier, which could be provided by architects and designers. Then he ominously concluded: "It is a question of building which is at the root of the social unrest to-day: architecture or revolution" (1986: 269).

Modernists like Le Corbusier were correct to see a domestic realm of mass consumption as a palliative for impending revolution driven by mass-production discontents. But they were mistaken to believe that such a realm could be constructed with the unaltered mechanical forms of mass-produced goods. Unlike bourgeois artists and architects, working-class people with an intimate knowledge of mass production could not be convinced that its products were beautiful. As one design historian notes, for them "a plain, functional form generally signified the often harsh necessities of work, and as such was tolerated in its place, but art, in the form of decoration and ornament, represented for many people a deep aspiration for a better life" (Heskett 1980: 49). In order to sell their products and ensure that the aspirations of workers for a better life were confined to consumption, manufacturers thus had to obscure their connection to the alienated labor process. They accomplished this superficially at first, with the application of elaborate external ornament, reminiscent of handicrafted goods, to mass-produced goods. For example, mass-produced Remington typewriters and Singer sewing machines had their black-enamel cases decorated with stenciled floral patterns, which not only concealed defects but also distracted from the mechanical look with organic forms that were more acceptable in domestic settings (Pulos 1983: 145–57; Heskett 1980: 56–57).

As the twentieth century progressed, however, industrial designers became more sophisticated in obscuring the alienating social relations of production by making products look natural. They progressed from applying distracting ornamentation to the surface of products to molding the entire form to erase the traces of mass production. Giving a manufactured product the look of a natural thing was often accomplished by enclosing the mechanism in a casing or shell. A smooth exterior shell conferred on the fragmented parts beneath the appearance of unity and integration, which could be achieved in reality only by reorganizing the labor process. And once the unpleasant reality of production relations was concealed, capitalists could mold and embellish the shell in forms that offered ersatz satisfactions for needs denied by those relations, thus postponing the struggle for change.

The American auto industry played a leading role in pioneering these unified, shrouded designs—known as streamlining—because it also pioneered the mass-production process whose problems it addressed. Despite the higher wages conceded to its contentious workers, the industry faced stagnant market demand by the mid-1920s. The once-large market of first-time auto buyers had been almost exhausted by prices lowered by mass production. In order to compete in this tight market it was no longer sufficient to offer merely basic transportation, as evidenced by the decline of Model T sales. New needs had to be mobilized to stimulate sales, needs that were denied by the labor process that the industry created, like freedom and individuality. But to offer such ersatz satisfactions automakers first had to obliterate any signs of the production process that blocked their real fulfillment. Streamlining emerged in the late 1920s to accomplish this task. This aesthetic trend gave cars a more "unified appearance," in the words of General Motors' Alfred Sloan (1972: 313), by carefully sealing over the discontinuities of fragmented production. "The body was extended in all directions in an attempt to cover some of the ugly projections and exposed parts of the chassis which were still in evidence" (Sloan 1972: 319). Over the same period the angles of the body became less sharp, as a gentle curvilinear form replaced the harsh rectilinear one, giving the automobile the appearance of a natural organism rather than a mechanical assemblage of parts. Such integrated, organic forms had long been the class-distinctive mark of luxury cars, which were crafted in a unified labor process in which skilled workers organized their own labor. The attempts of mass producers to superficially copy these forms thus also concealed the class differences to which these different styles bore witness (MacMinn 1984; Gartman 1994: 100–35).

This streamlining of automobiles and other transportation machines was often justified technically as an attempt to attain efficiency by reducing air resistance. But aerodynamic efficiency seems to have been the decisive factor only in aircraft, whose high speeds made air resistance a problem. On autos, streamlining was motivated more by style than efficiency. GM's president Alfred Sloan recognized this when he wrote to stockholders that the corporation's 1935 models reflected streamlined design even though "the contribution of streamlining is definitely limited to the question of styling" (quoted in Meikle 1979: 151). The definitive proof of this statement was provided during the 1930s, when many consumer products that did not move through a resistant medium were redesigned in streamlined style. In 1932 Henry Dreyfuss "streamlined" the Sears Toperator washing machine by integrating the previously separate tub and motor with a smooth sheet-metal shell. And in 1933 Norman Bel Geddes designed a stove for Standard Gas with a sleek sheet-metal casing that extended all the way to the floor and contained panels to cover burners and controls when not in use (Meikle 1979; Heskett 1980).

The popularity of streamlining was due in part to the association in the public mind between these sleek designs and progress. Streamlining had originated of necessity in the most advanced transportation technology—the airplane—and its spread to other products was an attempt to capitalize on its promise of progress. But people also perceived these shrouded designs as modern and progressive because they obscured the fragmented appearance of the alienated mass-production process. As designer Paul Frankl wrote: "Simple lines . . . tend to cover up the complexity of the machine age. If they do not do this, they at least divert our attention and allow us to feel ourselves master of the machine" (quoted in Meikle 1979: 153). This need to hide the complexities and alienation of the machine was particularly pressing during the Great Depression, which exacerbated the two forces that drove the reification of consumer products from the beginning—capitalist competition and class conflict. During this severe overproduction crisis many capitalists looked to new product designs to stimulate demand and alleviate competition. Further, rising unemployment and falling wages during this period dealt a crushing blow to the promise that ever-expanding consumption could compensate for the inhumanities of mass production. The alienating nature of this labor process stood unconcealed in the forms of speed-up, wage cuts, and lay-offs, and as a consequence class conflict escalated. Now, more than ever, the angular, fragmented products of mass production symbolized the repressive social relations of capitalism, preventing the increased sales of consumer goods that would solve the problems of underconsumption and class conflict. So capitalists were more than ever motivated to seal over these reminders of workplace alienation in products, and streamlining was the result.

THE ERSATZ SATISFACTIONS OF REIFIED CONSUMPTION

Once the enveloping shrouds of streamlining had obliterated the products' connections to the labor process, capitalists could manipulate designs to offer ersatz satisfactions for any number of needs denied by it. One of these was the need for progress or mobility. The rigid hierarchy of classes consolidated by the mass-production process allowed little movement between positions, thus denying the open, free mobility of individuals in the market that was an ideological bulwark of capitalism. But with the class hierarchy of production obscured by reified product design, it was possible for consumption to offer substitute mobility in a product hierarchy of consumer goods. Product hierarchies emerged in the mid-1920s, as each company began to offer a range of autos covering the entire market, from the inexpensive to the luxurious. At first based on mechanical differences, the distinctions between autos in these hierarchies became increasingly aesthetic, based largely on body embellishments and interior appointments tacked onto the same mass-produced components (Sloan 1972: 171–93; Rothschild 1974: 26–53). But consumers were induced by these invidious distinctions to move up the product hierarchies, thus experiencing an illusory sense of upward mobility in their lives. Auto ads of the era stressed the equation of social status with the possession of the right model, with the more expensive cars shown in front of fine estates crawling with servants. But the association was always between the auto and a standard of *consumption*, with all mention of owners' actual class standing, or position in *production*, carefully avoided. The seemingly fluid hierarchy of consumer lifestyles constituted by auto models diverted attention from the rigidity of the underlying class structure (Gartman 1994: 68–99).

The annual model change was a similar policy launched by the industry in the mid-1920s to create an ideological sense of not merely individual but social progress as well. Each year manufacturers introduced largely superficial, cosmetic "improvements" in each model—more chrome, different grilles, changed color schemes. The purpose of such planned obsolescence was to stimulate new sales by making consumers dissatisfied with the "old" models (Sloan 1972: 275–85; Rothschild 1974: 26–53). What is less recognized is that such policies also cultivated an ideology of technological fetishism or futurism. By offering regular incremental changes in automotive "technology," automakers created a vision of history as autonomous technological progress ushering in a future of prosperity for all. This ideology soared during the Depression, when the promise of an inevitable utopia created by technology compensated for the breakdown of social progress. One ad, for example, touted the 1935 Ford V-8 as "A Thoroughly Modern Car." "More and more, with each passing year, it becomes the symbol of progress and the newest, latest developments in automotive building. The Ford goes forward with the needs of the people" (Stern and Stern 1978: 33). This ideology of futurism was part of the larger phenomenon of reification, for it obscured the extent to which history is shaped by human struggles behind a vision of an inevitable future realized by technological progress.

This reified ideology of progress fundamentally shaped the design of consumer products. During the Depression designers began to borrow the look of the most advanced technology, especially the airplane, to lend other products like cars a sense of progress. Such borrowing rapidly escalated after the war, with designers plundering airplanes and rockets for design elements in order to convey a jet-age image not only of progress but also escape. The early promise of the automobile as a means of escape from the ills of the congested industrial city approached fulfillment in the postwar period. Government mortgage subsidies allowed American workers to flee en masse to the suburbs, where the auto became indispensable to the world of consumption they created there to compensate for the world of mass production. Consequently, auto designers began to build into automotive sheet metal connotations of escape by borrowing from the new world of flight.

One of the pioneers of adapting aircraft elements to auto design was Harley Earl, the head of General Motors' styling department. Describing his design philosophy, Earl once stated: "You can design a car so that every time you get in it, it's a relief—you have a little vacation for a while" (quoted in Sloan 1972: 324). During the 1950s Earl seemed intent on providing drivers with relief from alienated work by turning autos into earth-bound airplanes that conjured up fantasies of freedom, escape, and progress. And the whole industry was pulled along in his slipstream. Earl introduced the tail fin on the 1948 Cadillac, and modeled it on the vertical stabilizers of the twin- fuselage P-38 fighter plane. The fin grew and spread until the late 1950s, at which time nearly all American cars possessed soaring protrusions on their rear fenders. Other aircraft elements followed in the wake of the fin's success: gun ports, jet intakes and exhausts, propeller spinners, and curved windshields. Even auto interiors were filled with aircraft-style gauges, scopes, throw levers, and damascened panels. And to ensure that this imagery did not escape consumer attention, manufacturers used flight-inspired model names, such as Nash Airflyte, DeSoto Fireflite, Buick Airborn B-58, Aero Willys, and Oldsmobile Rocket 88. The drivers of such image-laden dream machines could thus be assuaged with fantasies of progress and freedom as they crawled along congested, smog-choked freeways toward their suburban retreats from alienated office and factory jobs (Bayley 1983; Earl 1954; Stern and Stern 1978: 74–75).

This ideology of technological progress and futurism was further reinforced by the auto manufacturers' policy during this period of building and displaying experimental "dream cars." Such cars were intended to gauge public reaction to possible design changes, but they also cultivated the notion that history is determined by laws of technological progress that are inexorable, but can be anticipated and accelerated by human effort. Thus, Harley Earl's first dream car for General Motors, the 1937 Y-Job, was promoted by the corporation as having "made possible better looking, more advanced cars produced years ahead of the time they would appear in normal evolution" (quoted in Bayley 1983: 55). Earl set the pace for postwar aeronautical designs with his second dream car, the Le Sabre XP-8, which was modeled after the F-86 Le Sabre fighter jet. The display of this car aroused so much public attention that GM president Sloan decided to launch an annual tour of new production and dream cars called the Motorama. Both Chrysler and Ford produced their own prototype cars, hoping to similarly tap consumer psyches with sheet-metal simulations of progress. Ford's dream cars were largely non-functional, and incorporated the pretense of such futuristic features as gyro-stabilizers, video displays, push-button steering, and compact nuclear propulsion devices. So in the process of marketing cars, the corporations also sold the future, convincing consumers that progress toward a technical utopia was inexorable and precluded the social conflicts of the past (MacMinn 1984; Gartman 1994: 157–60).

The basic logic of reification and displacement of desires would remain the foundation of consumer products, for the continuing problems of capitalist competition and class conflict created new contradictions that had to be resolved by consumer culture. Yet these solutions still required obfuscation of the relations of production and displacement of needs into the realm of consumption. In the 1960s, for example, the auto industry gradually abandoned the homogeneous flight fantasies of the 1950s to offer a greater range of styles targeted at specific lifestyles. Although this market diversification was made possible by growing incomes, which allowed families to buy multiple cars, its underlying cause was the emergence of social discontents with the standardized consumer culture that ignored the need for individual expression. For American youth in particular, this boring mass culture did not seem like sufficient compensation for the sacrifices made in bureaucratic universities training for bureaucratic business jobs. And during this period all Americans became aware of the escalating costs of the auto-driven consumer culture—environmental pollution, traffic gridlock, car accidents and deaths, and the waste and destruction of auto-driven development. Although some young people during this period attacked the real causes of these problems in the system of Fordist mass production, many merely embraced new, more individualized products—acid rock, Volkswagens, love beads, and Levis. Seeing this demand for more expressive and individual products, automakers responded with a plethora of new types of cars aimed at specific markets—sport and performance cars for the young, efficient compacts for the ecologically conscious, station wagons for suburban moms, personal luxury cars for commuting dads.

CONCLUSION

The 1960s rebellions were, however, once again largely contained within the limits of consumerism, leaving untouched the foundation of capitalist mass production. Its standardized, alienated relations of production, which turn humans into things in the service of others' goals, continued to be hidden behind a façade of products that seemed to address consumers' particular and individual needs. Yet this period also reveals that reification is a continually evolving process, which must be renewed and modified to address ever-shifting contradictions in production and consumption. Like the capitalist economy that gives birth to this imperative, the work of reification is never done, but must constantly find innovative forms to hide from its victims.

3 Culture as Class Symbolization or Mass Reification?
A Critique of Bourdieu's *Distinction*

The work of Pierre Bourdieu, perhaps the most influential analyst of culture in contemporary sociology, shares many of the assumptions and intentions of the Frankfurt School's reification theory. First, Bourdieu's theory also has a critical intent—it aims not merely to understand society but also to criticize and change it. Both theories recognize the injustice of class stratification in modern society and seek to eliminate or lessen it. Second, Bourdieu shares with the Frankfurt School the notion that culture legitimates or justifies this unjust system. The two theories differ, however, in postulating different mechanisms of cultural legitimation. Following Marx, the Frankfurt School holds that consumption of similar cultural goods across the class spectrum hides the real differences in power and wealth, thus making a hierarchical society seem leveled and democratic. By contrast, Bourdieu, following Weber, argues that the consumption of different cultural goods by different classes symbolizes their differences in power and wealth, and legitimates them by making the members of some classes seem individually superior to others.

Bourdieu's theory is presented in its most developed form in *Distinction*, which is superior to the earlier Frankfurt theory of reification in several respects. While the analysis of mass culture by Horkheimer, Adorno, and others is most often abstract and philosophical, Bourdieu's analysis of cultural taste is painstaking empirical, drawing on surfeits of survey data. And while the Frankfurt School paints impassioned portraits of cultural conspiracies, the French sociologist offers a cool blueprint of a structure of class and culture whose logic produces its effects behind the backs of individuals. But Bourdieu's objective, structuralist analysis of class and culture has its own gaps and weaknesses. First, he does not confront but ignores the Marxist theory of culture as reification, substituting for it a Veblenesque concept of culture as class symbols in a game of invidious distinction. And more important still, Bourdieu abandons any notion of people as agents engaged in actions capable of changing as well as reproducing the class system. He discounts any real agency in favor of a determinant class structure that is internalized in individuals and dictates cultural choices that automatically reproduce that structure.

In the following, I criticize Bourdieu's theory of culture for these two critical weaknesses. First, I argue that Bourdieu over-generalizes his model of class symbols in a game of distinction. Although such a Veblenesque conception may be valid for the nonmaterial culture of late capitalist society, the material culture more closely conforms to the Frankfurt School's notion of mass reification. Bourdieu ignores the leveling of material culture because his theory is largely ahistorical, failing to grasp the specificity of the culture of capitalism and its changing relations of production. But the Frankfurt thinkers conversely ignore the continued existence of class distinctions in nonmaterial culture because, while they recognize the effects of changing class relations on culture, they fail to specify the historically concrete factors that mediate these effects.

Second, I show that Bourdieu's failure to grasp the reification of material culture is grounded in a more fundamental flaw—a structuralist conception of culture that reduces cultural choices to passive reproduction of structural necessities. The Frankfurt School offers a more dialectical conception of culture as human praxis to realize needs that may transform as well as reproduce class structure. But critical theory fails to specify the concrete historical conditions under which this praxis becomes either reproductive or transformative. I conclude that both theories may be incorporated into a broader neo-Marxist theory of class legitimation that grounds the effects of class on culture in historical class conflict.

My critique of Bourdieu's theory of culture in this chapter is based on his works published before 1989. As I argue in Chapter 7, however, after this date Bourdieu's theory begins to change in ways that mark a convergence with the reification theory of the Frankfurt School. In his later works, which coincide with a period of escalating political engagement, Bourdieu recognizes and becomes critical of the leveling effect of mass culture in contemporary society, and argues that a critical, progressive culture may only emerge in the autonomous high culture that he previously criticized as protecting the privileges of the dominant class. Both these positions converge with the Frankfurt School's theory of culture. Further, unlike the cultural relativism of his early work, which holds that judgments of different cultures are impossible, his later work postulates, with the Frankfurt School, that certain cultural universals provide the grounds for privileging the high culture of autonomous intellectuals over the pecuniary mass culture. Finally, departing from the pessimistic structural determinism of the early period, the later Bourdieu clearly envisions possibilities for conscious action to disrupt the structure's reproduction and create change, setting him apart from the pessimism about social change embodied in Frankfurt School concepts like "one-dimensional man" and the "totally administered society." Thus, many of my criticisms below are successfully addressed by these revisions in Bourdieu's early theory of culture.

BOURDIEU'S THEORY OF CULTURE AS A
REPRODUCING STRUCTURE OF CLASS SYMBOLS

Distinction is the culmination of Bourdieu's project to reintegrate the realm of culture into the sociology of stratification and class. Here he seeks to reveal the indispensable contribution that the consumption of symbolic goods makes to reproducing class domination through legitimation and selection. For Bourdieu, self-interested behavior cannot be confined to the economic realm alone but must be theoretically generalized to cultural practice also. People pursue scarce goods and maximize their profits not only in economic "fields" of contest but also in cultural fields. As in economic struggles, people in cultural contests employ "capital" resources that they have acquired or inherited in their efforts to maximize their "profits." But in cultural fields of struggle these resources are "cultural capital"— symbolic abilities, tastes, and goods—and the returns are "symbolic profits," dividends of social honor or prestige (Bourdieu 1977: 177–83).

Bourdieu's formulation is similar to Weber's multidimensional conflict theory, with its separate but interpenetrating struggles of class, status, and power. Bourdieu acknowledges his general debt to Weber but distances himself from his specific formulations, stating that *Distinction* is "an endeavor to rethink Max Weber's opposition between class and *Stand*" (Bourdieu 1984: xii). In his historicist and nominalist framework, Weber postulates no universal relation between these two dimensions of stratification. Status, defined by lifestyle, may coincide with class, writes Weber (1968: 932), but the two normally stand in "sharp opposition." In his search for a general theory applicable to all societies, Bourdieu postulates an invariant relation of structural determination between economic position and cultural lifestyle. For him, classes always appear as status groups, whose culturally stratified tastes and goods legitimate the system of economic domination by presenting it in a misrecognized form. Naked acts of class interest are clothed with the mantle of the selfless pursuit of commonly recognized symbolic goods, making winners appear not as exploiters but as gifted individuals with superior cultural endowment (Bourdieu 1977: 163–65).

Bourdieu argues that the structure of economic positions is translated into and misrecognized as cultural symbols and lifestyles inherent in individuals through the mediating structure of habitus. The habitus is a system of durable dispositions that is socially conditioned by the objective structure of society. In the process of socialization, people in different class positions are exposed to different "material conditions of existence," which give rise to characteristic ways of perceiving and being in the world. This deeply rooted habitus gives rise to all specific tastes in food, clothing, art, and so on. The habitus is thus a generative structure that provides the unifying principle of the specific practices in different cultural fields. But it is a social structure—the class structure so deeply embodied in individual dispositions that they appear natural and obscure their social origins (Bourdieu 1977: 72–97).

The class structure of society becomes embodied in these habitus by determining the exposure of individuals to different material conditions of existence. Classes, Bourdieu states, are defined by different amounts and types of capital, both economic and cultural. Individuals with little capital are continually exposed to material scarcities and the consequent economic necessity of making a living, while those with greater capital share an objective distance from the material urgencies of life. The distance from economic necessity conditions different class habitus, which in turn generate different cultural tastes (Bourdieu 1984: 53–56, 169–75).

In *Distinction*, Bourdieu distinguishes three broad classes, each of which is unified by similar tastes and lifestyles: the bourgeoisie, the petite bourgeoisie, and the working class (peasants and industrial workers). The bourgeois class possesses a high volume of capital, which distances it from the economic necessities of life. These material conditions engender a "taste for freedom," a preference for cultural objects and practices that are removed from mundane material functions. This bourgeois taste determines an "aesthetic disposition," a propensity to stylize and formalize natural functions in order to lift them above mundane materiality and, in doing so, display distance from this realm of necessity (Bourdieu 1984: 18–63).

The bourgeois taste for freedom is defined in opposition to the working-class taste for necessity, which serves as a mere foil in the game of distinction. Having little capital, peasants and industrial workers must of necessity be concerned with the practicalities of material existence. But Bourdieu contends that this economic necessity becomes ingrained as a taste, an actual choice or preference for things that are functional, natural, unformalized, and sensual. Bourdieu paints workers as down-to-earth creatures who reduce practices to their functions and are unconcerned with games of distinction (Bourdieu 1984: 372–96).

Between these two main systems of class tastes is the petite bourgeoisie—those of moderate capital distinguished by their taste for pretension. The petite bourgeoisie aspires to bourgeois distinction but has neither the capital nor habitus to really achieve it. Hence, these pretenders seek to superficially adopt a lifestyle not their own, to become something they are not by borrowing the outward signs of legitimate culture (Bourdieu 1984: 318–71).

Bourdieu holds that the value society assigns each of these distinct class cultures is strictly arbitrary and determined solely by power. The dominant class is able to impose its lifestyle as the legitimate standard of judgment by sheer force or "symbolic violence" (Bourdieu and Passeron 1977: 4–8). But this arbitrary act of violence is hidden from view and thus accepted by the victims themselves. Consequently, those who possess the dominant culture have their power legitimated and reproduced. The economic power of their class is hidden behind a façade of individual cultural worthiness or giftedness, behind the "ideology of charisma."

As others have noted (Elster 1983; Miller 1987), Bourdieu's conception of culture is highly reminiscent of that offered in Veblen's *Theory of the Leisure Class*. Both Bourdieu and Veblen conceive of lifestyles as resources in a class contest for honor, which is won by the one displaying the greatest distance from economic necessity. Bourdieu uses Veblen's concept of "conspicuous consumption," arguing that the privileged display the abundance of their resources by ostentatious waste (Bourdieu 1984: 55, 281–82). And his analysis of education as cultural capital is anticipated by the last chapter of *Theory of the Leisure Class*, entitled "Higher Learning as an Expression of the Pecuniary Culture" (Veblen 1934: 363–400). But Bourdieu (1985; 1988–89) forcefully denies any similarity of his ideas to Veblen's theory. He argues that, unlike Veblen, he postulates no conscious, rational choice of goods in the pursuit of distinction. For him, cultural goods and practices are the product of the habitus, a practical sense that is not consciously formulated or chosen (Bourdieu 1988–89: 783). But their different emphases on intentionality should not disguise the similarity between their conceptions of culture. Both conceive of culture as necessarily oppressive, an inevitable support of the class system. Bourdieu thus shares what Adorno (1981b) calls Veblen's "attack on culture" as barbaric because of its involvement in class struggle.

CAPITALIST CULTURE AS MASS REIFICATION: THE CHALLENGE OF THE FRANKFURT SCHOOL

Distinction surprisingly ignores the cultural theory of the Frankfurt School, which offers a powerful challenge to the book's Veblenesque theory of class cultures. Although Frankfurt theorists like Theodor Adorno, Max Horkheimer, and Herbert Marcuse share Bourdieu's intent of integrating Weber's concern for cultural legitimation with Marx's class analysis, they offer a different theoretical solution—late capitalist culture legitimates classes by *obscuring* them altogether, rather than establishing a hierarchy of honor between them. Bourdieu contends that culture legitimates class by furthering a *misrecognition*. Symbolic behavior displays class differences, but in a form that diverts attention from their true origins in group power by making them appear as differences in individual worthiness. Frankfurt theorists, by contrast, argue that culture performs its ideological function for the class system by preventing any recognition of class differences, even a mistaken one. For them, culture makes classes *unrecognizable* by burying them beneath an indistinct mass culture shared by all.

The Frankfurt notion of class-obscuring mass culture is developed, as we saw in Chapter 1, from Marx's concept of reification in the capitalist economy (Marx 1967a: 71–83). He reveals that in capitalism the fundamental class relations between people appear as relations between things, commodities circulating in the market according to natural laws. Georg

Lukács (1971a) extends Marx's concept of reification to the cultural realm in *History and Class Consciousness*, arguing that capitalist culture legitimates exploitative class relations by hiding them behind unifying facades of nature. The Frankfurt School then applies Lukács's analysis of reified culture to modern consumer capitalism, in which the production of cultural goods is taken over by large, monopolistic industries whose sole motive is profits. Consequently, culture becomes a commodity, whose production and distribution is subordinated to the technological rationality of domination in the factory and marketplace. The culture industry subjects art, music, and literature to the standardization and homogenization of mass production in order to produce more profits. In the process, all critical distinctions and disturbing connotations are eradicated from cultural commodities, ensuring that they are palatable to the broadest possible market. This mass culture is offered to consumers as a substitute for the needs denied them in the degraded and alienated production process. Because all classes participate in this mass culture, although in unequal quantities, ostensible class differences are leveled by the consumption of its standardized commodities. Real qualitative differences in class power take on the appearance of merely quantitative differences in the possession of the same things (Horkheimer and Adorno 1972; Marcuse 1964; Adorno 1978).

Frankfurt School theorists thus argue that culture is ideological not because, as Bourdieu holds, it is "an expression of class standpoints" but because "the existence of classes is concealed by ideological appearances" (Adorno 1976: 68, 55). In his *Introduction to the Sociology of Music*, Adorno specifically criticizes the type of empirical research generated by Bourdieu's position, which seeks to associate specific cultural tastes with different class positions. "Inquiries into the social distributions and preferences of musical consumption tell us little about the class aspect" (1976: 56). Although here he is probably criticizing the empirical research of Paul Lazarsfled, in whose Princeton Radio Research Project he participated, it is almost as if Adorno were referring to Bourdieu when he ridicules this type of research as equating "pure science with knowing whether middle-income urban housewives between the ages of 35 and 40 would rather hear Mozart or Tchaikovsky, and how they differ in this point from a statistically comparable group of peasant women. If anything at all has been surveyed here it is strata defined as subjectively characterized units. They must not be confused with the class as a theoretical-objective concept" (1976: 56).

Adorno argues that the cultural preferences of these strata are actually created by the manipulative marketing strategies of the culture industry. In order to hawk more wares, corporations divide and subdivide markets by social variables, and then differentiate and stratify products to appeal to these market niches. But these product distinctions, which lend goods a pseudoindividuality to placate the need for real individuality denied in production, are in reality superficial differentiations of fundamentally similar goods. They do not correspond to but conceal class differences (Horkheimer and Adorno 1972: 121–24, 154–56).

The Frankfurt theorists hold that the differentiation offered consumers by the culture industry is superficial not only because its products are produced in a standardized production process but also because they are consumed in a standardized consumption process that cuts across all social categories. Bourdieu (1984: 100) sustains his theory of class cultures by holding that even when the same products are consumed by different classes they are appropriated and perceived differentially according to their respective habitus. By contrast, Frankfurt theorists support their theory of mass culture by arguing that even when different products are consumed by different classes they are appropriated similarly, thus leveling any cultural differences between classes. Bourdieu (1984: 588) offers what he thinks is a devastating criticism of Adorno's analysis of popular music by showing that legitimate music is also repetitive and passively consumed. But that is precisely the point of Adorno's (1978) critique of music produced by the culture industry. Despite the ostensible differences in content, both popular and classical music are consumed in the same fetishistic form, in which the popularity or market success of the composition is valued over its intrinsic worth as art. In material products like automobiles, consumption focuses not on the intrinsic quality of the mechanism but the fetish of the trademark, which testifies to the car's standing in the artificial prestige hierarchy. Such consumption offers people ersatz satisfaction of their unfulfilled needs and conceals the real differences in class power beneath a mass of artificiality differentiated commodities.

The Frankfurt School's theory of mass culture has been justly criticized for certain weaknesses. Bourdieu (1984: 386) correctly points out that critical theorists often commit the short-circuit fallacy—establishing a direct, unmediated link between economic structure and cultural practices. They do not make explicit how and why the reified, class-obscuring logic of capitalism infiltrates and dominates culture. Their implicit answers are rather functionalist and essentialist. The capitalist system requires a mass culture that hides class divisions to reproduce itself, so it emerges. This functionalism often degenerates into crude instrumentalism, in which omnipotent elites consciously manipulate culture to perpetrate the domination of the masses, who passively accept whatever is foisted on them (Kellner 1984–85; Miller 1987).

Despite these problems I think that critical theory's conception of a mass culture that obscures class differences is a powerful and indispensable tool for understanding the legitimating role of culture in late capitalism. But it should be conceptualized as a complement, not as an alternative, to Bourdieu's conception of a culture of class symbolization. Both theories capture part of the cultural reality of late capitalism but err in generalizing from this part to the cultural whole.

CLASS CULTURE OR MASS CULTURE: EMPIRICAL ARGUMENTS

There is good empirical evidence from a variety of sources to at least partially validate both Bourdieu's idea of culture as symbolizing class differences and the Frankfurt School's notion of a mass culture obscuring class differences. Although this evidence may seem at first contradictory or at least inconsistent, a close examination reveals that it is drawn from different parts of the culture of late capitalism. To bring the empirical data to bear on this debate, first we need to clarify the exact nature of the disagreement between the two theories. Both postulate differences of attitudes and outlooks between classes, and there is ample evidence that documents these subjective differences (for a summary, see Collins 1975: 67–87; 1988: 208–20). The two theories differ, however, on how and whether subjective class differences are objectified in cultural consumption and lifestyle. Bourdieu argues that class differences produce visible cultural differences in all fields, but because these differences are mistakenly perceived as originating in individual worthiness rather than class position, they end up legitimating the class system. The Frankfurt theorists contend that subjective class differences are obscured by the objective homogeneity of mass culture, which legitimates the class system by making its real differences invisible.

Bourdieu offers a great deal of empirical data from his and others' surveys that purport to reveal objective differences in cultural consumption between the classes. But upon close examination these data do not unequivocally support his broad generalizations. The evidence for class differences is systematically stronger in fields of nonmaterial culture like visual art, music, and literature than in fields of material culture like food, clothing, and furniture. Thus, for example, in the field of music, class is clearly and strongly associated with knowledge of and preference for legitimate or classical music. When asked which musical compositions they preferred, 1% of the working class chose the legitimate works, as opposed to about 30% of the upper class. And when asked to identify the composers of sixteen classical works, none of the manual or clerical workers but over 20% of the upper class named more than twelve (Bourdieu 1984: 15, 64). In the field of visual art, the upper class displayed its formal aesthetic by stating much more frequently than the working class (20% and 6%, respectively) that an object socially designated as meaningless, like a cabbage, could make a beautiful painting. The working class revealed its functionalist aesthetic by stating a greater preference than the upper class (88% compared to about 60%) for superficially pretty subjects like a sunset over the sea (Bourdieu 1984: 37–38).

Bourdieu's data in these fields are supported by other studies, which also found a positive correlation between class position and preference for and participation in the high arts (DiMaggio and Useem 1978a, 1978b, 1982; Blau 1986; Hughes and Peterson 1983; Gruenberg 1983). Research by Paul DiMaggio and his associates also seems to support Bourdieu's thesis that cultural capital in this area of high arts acts as a means of class selection and reproduction. They have demonstrated that interest in and familiarity with high arts is positively related to student grades, educational attainment, and the status of future spouses (DiMaggio 1982a; DiMaggio and Mohr 1985).

The data do not, however, seem sufficiently strong to support Bourdieu's contention that class lifestyles are sharply segmented and insular. There appear to be no rigid class boundaries between popular culture and high culture. Although the upper class clearly has more knowledge of and participation in high culture, research has also shown consistently that its members also participate in the popular culture, often at levels commensurate with the lower classes (DiMaggio and Useem 1978a; Wilensky 1964; Bennett et al. 2009). This has led Richard Peterson to coin the term "omnivores" to describe the upper class, and to argue that it is set apart from the lower classes not by a specific type of culture but by the broader range of cultures it incorporates into its repertoire (Peterson and Simkus 1992; Peterson and Kern 1996). Bourdieu's own data seem to reflect the existence of this mass culture, in which all classes participate, alongside the high culture dominated by the upper class. For example, although a much larger proportion of the upper class (20%) stated that a cabbage could make a beautiful painting than did the working class (5%), a majority in all classes stated that a sunset over the sea made a beautiful painting. And while the upper class expressed a greater preference for legitimate music than the working class, a substantial proportion of all classes expressed a preference for popular music (Bourdieu 1984: 64, 37–38).

The existence of a common, mass culture seems even more prominent in the area of material culture. While Bourdieu claims that class habitus dictate the consumption of different types of physical products, his data belie this generalization and indicate class differences significantly smaller than those revealed in nonmaterial culture. In the field of food, for example, Bourdieu claims that the working-class taste for necessity dictates foods that are fatty and heavy, while the bourgeois taste for freedom dictates lighter, leaner foods. Yet the data on the distribution of expenditures among the various food categories are surprisingly similar across classes. Manual workers spent on average 2.4% of their food budgets on fresh fruit, while senior executives spent 3.1%; on fats, workers 5.3%, executives 4.3%; on beef, 8.1% versus 9.8%; on fresh vegetables, 5.4% versus 5.5%; on cereals, 8.9% versus 7.5% (Bourdieu 1984: 181–82, 188–89). We are told that the working-class meal stresses informality and abundance, while the bourgeois meal stresses formality and ceremony. But the data presented reveal that differences between the classes are small. Even when entertaining, the majority in all classes preferred to offer guests a full meal rather than a buffet, liked their guests to dress casually rather than elegantly, and preferred for guests to choose their own places rather than designating places. And while working-class people answered more frequently than the middle or upper class that the most important aspect of spontaneous entertaining was having enough to eat (34%, 28%, and 26%, respectively), nearly an identical proportion of workers (33%) also answered that it was important that guests not be bored (Bourdieu 1984: 198–99).

In the field of domestic furnishings, Bourdieu tells the reader that the working-class taste for necessity is expressed in the preference for homes that are clean and practical, while the bourgeois taste for freedom imbues a preference for the studied and imaginative interior. The data reveal that higher occupational groups did describe the ideal domestic interior as "imaginative" and "studied" more often than the lower groups, who were more likely to mention "clean" and "practical" in their descriptions. But the adjectives most frequently used by nearly all groups, high and low, were "comfortable" and "cozy" (Bourdieu 1984: 247–48).

David Halle's (1984) ethnography of blue-collar workers lends credence to this notion that a mass culture shared by all classes and centered largely on material commodities exists alongside a high culture dominated by the upper class and focused on nonmaterial arts. In his study of chemical workers in one New Jersey refinery, he found that their distinctive position at work led to subjective attitudes and beliefs that were clearly different from while-collar employees. The blue-collar workers were generally dissatisfied with their work and resentful of their immediate bosses and corporate power in general. They held few aspirations for individual advancement but pinned their hopes for the future on collectively won gains in wages and benefits. So on the job Halle's workers saw themselves as "working men" and, with a certain amount of class consciousness, marked themselves off from white-collar employees and managers. But outside of work these subjective attitudes were not objectified in a distinctive class style of cultural consumption. These well-paid blue-collar workers led leisure lives rather similar to white-collar employees, for their overlapping incomes allowed them to purchase similar goods and services. Halle (1984: 294) concludes: "In modern America there are no 'working-class' cars, washing machines, video recorders, or even, with some exceptions concentrated on the young, styles of dress. In an urban department store or a suburban shopping mall, it is hard to know if a customer has a blue- or a while-collar occupation."

In the world of cultural consumption these chemical workers did not see themselves as a distinct group but as part of a broad "middle class" in a continuum of consumption that overlapped and blurred the class oppositions of work. In a study of similarly affluent manual workers in England, Goldthorpe et al. (1969: 147) also found that their privatized and materially abundant leisure lives caused them to view themselves as part of a large central class defined not by power or prestige but by income and material living standards. Coleman and Rainwater (1978: 24–33) similarly found that a majority of all Americans perceived the class system not as a rigidly delineated structure of power but as a complex, infinitely graded hierarchy of income and consumption. And positions in the imbricated hierarchy were legitimated by beliefs in differences not of natural giftedness or merit, as Bourdieu contends, but of effort and ambition (1978: 241).

In detailing the participation of blue-collar workers in a broad mass or "middle-class" culture, Halle lists mainly material commodities they shared with others. He found, however, that these chemical workers did feel distinct and inferior with respect to some forms of nonmaterial culture—namely, the high arts and education. Few of these workers had any interest in classical music, ballet, opera, or literature. And they felt uneasy and inadequate about their lack of formal education. Most described their experiences in school as humiliating and were openly hostile to the teachers who judged them as inadequate. The part of their education that many felt most uncomfortable with and hostile toward was the high arts. Thus, in the fields of high arts and education culture seems to mark out class distinctions, as Bourdieu contends. By doing so, it legitimates the class structure by making the lower classes feel inadequate, and reproduces it by selecting for educational success only those already inculcated with cultural capital (Halle 1984: 48–50, 130–32, 169–70, 208, 295).

The empirical evidence reviewed thus far reveals that both Bourdieu's theory of class symbolization and the Frankfurt School's theory of mass reification have validity, but for different aspects of the culture of late capitalist societies. Distinct differences do appear to exist in the consumption of nonmaterial culture, especially the high arts, which objectify and legitimate class positions. But in the realm of material commodities, there exists a qualitatively indistinct mass culture, which obscures class divisions behind a mass of material goods that distinguish individuals solely by the quantity of their income. My own study (Gartman 1994) of one prominent artifact of contemporary material culture, the automobile, further demonstrates the limits of Bourdieu's generalizations about class cultures.

Bourdieu (1984: 231) writes that consumer goods are produced in a variety of forms that express the distinct tastes of classes and class fractions because each group has it is own producers. The competitive struggle between producers in the marketplace leads each to produce a distinct product. And each supply finds a matching demand, both because producers and consumers come from the same class, and thus have similar habitus that dictate tastes, and also because producers' positions in the field of production—e.g. established versus outsider—are homologous to the class positions that consumers occupy in the field of consumption (Bourdieu 1984: 230–34; 1993b: 44–45; 1993d: 82–93).

But these generalizations do not seem true of the automobile, which Bourdieu uses to exemplify his theory (1984: 128–29, 278–79, 548–51). His theory assumes a highly competitive market in which numerous producers jockey to find consumers, but the market for American automobiles, like many other material commodities, is unquestionably oligopolistic. The handful of large corporations that dominate production do not specialize in one market niche but offer a wide range of products that blankets all markets, from the cheapest to the most expensive. And the different automobile models offered by each oligopolistic corporation cannot appeal to specific class tastes because they are all designed by the same designers. Typically, the automobile designers of a corporation are not responsible to one of its several model-producing divisions but are grouped in a staff department directly responsible to top corporate managers. Often working in a separate center geographically and organizationally removed from divisional managers, this design staff is responsible for the aesthetics of the entire range of corporate products, from the cheapest to the most expensive. Although there is usually a separate studio for each division, this separation exists not to create products that differ fundamentally in aesthetics to appeal to different class tastes but to superficially differentiate the few structural foundations from which all corporate cars are produced. The different automotive nameplates of each corporation generally share the same few body shells, which are given distinct divisional identities by the addition of largely superficial details, such as fenders, grilles, headlights, and taillights.

The empirical facts of automobile design reveal that these artificially differentiated models do not and cannot appeal to a variety of distinct class tastes. If this were the aim, design personnel would have to be rigidly specialized by division, spending their entire careers cultivating a specific class style. But in most corporations designers are juggled around constantly. And independent designers who contract with corporations also design a variety of automobiles across the entire price spectrum. In addition, my interviews with auto designers reveal that they do not apply different aesthetic standards to different lines of autos. They try to accomplish the same basic look in all lines. For example, economy cars, which generally sell to lower-income groups, are not designed specifically to appeal to the "functionalist aesthetic" that Bourdieu argues characterizes this group. Designers know that no one wants a car that looks cheap, that screams stripped-down functionality. So they attempt to make economy cars look as much like their expensive corporate relatives as is possible within the cost restraints given them and while maintaining the separate identities of the lines. The quantity of features and embellishments on the various makes in the automobile hierarchy are varied by designers to justify the price differences. But the quality of aesthetics is basically the same across the hierarchy, so the graded models cannot testify to distinct class tastes. More expensive cars offer those with more money to spend not qualitatively different aesthetics to testify to superior tastes but merely more of what everyone has a taste for (Gartman 1994).

Empirical evidence on automobiles and other artifacts of material culture is more compatible with the Frankfurt School's arguments that modern culture legitimates class by obscuring rather than symbolizing class differences. The qualitative hierarchy of class power is obscured by a quantitative hierarchy of material consumption in which people are differentiated by the income rewards of a seemingly equitable market. Hierarchies of material products like autos ideologically transform the *contradiction* of class power into a *continuum* of consumption, in which position is legitimated not by inborn taste but by individual market efforts, as surveys routinely reveal (Coleman and Rainwater 1978: 24–33, 241; Goldthorpe et al. 1969: 146–56).

HISTORY, CLASS, AND CULTURE

The empirical evidence shows that there is a partial truth to the theories of both Bourdieu and the Frankfurt School. While the material culture of consumer commodities in late capitalist society seems to obscure the differences between classes, the nonmaterial culture, especially the high arts, demonstrates distinct cleavages that symbolize classes. I believe the partial vision of each is explained by their respective approaches to historical development. Bourdieu's basically ahistorical theory projects onto capitalism a model of class and culture derived from a precapitalist past, and thus fails to capture the cultural dynamics introduced by the specific class relations of capitalism. The Frankfurt School's essentialist theory overgeneralizes the historical trends introduced into culture by capitalist commodity relations and thus fails to recognize the persistence of certain precapitalist cultural relations. I propose to correct both theories by a neo-Marxist approach to culture that focuses on the mediating factor of historical class struggle.

Bourdieu (1984: xii) asserts that the relationship between class and culture presented in *Distinction* is "valid . . . for every stratified society." He acknowledges some historical variation in modes of class domination and their legitimation. But his theory of historical development is a severely truncated, two-stage model in which the relation between class and culture changes only in form. Bourdieu distinguishes between precapitalist and capitalist society on the basis of the degree of objectification and autonomy of economic and cultural capital. In precapitalist society, economic and cultural resources are uninstitutionalized and undifferentiated from each other. Relations of economic domination are direct and personal, reproduced in daily interaction through the exercise of violence. To secure legitimation, the economic capital used to dominate others is continuously translated into and disguised as the cultural or symbolic capital of honor in personal ceremonies like potlatches and gift exchanges (Bourdieu 1977: 171–97).

With the coming of industrial capitalism, however, the market institutionalizes economic capital, making it objective and impersonal. Industrialization also renders cultural capital autonomous from economic capital. The increasing income and education of the common classes (bourgeoisie and proletarians) create a large, culture-consuming public and, consequently, frees cultural producers from dependence on aristocratic patrons.

Producers in this subfield of large-scale cultural production are motivated by economic profit to seek the largest possible market and hence reduce standards to the lowest common denominator. Alongside this subfield, however, emerges a separate cultural subfield of restricted production, where producers are motivated not by economic profit but by the symbolic profit or prestige of recognition by other cultural producers, gained by adherence to autonomous aesthetic standards. Bourdieu states that the emergence of this autonomous subfield of art results from the oversupply of artists crowding into the cultural field from bourgeois and working-class backgrounds, who can find no employment elsewhere. This large group of underemployed bohemian artists provides a market for the production of artists who cater not to the public at large but to other artists, thus creating autonomous art (Bourdieu 1996a: 47–140).

Bourdieu contends that in early capitalism there is no need for cultural legitimation of economic inequalities. The objective mechanism of the market itself hides these inequalities, so there is no need for a symbolic veil of misrecognition. But this early stage ends when, as Bourdieu vaguely states, the ideological effects of the market are uncovered and neutralized. Consequently, legitimation of class domination requires a return to cultural misrecongition of economic capital through its conversion into symbolic capital (Bourdieu 1977: 196). This misrecognition is accomplished by the bourgeois consumption of cultural products from the subfield of restricted production, to which their habitus naturally inclines them. Such consumption not only distinguishes the bourgeoisie from the working class but also consecrates it with the air of disinterestedness and personal worthiness that accompanies this cultural realm autonomous from the economic market (Bourdieu 1993b: 42–43, 55–57; 1993c: 119–20, 128–31). So after a brief separation of economic and cultural capital in early capitalism, once again the two are integrated in a system of legitimation in which class power is misrecognized as individual giftedness or charisma. Bourdieu's history of class ideologies is not really much of a history at all, but the story of an eternally occurring relation that changes only in form.

This essentially ahistorical formulation fails to recognize the historical specificity of the culture of capitalism and the relations of reproduction on which it is based. Bourdieu generalizes the peculiarly precapitalist ideology of charisma into capitalist society. Following Weber, he uses the concept to denote a system of beliefs that legitimates differences in power by reference to the intrinsic qualities of individuals displayed in distinctive lifestyles. But Weber confines charismatic authority mainly to precapitalist society, in which personal power relations require ideologies that justify the person as superior. He argues (1968: 241–54) that the rationalization process brings the impersonal rule of economic and political bureaucracies, in which authority is justified by the rationality of the structure, not the worthiness of individuals.

Bourdieu ignores this change in the nature of cultural legitimation largely due to his conceptualization of class, which rejects the Marxist emphasis on positions in production in favor of a Weberian emphasis on positions in the distribution of goods. He defines class as a structural position in a distributional space of two resources: economic capital and cultural capital. An individual's combined resources in these two fields determine his or her class position. In modern society, primary class differences are determined by the overall volume of combined capital, with secondary differences (class fractions) derived from the relative proportion of the two different capitals held (Bourdieu 1984: 99–125).

This definition of class, however, has a tautological relation to culture, the variable it is constructed to explain. Bourdieu explains variation in culture and lifestyle by class position, yet he defines class in part by the distribution of cultural capital. Since the latter is acquired through socialization in the family or school, the explanation degenerates into simplistic cultural transmission—classes have different lifestyles because they learn different lifestyles at home or in school. This argument begs the question of how these transmitted class lifestyles originate to begin with and ignores what is supposedly the intervening variable between class and lifestyle—habitus engendered by conditions of material existence.

Bourdieu sidesteps this tautological problem in places by giving subtle primacy to economic over cultural capital in determining lifestyle. He states in one passage (1977: 83), for example, that class habitus "are engendered by the objective structures, that is, in the last analysis, by the economic bases of the social formation in question." And in *Distinction* (1984: 115, 136), positions in the economic base are defined mainly in terms of income. For Bourdieu it is income from one's economic role, not the power or knowledge entailed by it, that asserts the predominant influence on culture, determining one's relative distance from economic necessity, that is, how preoccupied one is with securing the resources for material existence. So in the last analysis Bourdieu argues that income engenders habitus, which in turn determine cultural consumption (1984: 53–56, 375).

Bourdieu's analysis of class as position in economic *distribution* fails to capture the historical changes in economic *production* that condition culture. Because the distribution of resources remains similarly unequal across capitalist and precapitalist society, he postulates cultures that similarly symbolize this inequality. Marxism's focus on class as relations of production makes it potentially more cognizant of historical changes induced in culture. For Marxists, the distribution of market incomes in capitalism is epiphenomenal, the surface appearance determined by the relations between classes in production. At this level exists the more fundamental inequality of power to control the process of social labor.

The Frankfurt theorists of mass culture focus on this Marxist conception of class inequality to explain the historically variant forms of cultural legitimation. Following Marx (1967a: 77–78) and Lukács (1971a: 83–110), they argue that the relations of labor control in precapitalist society are direct and personal. Precapitalist culture bears the marks of these direct relations of subordination, for it is obviously the exclusive preserve of the dominant classes who alone have the power and resources to cultivate and appropriate nonessential goods. However, with the rise of capitalism the relations of power in production become indirect, with workers subordinated to capitalists through the impersonal exchange of labor power for wages. Thus, class relations become reified, appearing not as human power relations but as relations between things exchanged in the market. With Lukács, critical theorists argue that the reified relations of production are extended to culture as it becomes produced by large-scale, commercial enterprises. Mass production reduces the distinctions of cultural products, thus hiding the real differences in class power behind a façade of standardized things consumed by all.

While their historical focus on changing forms of class domination in production makes critical theorists more cognizant of changing forms of class legitimation, their use of history is flawed by its essentialism. Heavily influenced by Hegel, the Frankfurt School gives us a history of class and culture that reads like the unfolding of an essence inherent in capitalism. The concrete, mediating mechanisms that account for the spread of economic reification into the cultural realm, are not specified, as Bourdieu points out. This essentialist inattention to historical mediations leads critical theory to ignore the differential effects of reification on culture.

Bourdieu's ahistoricism leads him to postulate the persistence of a basically precapitalist culture of class symbolization, while the Frankfurt theorists' essentialism leads them to postulate the universal reification of all capitalist culture. A more powerful theory of class legitimation requires a historical model that recognizes the effects of changing class relations on culture but specifies the concrete mechanisms that explain their different effects. The corrective to both theories is a model of cultural legitimation in which historical human praxis—that is, class conflict—provides the crucial mediating link between class structure and cultural production.

CULTURE AS STRUCTURE OR CULTURE AS PRAXIS

Beneath Bourdieu's ahistorical analysis lies a more fundamental problem that prevents him from recognizing the partial reification of capitalist culture—his conceptualization of culture as a structure that inevitably reproduces social relations. Bourdieu's structuralist approach conceives of classes as the passive recipients of a culture that reproduces the structure of domination and carries little potential to transform it.

Bourdieu claims his theory offers a theoretical middle ground between structuralism and philosophies of action by specifying the conceptual link of habitus between objective structures and subjective actions. People chose their actions but not freely, for the dispositions internalized from their structural positions govern their choices (Bourdieu and Passeron 1977: 203–4, 217 n. 31). So Bourdieu's actors do not really act or choose anything— "these enacted choices imply no acts of choosing"—for their actions and choices are predetermined by their habitus (Bourdieu 1984: 474). Aesthetic tastes and consumer preferences are really determined by class position— people choose what they are already condemned to. "Taste is *amor fati*, the choice of destiny, but a forced choice, produced by conditions of existence which rule out all alternatives as mere daydreams and leave no choice but the taste for the necessary" (Bourdieu 1984: 178). Consequently, these tastes and the cultural practices they motivate inevitably and inexorably reproduce the structures that produce them.

There is contest and struggle in Bourdieu's theory. He postulates that people are incessantly, but not necessarily rationally, pursuing strategies to optimize the returns from their capital within a given field. But these struggles take place solely within the predetermined confines of the field and rarely challenge the rules of the game themselves (Di Maggio 1979: 1470). Class conflict in Bourdieu never seems to contradict or change the class structure because it is largely limited to intraclass struggle within the bourgeoisie. He confines his attention almost exclusively to the struggle for power between the dominant and the dominated fractions of the bourgeoisie and the struggle for symbolic capital within the latter fraction (Bourdieu 1993b: 37–45). This intraclass strife never fundamentally challenges the class structure of capitalism, since all bourgeois fractions have an interest in their joint domination of the working class.

Bourgeois struggles for symbolic capital within fields of restricted cultural production do often transform these fields and lead to changes in literature, education, and art. Historic shifts in the relative scarcity of resources within fields disrupt the equilibrium established between the objective opportunities for success within it and the subjective expectations (habitus) of individual participants. Such disruptions give rise to cultural struggles between established and parvenu cultural fractions that change a field. In *Homo Academicus* (1988), for example, Bourdieu argues that in the field of education the increase in the number of students and teachers in the 1960s caused a devaluation of their credentials on the job market. This, in turn, produced a discrepancy between the career expectations they internalized under the previous structure and the objective opportunities that credentials afforded in the changed structure of the field. The result of this discrepancy was the revolt in the universities culminating in May 1968.

Such challenges to established bourgeois cultural authorities often find resonance within the dominated class due to its homologous position of exclusion and domination. In the May 1968 revolt, for example, upstart students and teachers found temporary support among industrial workers, who were similarly degraded by established educational authorities.

However, the course of events usually reveals that bourgeois intellectual challengers have no interest in eliminating cultural authority per se, but merely securing a greater share for themselves. So interclass alliances ultimately dissolve, and temporary "breaks in equilibrium" are restored to the field as the transformed structure of opportunities is internalized in agents (Bourdieu 1988: 156, 167).

So, for Bourdieu, cultural changes are caused not by fundamental struggles between classes with inherently divergent interests but by shifts in resources between individuals and class fractions maneuvering in cultural markets to monopolize symbolic capital. He depicts the dominated class of capitalism as almost completely passive and powerless. Workers actually have a taste for the cultural practices and goods forced upon them by their subordinate class position. In contrast to the bourgeois taste for freedom, the working class has a taste for necessity, for undisguised objects and practices that do not seek to hide their relations to animal functions. Workers have so thoroughly internalized their own domination that they must rely on the symbolic tools supplied externally by bourgeois intellectuals to organize and express their interests. But because these tools are bourgeois in origin, they are limited in their challenge of the totality of bourgeois society (Bourdieu 1985: 735–44; 1984: 397–465).

Bourdieu's conception of the working class is at once degrading and exalting. He degrades it to the level of an unreflective, animal existence. Workers are "natural" creatures who, because they are reduced to sheer physical labor by the class system, develop a taste for base and animal pleasures (Bourdieu 1984: 32). But having thus reduced workers to simple animals, Bourdieu then exalts this animality as the natural form of existence and uses it to launch an attack on the hypocrisy of bourgeois culture. Workers play the role of Rousseau-like noble savages, who are unsullied by the games of cultural distinction played by the bourgeoisie and its "petite" pretenders. Their popular realism "inclines working people to reduce practices to the reality of their function, to do what they do, and be what they are . . . , without 'kidding themselves.' . . . [It is] the near-perfect antithesis of the aesthetic disavowal which, by a sort of essential hypocrisy . . . masks the interest in function by the primacy given to form, so that what people do, they do as if they were not doing it" (Bourdieu 1984: 200).

In contrast to Bourdieu's structuralist theory of culture as a reproducing structure, the critical theory of culture as reification is based upon a conception of culture as praxis, a struggle to realize human needs that may fundamentally transform as well as reproduce class structure. For critical theorists, cultural action may contradict and change the social structures in which it is exercised because it has an ontological basis in human needs that are transhistorical, even though they are always expressed in historical forms. They follow the early Marx in postulating that human beings are by nature social creatures whose consciousness gives them the potential for self-determination or freedom. The historical mode of production constrains and limits the realization of these needs, but it can never totally suppress the natural desires for freedom and sociality. While Bourdieu postulates that the pursuit of freedom is a structurally conditioned taste of the dominant class alone, critical theorists hold that the praxis of all people is underwritten by a basic desire for freedom (Marx 1964; Marcuse 1966).

For critical theorists, culture is a realm of praxis that expresses these transhistorical needs and cannot be simply reduced to the social function of reproducing the class structure, as Bourdieu seeks to do. Historically, culture has served a utopian function—it has expressed and maintained in the collective consciousness the longing for fulfillments which the existing society does not provide, but could if organized differently. The Frankfurt School holds, however, that to perform this critical function culture must remain autonomous from society's practical, economic function of providing for people's immediate needs. In order to be "practical" and serve immediate needs, culture would have to adjust to the repressive demands of the existing society that denies humanity their more basic needs for freedom and sociality. Thus, in most socially differentiated societies beyond the tribal stage there exists a "high culture" performing this critical function, which is exempted from the practical demand to make money by the sponsorship of aristocrats or the state. But alongside this impractical culture of the few there exists a popular culture that addresses these practical demands of the many for immediate gratification. The Frankfurt theorists thus agree with Bourdieu that culture has historically been bifurcated and thus symbolized class divisions, although they dispute his relativistic claim that each half is equally valid (Marcuse 1968, 1978; Horkheimer and Adorno 1972: 135–36).

Critical theorists argue, however, that modern monopoly capitalism destroys this bifurcated culture by reducing autonomous, critical high culture to the level of popular culture, demanding that it too make money by providing immediate gratifications. During the early twentieth century large-scale, bureaucratic corporations arise that increase profits by standardizing goods into a few basic types, and then mass-producing these types on specialized machines operated by deskilled workers. When these corporations seize the production of culture, they necessarily eliminate the differences between high and popular culture that symbolize class divisions, giving all consumers a leveled mass culture with standardized gratifications. These mass-produced cultural goods provide merely superficial satisfactions of real needs, and reconcile people to an oppressive system. Thus, culture becomes reified—the real relations of class domination on which the system is based are obscured behind a facade of homogenized things consumed by all. In the consumer market of standardized mass culture, the qualitative differences between people in class power are hidden behind merely quantitative differences in the possession of the same goods. Some people just have more of what everyone wants, supposedly because they contribute more value to the market through their labor.

The weakness in the Frankfurt School's formulation of culture is that it is historically underdetermined. Critical theorists tell us little about the specific historical conditions under which cultural praxis becomes either critical or ideological. Specifically, the transition from a critical and autonomous high culture to a leveled and reified mass culture is sometimes portrayed as if it were the inevitable result of the technology of mass production, with little intervention by humans themselves. But at other times they paint the rise of mass culture as a conscious conspiracy by the savvy capitalists of the culture industry. This weakness can be corrected, however, by replacing their vague, socially dislocated and historically unspecified praxis to realize human needs with concrete, historical class conflict. The mediating factor that determines the effect of the class structure of a society on its cultural productions is neither Bourdieu's inexorable reproducing habitus nor critical theory's dislocated praxis, but the socially located, historically specific conflict of dominant and dominated classes. Such an approach is embodied in the pioneering work of Georg Lukács.

In several places Bourdieu (1993b: 56; Bourdieu and Wacquant 1992: 69) includes Lukács in his criticism of Lucien Goldmann and other Marxist literary critics for their short-circuit fallacy—that is, making direct and naïve connections between the class positions of writers and their cultural productions. Although this fallacy may be characteristic of Goldmann and some Frankfurt theorists, it is not relevant to Lukács, who does not reduce the form or content of a cultural production to the class position of its producer. If truly guilty of such a simplistic reductionism, he would have no grounds for praising the works of some bourgeois writers over others, or for condemning the production of some proletarian writers (Lukács 1973a, 1973b, 1962, 1980a, 1980b). Lukács, like Bourdieu, postulates an important mediating factor between a writer's class position and the nature of the work. But his mediating factor is not a static, reproducing habitus but the dynamic, historical conflict of classes.

Lukács postulates that the interests of a writer's class position impose cognitive limits on his or her productions, but the nature of these interests is determined by the class's changing relation to humanity's progressive struggles for freedom. So, for example, he argues that the narrative style of bourgeois realists like Balzac, Dickens, and Tolstoy, which depicts reality as a historical creation of human strivings, is the consequence of the bourgeoisie's progressive struggle against the feudal order in the formative stages of capitalism. Because at this time the bourgeoisie was engaged in the struggle against feudalism—a struggle that served not only its particular interest but the general interest of humanity in freedom—its cultural producers were able to see the reality of society as a human creation and embody it in narrative about active characters.

After the revolutions of 1848, however, capitalism was consolidated in most Western European societies, and the bourgeois ruling class had an interest no longer in progressive change but in reactionary protection of its rule against the class to whom history passed the interest in freedom, the proletariat. The cultural result of this changed position with respect to class conflict was the descriptive style of bourgeois modernists like Joyce and Flaubert. No longer having an interest in progressive change, bourgeois writers were blinded to the nature of reality as a human creation and began to depict the world as a static, reified thing. In their novels, these writers merely described the established facts of society and created characters who passively adopt various subjective attitudes toward them. People and their relations are not developed but merely described as already constituted products of forces beyond their control. The reality of class and struggle is thus obscured behind this impenetrable façade of static things (Lukács 1973a, 1973b).

In this Lukácsian formulation, cultural works are understood as reflecting not static class position but active interventions in historic class struggles that may transform, not merely reproduce, social structures. In their productions, cultural producers resolve in formal, imaginary ways the problems and dilemmas of a class in conflict. These interventions are always political, although usually unconsciously so, since they are the product of, first, the class position of the producer and, second, the historical relation (progressive or reactionary) of that class to the struggle for human liberation (Jameson 1971: 375–400). This theory of culture is in a better position than either Bourdieu or the Frankfurt School to capture the complexities of modern capitalist culture. Unlike Bourdieu's theory of a reproducing structure, it grasps culture as an active praxis that may transform society. And unlike the Frankfurt School, this more historically grounded theory also specifies through the mediating factor of class struggle how this praxis produces a reified mass culture that obscures and compensates for the real human relations of exploitation and oppression that organize society.

In Chapter 2, I used this variant of reification theory focused on class conflict to explain the historical development of class-obscuring, reified automobile designs. In Chapter 4, I develop this theory further, focusing once again on the case of American automobile culture. There I seek to demonstrate that conflict-oriented reification theory can incorporate and explain Bourdieu's class symbolization theory as generated by and appropriate for an early historical stage in capitalist culture, before class struggle produced the transition to the stage of a consumer culture of mass reification. I also argue that this theory explains a later stage of postmodern development beyond mass reification, in which obscuring the relations of production is accomplished by a consumer culture differentiated into a diversity of subcultures and lifestyles. Thus, I hope to demonstrate that reification theory sensitive to continuing class conflict is not static but contains the conceptual tools to explain the vicissitudes of contemporary capitalist culture.

4 Three Ages of the Automobile
The Cultural Logics of the Car

In this chapter I once again use the empirical case of the automobile to inter-rogate the issues and problems of a critical theory of culture. Here I am par-ticularly concerned with developing a historically grounded critical theory that views the culture of capitalist society not as a static structure but as a dynamic, contradictory constellation subject to change. As we saw in the Chapter 3, there are elements of truth in the cultural theories of both Pierre Bourdieu and the Frankfurt School. Yet both seem blind to the dynamics of change, as they generalize from a specific historical period to explain capitalist culture as an unchanging type, in all times and places. I seek here to use the history of the automobile as a cultural artifact to demonstrate the inherent instability of all cultural constellations within capitalism, and the inevitability of cultural change. The foundation of this instability is the contradiction between inherent human needs for sociality and freedom and capitalism's constitution of people as individuals subjected to its alien logic of production and the market. This contradiction creates human conflict that destabilizes culture and pushes it on toward new legitimations under-written by new cultural logics.

In the following, I argue that there have been three ages of the automobile in the twentieth century, each defined by a unique cultural logic of meaning and identity. To conceptualize these different logics I draw on three socio-logical theories of cultural consumption. Pierre Bourdieu's theory conceives of consumption as a game of distinction, in which different classes compete for cultural capital or status honor. For him, the automobile is a distinctive status symbol, marking off but ultimately misrecognizing the inequalities of class society. By contrast, the Frankfurt School argues that the culture of mass consumption legitimates class differences not by displaying these differences in a symbolic hierarchy, but by hiding them altogether. For these theorists, consumer commodities like the automobile obscure the class rela-tions of their production behind reified facades of mass individuality, giv-ing consumers different quantities of the same illusions to compensate for the denials of mass production. Finally, theorists of postmodernism argue that the diversity and individuality of consumer commodities undermines old class identities and gives rise to a multitude of fragmented subcultures.

For postmodernists the car and its subcultures are part of a fragmented, liberated society of "difference" that follows the collapse of modernity.

Although each theory claims to capture the cultural logic of consumerism in capitalist society, I hold that, with respect to the automobile at least, each is valid for only a specific historical period or age. This does not mean that these successive logics are totally independent and completely annihilate the preceding ones. The relationship between them is best conceived as dialectical, in the original Hegelian sense (see Marcuse 1960). Each stage and its logic represent not a replacement but a development of the preceding one. The problems and contradictions of the earlier stage are incorporated into and overcome by a higher stage of development, without being solved in any final sense. So the old logic survives in the new, but in a higher form of development. Thus, I postulate not a succession but a *progression* of stages, without postulating, as do Hegel and Marx, some end point or purpose to this historical progression. There is, however, a common theme or impulse underlying all three stages—the search for individuality within a capitalist society that holds out the promise of autonomy but simultaneously denies it in the heteronomy of the economy.

The periodization of these three ages is based mainly on my research on the automobile in American society (Gartman 1994). But I also cite studies that lead me to believe that a similar progression of cultural ages occurs in other countries, especially Britain, although the timing may be different.

THE AGE OF CLASS DISTINCTION: BOURDIEU AND CRAFT PRODUCTION

The automobile entered American society in the late nineteenth century, a time of economic crisis and class conflict with which the vehicle was inevitably associated. The auto marked out these increasingly contentious class divisions, for its high price ($600 to $7500) put ownership beyond the reach of all but the high bourgeoisie. These prices were the result of a skilled, craft labor process, in which the aesthetic appearance of these cars was as important as their mechanical function. Auto bodies, in particular, were works of the coach-building art, produced in elaborate styles to match the tastes of the upper classes. Not only the production but also the use of these early cars solidified their association with class privilege. In the United States, where freedom had always been conflated with geographic movement, autos gave their wealthy owners the freedom of a rapid, flexible, and individual form of mobility, unencumbered by the collective regimentation of railway timetables and itineraries. But these beautiful, expensive vehicles were more often used not for practical transport but for leisure activities and public ostentation. They became an essential accessory of the leisure class, which used them for touring, racing, and parading down fashionable boulevards. Consequently, the automobile quickly became defined in American culture as an instrument of freedom and leisure, and a symbol of the wealth which removed an entire class of people from the mundane concerns of work and functional effort.

The lower classes reacted to this symbolism with hostility and resentment. Farmers resented the "freedom" of wealthy auto owners to intrude into rural communities, not only for the damage they did to land and livestock but also because they symbolized urban big-business interests, whose abuses caused radical agrarian protests during this period. Urban workers also resented bourgeois automobilists on city streets, where they disrupted street life and symbolized this class's arrogant disregard for workers' lives and livelihoods. At the same time, workers envied this possession of the rich, as indicated by the crowds that were attracted to movie theaters by early films featuring auto races and parades. In 1906 Woodrow Wilson worried about the class-divisive effect of the car, stating: "Nothing has spread Socialistic feeling in this country more than the use of automobiles. To the countryman they are a picture of arrogance of wealth with all its independence and carelessness" (*New York Times* 1906). Sean O'Connell (1998: 11–42, 77–111) finds similar meanings of class privilege, leisure, and freedom of mobility in the early period of the car in British society.

These early cultural meanings of automobility, conditioned by the car's production and use, are congruent with Pierre Bourdieu's theory of consumption as class distinction, developed in *Distinction* (1984). Building a structural theory on the simple conception of consumer goods as status symbols, he argues that cultural objects carry socially constructed meanings that testify to an individual's class position. The symbolic connection between economic class and cultural taste is not direct, however, but mediated by an embodied habitus, a set of durable predispositions and ways of seeing the world. Thus, for example, the ample economic capital of the bourgeoisie determines a life removed from mundane material needs and the functions of things. This life determines a habitus that inclines members of this class toward cultural goods that reveal this distance from necessity by their formalization and aestheticization. By choosing goods that privilege aesthetic form over material function, the bourgeoisie unconsciously indicates that it has sufficient resources to be unconcerned with mundane functions and needs. The bourgeoisie's formalized culture distinguishes it from the working class, whose consumer goods are focused exclusively on immediate material needs and gratification. Lack of economic capital dictates that workers have to be constantly concerned with meeting material necessities, which ingrains in them a habitus that inclines them toward goods that privilege material function over aesthetic form. Thus, cultural consumption marks off class identity, and consuming the "legitimate culture" of the bourgeoisie brings the additional resource of cultural capital or honorability, which disguises and justifies the economic capital on which the class system rests. Cultural capital testifies to refined tastes and creates the illusion that its upper-class possessors are personally superior to others and thus deserving of their superior economic resources. Culture thus symbolizes class, but in such a way as to cause a misrecognition of its real basis.

Early automobiles clearly conveyed cultural capital on the high bourgeoisie in American society by testifying to its removal from necessity. The beautiful forms of their craft-built bodies made it clear that these expensive vehicles were not merely mundane machines of transportation but also works of art, testifying to refined cultural tastes. And their use in leisure activities testified to a life free from the mundane, material concerns of earning a living. Another fact of this early period of automobility explained by Bourdieu's theory is the diffusion of ownership. Bourdieu argues (1984: 251–52) that in an attempt to accumulate cultural capital for themselves, members of the petite bourgeoisie or middle class seek to appropriate the prestigious goods of the bourgeoisie. But lacking both the economic means and the cultural habitus of the latter, they settle for cheap imitations, which seem satisfactory to them but give away their inferior resources to their class betters. This process of class imitation explains the diffusion of autos to middle-class professionals and managers by the first decade of the twentieth century in the United States. Anxious to mark their own growing prosperity, these petite bourgeois borrowed the automotive symbol of wealth, leisure, and freedom. This growing but less prosperous market for cars stimulated automakers to add less expensive models to their product lines. Finding few lower limits to the demand for automobility, a few visionary producers like Ford and Olds were stimulated to pioneer mass production. In 1908 Ford Motor Company introduced its inexpensive Model T, and over the course of the next two decades pioneered a production process of specialized machines and assembly lines that brought the price of the car down within reach of the rising incomes of most of the petite bourgeoisie and even the top strata of the working class. In Britain, however, the advent of mass production seems to have been impeded by a class system more rigid in both economic and cultural boundaries, leading automakers to shun standardized production for fear it would undermine the distinction of auto ownership (O'Connell 1998: 18–38).

Mass-produced American cars were clearly distinguished from the grand luxury makes driven by the rich. But initially these differences did not seem to concern their buyers. Ownership of a car of any kind was still sufficiently rare to constitute status symbol in itself. But as mass production spread cars further down the class hierarchy, mere ownership lost its ability to convey distinction. Increasingly the type of car owned conveyed status, and the simple, functional, mass-produced cars were clearly degraded and stigmatized relative to the luxury makes. The latter became the true mark of automotive distinction, testifying to the great wealth and refined tastes of their high-class owners. Their quantitative superiority in size and power immediately marked them off from mass-produced cars. But the refined eye also noticed qualitative differences in aesthetics and mechanics. The luxury classics were, due to superior engineering and careful hand-fitting, mechanically tighter and drove more smoothly. Their engines ran quietly, their transmissions shifted effortlessly, and their brakes functioned at a touch, creating a refined, relaxed driving experience befitting the ostentatious ease characteristic of the upper-class habitus. The aesthetics of these cars, however, denied and negated their mechanical function in the name of art. Their wooden bodies were lavished with hundreds of hours of craft labor and molded into curving, often rococo forms. And their lustrous surfaces were finished with up to twenty coats of slow-drying varnish paint. The resulting cars were unified, elegant works of art, which raised the mundane function of transportation to a formal, aesthetic experience testifying to the removal from necessity conveyed by great wealth.

The mass-produced cars, by contrast, were marked by a mundane concern for function and efficiency, which characterizes working-class consumption, according to Bourdieu. The mass-production process was designed to produce simple, functional cars as quickly and as cheaply as possible, and these criteria were painfully obvious in the appearance and operation of its products. Cheap engineering and quick assembly led to loud, rough-running engines, laborious transmissions, and vibrating frames and bodies. These cars required considerable labor to drive, testifying to their owners' physically-demanding occupations. Their fragmented, unintegrated appearance also testified to a hurried, unskilled labor process that wasted little time on fit and finish. The bodies were rigidly rectilinear and flat, for curved panels created problems for machines. And the drab, unimaginative black finishes, dictated by quick enameling, spoke of an unconcern for aesthetic variety. Everything about these cars symbolized the immediate concern for cost-cutting efficiency and function that characterized the lives of classes with few resources to waste on luxury. In contrast to the luxury classics, these cars were seen in the 1920s as degraded and stigmatizing. While Ford's Model T was welcomed in the 1910s as an instrument of democracy, bringing automobility to the masses, by the 1920s it was commonly ridiculed as ugly and poorly built. One contemporary joke asked why a Model T was like a mistress. The answer: because you hate to be seen on the streets with one.

In this early period of automobility, qualitative differences in cars symbolized and legitimated not merely the inequality of class but the inequality of gender as well. Both in the United States (Scharff 1991) and Britain (O'Connell 1998), automobile production and use were influenced by the gender ideology of separate spheres. In general, automobiles were defined as masculine, both because they provided mobility in the public sphere and because they were utilitarian and mechanical objects of production. Women were supposed to confine themselves to the private, domestic sphere and to the nonutilitarian concerns of consumption and aesthetics. Consequently, car ownership and operation were considered culturally appropriate mainly for men. However, even when women in this early period gained access to automobility, gender ideology segregated them in a different type of automobile, the electric car. Gasoline-powered cars were said to be too smelly, noisy, powerful, and difficult to operate and maintain for women. Cars powered by electric motors were considered more appropriate for women, for they were quieter, cleaner, and less mechanical. The major limitation of electric cars—their short range of travel between battery charges—was held to be unproblematic for women, since they were forbidden to stray far from home anyway.

When a combination of women's demands and gas automaker's self-interest finally brought the death of electric cars, gender ideology was reinscribed within the market for gas cars. The larger, more luxurious, higher-priced cars, with their concerns for aesthetics and comfort, were defined as more feminine, while the smaller, cheaper, mass-produced cars, with their concerns for utility and efficiency, were defined as masculine (Scharff 1991: 49–58). So there was a definite superimposition of class and gender connotations in the culture of early automobility. And this was not only because women with more income were more likely to drive than those with less. Bourdieu (1984: 382–3, 402–04) recognizes a cultural basis for this confluence, arguing that class distinctions are naturally gendered. In general, the bourgeoisie is considered more feminine, because both the men and women of this class are removed from the realm of physical production and emphasize aesthetics and form. By contrast, the working class as a whole is defined as more masculine, due to its involvement in physical work and unconcern for beauty. Consequently, during this period the distinction between luxury cars and mass-produced cars served simultaneously as a class and a gender marker, legitimating both inequalities.

By the mid-1920s, the class-stigmatizing characteristics of mass-produced cars had extended the imitation process from mere auto ownership to aesthetics as well. As the upper working class began to purchase mass-produced cars, the petite bourgeoisie lost its automotive distinction vis-à-vis this class. Consequently, a clamor arose in the auto market for something different from and better than mass-produced cars, an inexpensive car with more "class." General Motors head Alfred Sloan sensed the emergence of what he called this "mass-class market" in the mid-1920s, arguing that many buyers were now willing to pay a bit more for a car beyond basic transportation. His corporation began to compete with Ford's Model T by creating mass-produced cars with the superficial style of the luxury classics. One of the most successful of these was the 1927 La Salle, a smaller, cheaper model of the corporation's luxury car, Cadillac. Unlike the craft-built Cadillac, the La Salle was mass-produced to lower its price. But to borrow the prestige of the nameplate, Sloan wanted the car to have the look of handcrafted luxury. To design this "imitation Cadillac," he hired a Hollywood coachbuilder, Harley Earl, who created custom auto bodies for the movies and their stars. Earl was so successful in capturing the superficial look of unity and integrity for the mass-produced La Salle that he was hired by Sloan to do the same thing for the entire line of GM cars. In 1927 Earl joined General Motors as the head of the new Art and Color Section, later to be renamed Styling.

Earl's subsequent work at GM, however, raises questions about the validity of Bourdieu's model of class distinction. He was not content to merely design imitation Cadillacs for the pretentious and upwardly striving petite bourgeoisie. At the behest of Sloan, Earl brought the look of the craft-built luxury cars to the entire hierarchy of GM cars, from the cheapest to the most expensive. This extension of style to even the lowest-priced cars undermines Bourdieu's theory, which holds that workers have an ingrained taste for the simple and functional. The surge in sales during this period of the inexpensive Chevrolet styled by Earl revealed that workers also wanted goods with the aestheticized forms of the high bourgeoisie. This indicates that Bourdieu is mistaken to exempt workers from the game of distinction. The working class also wanted to appear distinctive and superior and, given the chance, imitated the goods of the bourgeoisie to do so. Workers may have initially consumed simple, functional cars because they could afford nothing else, not because they had an ingrained taste for them. The rising incomes of American workers during the 1920s, however, allowed them to abandon these goods and demand cars with style, thus entering the game of distinction for the first time.

The diffusion of cars with style and beauty beyond the bourgeoisie threatened, however, to breach rigid conceptions of separate gender spheres. While it may have been culturally acceptable for the "effeminate" men of the upper class to be interested in aesthetics and beauty, these traits threatened the more masculine self-images of middle- and especially working-class men. Indeed, in both the United States and Britain during this period there emerged fears and admonishments that automobiles were becoming feminized, as concerns for appearance and fashion began to outweigh those for engineering function and efficiency. But, conveniently, the same gender ideology that seemed threatened by this attempt of lower-class men to grab the distinction of upper-class goods also provided them with an alibi for this consumption decision. Men blamed their preference for stylish cars on their wives. Backed by the unproven assertions of marketing experts, males claimed that women exerted increasing influence on family auto purchases due to their dominance of the sphere of consumption. Consequently, men could buy the cars that brought them distinction while avoiding the taint of femininity that came with them (Scharff 1991: 57–66; O'Connell 1998: 63–70).

Although gender distinctions remained largely intact, the extension of the game of automotive distinction to larger and larger numbers ultimately contradicted the cultural logic of class distinction. Bourdieu's logic of distinction depends on real qualitative differences between cultural goods to symbolize qualitatively different class positions. Formalized goods symbolize a position of command that exempts its holders from work, while functional goods symbolize a subjection to efficient effort commanded by others. The mass production of superficially styled or aestheticized cars began to undercut these qualitative differences within the auto market. Increasingly there was little symbolic advantage to owning and driving an expensive luxury car produced by the craft process when inexpensive, mass-produced cars looked superficially just as good. The distinction of a qualitatively superior car disappeared among the throngs of look-alikes driven by the lower classes. Further, the divided and deskilled process of mass production undermined the sensibilities necessary to distinguish qualitatively different machines. Consequently, the handcrafted luxury makes began to decline in the mid-1920s. Some, like Cadillac and Lincoln, were acquired by mass-production firms and integrated into their product line-ups. Others downgraded their products to compete with mass producers or went out of business entirely, especially during the Great Depression of the 1930s, when the demand for luxury cars dropped precipitously. Luxury automakers found it almost impossible to compete with the large mass producers, with their market power and economies of scale. By the mid-1920s the three largest mass-production automakers in the U.S. accounted for 72% of total automobile output. Consequently, there were very few qualitative differences within the market to symbolize superior taste and convey cultural capital. The car as a symbol of real, qualitative class differences was finished in America.

In Britain, however, a similar qualitative leveling did not occur in the car market until the post-World-War-II period. Some manufacturers like Morris started on the road to mass production in the mid-1920s, but full mass production was hindered by a more unequal income structure as well as more rigid cultural boundaries between the classes. Consequently, no great demand emerged among the working class for mass-produced cars with the look of luxury. Workers were generally forced to settle for second-hand autos from the middle class (O'Connell 1998: 19–38).

THE ERA OF MASS INDIVIDUALITY:
THE FRANKFURT SCHOOL AND FORDISM

The collapse of distinctive, qualitative differences between cars did not mean, however, that the market dominated by mass-producers became homogenized. Indeed, the large American automotive firms began in the late 1920s to offer a large variety of models that, although qualitatively similar, were superficially differentiated by aesthetics and accessories. All these mass-produced cars imitated the smooth, integrated look of the increasingly rare luxury cars, but they were differentiated into price grades by the quantity of valued attributes, like chrome trim, size, and power. Why take the trouble to create artificial differences among qualitatively similar cars?

The answer lies in the demand for cultural legitimation of the new system of mass production. As Regulation theorists like Michel Aglietta

(1979) argue, the new process of mass production required a new mode of mass consumption to distribute and consume all of the goods pouring off of specialized machines and assembly lines. They label the combination of the new organization of production with the new organization of consumption "Fordism," for they attribute the initiation of both to Henry Ford. In 1914, shortly after introducing the assembly line, Ford instituted the Five Dollar Day program, drastically increasing the wages of his workers and thus creating thousands of new consumers for his cars. But this program was an attempt not merely to create more consumers but also to produce more stable and compliant workers. As I argued in Chapter 2, this wage increase was implemented largely to quell the wave of worker conflict instigated by his new, more intense and exploitative production methods. In return for the Five Dollar Day, Ford demanded that workers acquiesce to mass-production methods as well as adopt a stable home life centered around major consumer durables that made them dependent on their high-paying jobs (Meyer 1981).

But what kind of consumer goods would workers consider sufficient compensation for their increasingly alienated and exploited work? This was the question that the American automobile industry was trying to answer beginning in the late 1920s. Harley Earl and other auto designers were bringing the look of luxury cars to mass-produced vehicles to satisfy not merely the masses' desire for distinction but also their demand for escape from the dehumanizing aspects of mass production. During this period the American working class was beginning to use its higher wages to construct a separate realm of consumption in the home, where they could find respite from and compensation for the realm of work. The automobile was the keystone of this narcotizing edifice of consumerism. Social reformers and capitalist philanthropists argued that automobility would solve labor and social problems by allowing workers to escape from urban congestion into the countryside for recreation and relief. They also hoped that auto ownership would overcome class tensions by turning workers into "property owners," thus giving them a stake in capitalism. But neither could be accomplished as long as the autos workers purchased brought with them into the realm of consumption symbolic reminders of mass production. The rectilinear, fragmented homogeneity of mass-produced cars was a symbol of the rigid, boring, heteronomous production process workers sought to escape at home. By molding the surface of these cars into the smooth, rounded, varied shapes of luxury cars, car stylists like Earl covered over the offending reminders of work and allowed them to perform their escape function unobtrusively. As Earl put it, he tried to "design a car so that every time you get in it, it's a relief—you get a little vacation for a while" (quoted in Sloan 1972: 324).

But auto consumers wanted their goods not merely to obscure work but also to fulfill needs denied them there. And one of the most important of these was individuality. The mass-production process reduced work to standardized, repetitive tasks with little room for the expression of personal uniqueness or difference. Not surprisingly, then, people subjected to this process sought to compensate in their consumption lives by buying goods that were individual and unique, that made them seem different from but not necessarily superior to others, as in Bourdieu's notion of distinction. As GM's Alfred Sloan stated in 1934: "People like different things. Many people do not want to have exactly the same thing that the neighborhood has" (Sloan 1972: 207). Consequently, it became the policy of GM and other mass producers to build many different types of cars to accommodate consumer demand for individuality, or, as Sloan put it, to produce "a car for every purse, purpose, and person" (1972: 520). One method used by automakers to create individuality was to produce several makes of cars that were graded by price. Thus, for example, in the mid-1920s Sloan carefully arranged General Motors' makes in a price hierarchy to appeal to consumers of all income levels. Cadillac was at the high-priced end, followed by Buick, Oldsmobile, Pontiac, then Chevrolet, which occupied the low-priced extreme. There were few differences of real quality between them. All were mass-produced, even the Cadillac, and the different makes shared some of the same components. But styling allowed automakers to differentiate these models and still meet the high-volume demands of mass production.

When Sloan hired Earl in 1927, he instructed him to maintain a strict stylistic division between GM's makes in order to justify differential pricing. All the makes were given the unified, rounded look of luxury, which covered over the signs of mass production. But in addition to this, the brands in the price hierarchy were differentiated by relatively inexpensive styling cues, such as chrome strips and grilles. These arbitrary features made the mass-produced body shells shared between the makes appear different. Beyond these cues, what differentiated the top makes from the bottom ones was not quality, but the quantity of their features—they had more of what everyone wanted. The high-priced Cadillac was longer and heavier and had more cylinders and accessories than the low-priced Chevrolet. So the Cadillac buyer felt not only different but somehow "better" than the Chevy buyer, not due to superior taste but because he or she could afford more of what everyone recognized as desirable.

A second policy devised by Sloan and implemented by GM's styling department provided consumers with a superficial substitute for another desire denied in production—progress. Sloan knew that consumers wanted not merely different things but also products that were constantly changing in order to symbolize progress. The solution that Sloan devised to deliver symbolic progress was the annual model change. Each year the appearance of every model was slightly changed through the manipulation of the body and accessories, thus giving it a new look. Beneath the surface, however, the mass-produced mechanical parts stayed the same for years. Harley Earl coordinated these annual model changes with the hierarchical differentiation of the makes into an ingenious trickle-down scheme that played upon consumers' desire not merely for progress but also for social mobility. In the first year of the cycle, Earl introduced a style feature in the top make of GM's product hierarchy, Cadillac, thus associating it with prestige and high income. In the following year, he transferred it to the next lower make, Buick, thus lending this car some of the Cadillac's prestige. He continued this trickle-down styling in successive years, until the feature reached the cheapest make, Chevrolet, and thus became commonplace, at which time he introduced a new feature at the top, starting the cycle anew. Consumers of the lower makes were thus persuaded that their cars were getting better because they looked more like Cadillacs and, thus, that their lives were getting better as well.

These developments in the industry further undermine the validity of Bourdieu's theory of consumption as determined by habitus and ultimately symbolic of class position. In his theory, the production of goods to match the habitus of different classes is the result of an unconscious, structural homology of the positions of goods producers and consumers. Each class has its own producers, which stand in the field of cultural production in a similar position—insider versus outsider, new versus old—as that of its consumers in the field of social classes. As a result, these producers are motivated by competition with other producers to provide the type of goods that match the habitus of a class that is competing against other classes for cultural capital (Bourdieu 1984: 230–34). But this was clearly not the case for the different car makes of this period. Almost all of these were produced by the same large, mass-production firms, and within each firm the different makes in its hierarchy were designed in the same styling department. There stylists *consciously* manipulated the makes' designs to differentiate them, but not by appealing to different habitus. The same stylists with the same class habitus could not, according to Bourdieu, appeal to different consumer habitus. What these stylists appealed to, in all of the makes they designed, were the same needs denied all classes, albeit in varying proportions, by the system of administered mass-production. The higher classes could just afford more of what everyone wanted, especially individuality and the concealment of the telltale reminders of mass production.

Bourdieu's theory does recognize the type of style cycle implemented in the auto industry, in which the distinctive features of upper-class products are imitated by the lower classes in order to borrow their prestige. When these features become so widespread that all distinction is lost, the bourgeoisie goes back to the field of culture to appropriate new innovations unsullied by the taint of commonality and commercialism (Bourdieu 1984: 372–84). But for Bourdieu, the cycle is an unintended, uncoordinated outcome of the competition between classes for distinction. He does not provide for the possibility that this cycle could become a conscious policy, intentionally manufactured to provide consumers with a sense of progress and mobility in a society whose fundamental structure remains the same (see Chapter 3).

The theory of consumption of the Frankfurt School better captures the cultural logic of this Fordist stage of automobility. From the beginning, Max Horkheimer and Theodor Adorno conceptualized the products of mass consumption not as means to satisfy lower-class status striving but as means to compensate workers for the inhuman conditions of mass production. They write in "The Culture Industry" that the products of mass amusement are "sought after as an escape from the mechanized work process, and to recruit strength in order to be able to cope with it again" (Horkheimer and Adorno 1972: 137). These consumer products offer satisfactions, but only inauthentic, substitute gratifications for the needs denied by an alienated production process. "Whatever remained unsatisfied in them [consumers] through the order which takes from them without giving in exchange what it promises, only burned with impatience for their gaoler to remember them and at last offer them stones in his left hand for the hunger from which he withholds bread in his right" (Adorno 1974: 148). And what hungers are these that are denied by the system's right hand of production only to be placated with empty substitutes offered by the left hand of consumption? Foremost among these are freedom, individuality, and progress, all casualties of "the administered society" of capitalist mass production.

Frankfurt School theorists realize that this attempt to provide in consumption satisfactions for needs denied in production raises an immediate dilemma. Consumer goods are themselves mass-produced and necessarily bear all the marks of this production process, including standardization, homogeneity, and unchanging design. When mass production seizes culture and subjects it to the imperatives of exchange value, the result is the leveling of offerings, reducing the qualities of products to the lowest common denominator in order to facilitate long runs of standardized goods on machines. One of the prime examples of such cultural leveling cited by Adorno is the automobile. He recognized in the mid-1940s that there were few real, mechanical differences between the cars in the hierarchies of mass producers, and that the craft-built luxury cars were increasingly extinct as a breed.

> While a Cadillac undoubtedly excels a Chevrolet by the amount that it costs more, this superiority, unlike that of the old Rolls Royce, nevertheless itself proceeds from an overall plan which artfully equips the former with the better cylinders, the latter with the worse cylinders, bolts, accessories, without anything being altered in the basic pattern of the mass-produced article; only minor rearrangements in production would be needed to turn the Chevrolet into a Cadillac. So luxury is sapped. (Adorno 1974: 119–20)

This passage raises a deeper question about the function of culture that sets Adorno and the Frankfurt School apart from Bourdieu. For the latter, luxury goods have no inherent value beyond the maintenance of class inequalities. For Adorno, however, luxury, the needlessly and uselessly beautiful and refined, is the epitome of culture, and naturally plays a subversive role in society. For him, culture is the "promise of happiness" in an unequal and oppressive world, and provides an implicit critique of an ugly society that denies human desires (Adorno 1984: 17–18). In capitalism, culture is a valuable counter to the market's tendency to reduce all people and things to their immediate "usefulness" in exchange. The superfluity of the beautiful and luxurious in culture counters the quantitative reductionism of the market and asserts human qualities that cannot be fulfilled through exchange. For Adorno, consequently, the loss of luxury in mass production is not progressive but reactionary; it is the subsumption of the last contradictory force into a repressive capitalist society (Adorno 1974: 120).

If luxury is leveled, however, and becomes just another homogenized exchange value on the market, how can the mass producers of culture provide their consumers with substitute satisfactions for the real needs denied them in production? The answer, Adorno tells us, is artificial, manipulated differentiation of the type offered by the auto industry. "The same thing is offered to everybody by the standardized production of consumption goods. But the commercial necessity of concealing this identity leads to the manipulation of taste and the official culture's pretense of individualism, which necessarily increases in proportion to the liquidation of the individual" (Adorno 1978: 280). Legitimation of the system is secured by providing consumers of all classes with the illusion of free choice between seemingly different goods, while beneath the surface the mass-production process levels the real qualitative differences between things as well as people. Adorno holds that the need for such illusory compensation for denied needs is characteristic of even the high bourgeoisie, the so-called ruling class. While it may be true, as Bourdieu holds, that this class was once distinguished by its removal from economic necessity, Adorno argues that "[high] society life is . . . thoroughly stamped by the economic principle, whose kind of rationality spreads to the whole" (1974: 187). The bourgeoisie's formalization and aestheticization of life, he states, represents not a removal from economic necessity but an attempt to escape from the boredom and heteronomy that results from its own subjection to the system of exchange, which it shares with all other classes. This class is now distinguished from others only by its greater means to effect this escape (1974: 187–90).

The Frankfurt School's theory of consumption as mass individuality and progress argues, like Bourdieu, that the ultimate result of this culture is to legitimate and maintain the class system of capitalist society. But it postulates that legitimation is secured in a different way. For Bourdieu, consumption prominently displays the economic inequalities between classes, but in a symbolic form that *misrecognizes* their origins. Legitimate consumption tastes, determined by internalized class habitus, seem to testify to the personal superiority of their individual bearers, thus justifying their larger share of economic resources. The Frankfurt School, by contrast, argues that consumption legitimates classes by obscuring their real differences altogether, making them *unrecognizable* by burying them beneath an indistinct mass culture shared by all. As Adorno writes (1976: 55), "today the existence of classes is concealed by ideological appearances." The culture industry eliminates the qualitative differences between goods, which testify to different class tastes, and substitutes for them artificially manufactured, quantitative differences of the same compensating characteristics demanded by all. What these quantitative differences symbolize is not class, properly speaking, that is, qualitative distinctions of social power rooted in production, but mere "strata," that is, quantitative distinctions of market income rooted in consumption. Thus, for the Frankfurt School, mass culture legitimates class structure by reifying it, by hiding social relations behind the relationships of things, commodities in the marketplace (see Chapters 2 and 3).

Although the Frankfurt School does not explicitly extend its theory of consumption as reified, mass individuality to gender relations, it is possible to do so, as revealed by the insightful work of scholars like Susan Willis (1991). The automobile reveals the empirical validity of such an extension. The age of mass individuality saw the narrowing of gender differences in both the use and consumption of automobiles. As the benefits of automobility became clear, more and more women took the wheel. By the post-World-War-II era in America, the suburbanization of the population facilitated by the car also made it an essential tool for fulfilling women's domestic role in the newly dispersed landscape. The suburban housewife who did not drive was a rarity. Further, as styling and beauty became the primary means of competition in an increasingly oligopolistic automotive market, it became difficult to maintain the notion that women alone were concerned with aesthetics. This did not mean that notions of automotive gender differences disappeared, just that they were redefined as quantitative rather than qualitative. Men were increasingly willing to admit that they too liked style, beauty, and comfort. But, judging from auto ads, it was assumed that women preferred and demanded *more* of these characteristics. So, for example, ads of the 1940s and 1950s often promoted the general style and comfort of the car interior in gender-neutral terms, but when they touted the fashionableness of specific colors and fabrics, they addressed women alone. When General Motors launched a marketing campaign to target women in the late 1950s, it commissioned a series of "Fem" show cars from its few women designers. These cars did not differ qualitatively in style from GM production models; they simply offered a quantitative excess of stylish accessories. One had four sets of seat covers to change with the seasons. Another "Fem" car was furnished with a set of luggage to match the pastel upholstery, while a third was painted in metallic rose with upholstery of red and black leather with plaid inserts (Bayley 1983: 99–108). More accessories, brighter paint, more multi-colored upholstery—this was what women were thought to want. So the qualitative, social differences between the genders in power, occupation, and opportunity were reified, reduced to merely different quantities of the same commodities, so as to better capture them for the marketplace.

Just like the cultural logic of class distinction before it, however, the extension and intensification of the logic of mass individuality produced contradictions that ultimately spelled its transcendence. By the late 1950s there were signs that all was not well with the program of trickle-down individuality offered by the quantitatively differentiated product hierarchies of American automakers. The Fordist system of automobility was falling victim to its own success. The Keynesian demand management policies of postwar Fordism were enormously successful in increasing and equalizing incomes, bringing millions of working-class consumers into the market for new cars. This more equitable market exerted a leveling effect on the quantitative differences between makes in corporate hierarchies. The largest market was now comprised of the lower-priced makes like Chevrolet and Ford, and to increase their profit per car in this market, automakers began to upgrade these autos. The low-priced cars added more size, power, and accessories until the gap between them and the expensive cars was minimal. The same leveling pressure was also exerted on automotive style. The orderly passing of individual style traits down the hierarchy of makes fell victim to both consumer demand and producer competition. Working-class consumers anxious for symbols of their new prosperity clamored for the look of individuality exemplified by the pricier makes. Each manufacturer knew that if its stylists did not quickly give these consumers what they demanded, its competitors would. GM's Harley Earl tried, for example, to maintain an orderly trickle-down of the tail fin, a feature introduced on the 1948 Cadillac to borrow the connotations of technological progress and escapism associated with aviation. He slowly brought it down to the Buick and Oldsmobile makes in the early 1950s. But working-class consumers of low-priced makes were impatient for this symbol of aeronautical freedom, and Chrysler tapped this pent-up demand by offering soaring fins on all its makes beginning in 1956. The style wars that ensued ultimately undermined the system of quantitative differentiation between cars.

Under competitive pressure to quickly bring prestigious traits to the lucrative lower-priced market, stylists abandoned incremental changes in the late 1950s and vied with one another by making bold innovations. Fins soared, bodies lengthened, and chrome proliferated in an unprecedented orgy of automotive change. All semblance of aesthetic difference between makes in the corporate hierarchies was lost. The implications of this aesthetic leveling were evident in the colossal failure of the new make launched by Ford in 1958, the Edsel. In order to make their new car stand out in an overcrowded market, Ford executives instructed their stylists to create a car that looked unique from every angle. Thus, the Edsel was given concave sides to counter the usual convex ones; horizontal fins to counter the vertical ones; and a vertical grille to counter the horizontal ones. Taken separately, these styling elements were not that bizarre or different. But the combination of all this cloying, attention-grabbing newness was too much. The Edsel protested its difference so loudly and superficially that it exposed the underlying similarity of all Detroit's large, lavishly decorated family sedans. The car became a lightning rod for consumers' gathering discontents with the automotive excesses of the decade. Sales were so low that the make was forced off the market in three years. This episode indicated that consumers were beginning to see through the aesthetic disguise of mass production, a trend also apparent in the popularity of exposés like Vance Packard's *Hidden Persuaders* (1957) and John Keats's *Insolent Chariots* (1958). The aesthetic and structural convergence of American autos provided consumers so little individuality that a growing number began to buy imported cars. The cultural elite ridiculed the "balloon-like chromium-encrusted bodies" of American cars as the pretentious status symbols of middle-class housewives, and expressed a preference for lithe European sports cars (*Fortune* 1947: 184). Well-heeled businessmen appropriated European luxury makes like Mercedes-Benz to individuate themselves. Even working-class youth rejected homogenized American sedans and sought difference and individuality by modifying stock cars, touching off the hot-rod and custom-car subcultures. Some middle-class youth and adults embraced the simple, unchanging Volkswagen as a mark of difference, turning it into the "anticar" in American culture.

The contradictions of the Fordist age of mass individuality were not confined to consumer aesthetics but also spilled over into use. When all Americans sought to express individual freedom and escape from mass production by taking to the roads, they created unintended collective effects that undermined these pleasures of automobility. Crowded roads increased breakdowns, accidents, noise, and pollution, and generally despoiled the pristine countryside to which motorists sought to escape. By the 1960s several movements emerged to fight these consequences of the automobile, most importantly, the environmental movement and the consumer movement. The automotive age of mass individuality was drawing to a close, collapsing under its own contradictions. Out of these struggles and contradictions, however, emerged a new synthesis of elements, a new era of production, consumption, and use which would carry the automobile into the new millennium.

THE ERA OF SUBCULTURAL DIFFERENCE: POSTMODERNISM AND POST-FORDISM

Beginning in the 1960s both the American government and the automobile industry responded to the contradictions of Fordist automobility. The U.S. Congress responded to the environmental movement in 1965 by passing the Motor Vehicle Air Pollution and Control Act, which set emission standards for automobiles. And addressing the safety concerns of the consumer movement, Congress passed the National Traffic and Motor Vehicle Safety Act of 1966, which empowered a federal agency to set safety standards for new cars. While simultaneously fighting these governmental regulations, American automakers undertook changes in their products to stem their loss of market share to foreign competitors. Sensing that the ultimate problem was the lack of product individuality, they abandoned the Fordist emphasis on mass-produced but superficially differentiated autos and began to offer a greater variety of cars that differed fundamentally in structure and engineering. Between 1960 and 1970 American manufacturers increased model offerings by 50% and, in the process, introduced a plethora of totally new types of vehicles: compacts, subcompacts, intermediate-sized cars, muscle cars (powerful performance cars), pony cars (sporty, youth-oriented cars), sports cars, and personal luxury cars. Each type was targeted not, as before, to a broad income group but to a small, more specific market niche, based on nonclass characteristics like age, gender, and family status. Many of these types were based on preexisting automotive subcultures like hot rodders, customizers, and anticar dissenters. Thus, the artificially differentiated and hierarchical mass market that obscured real class differences broke up into a plethora of leveled but distinctive niche markets. On this flattened playing field, aesthetic distinctions no longer spread from higher to lower products, but from peripheral subcultures to mainstream markets (see Chapter 6).

It became quickly evident, however, that this new, more differentiated mode of consumption of automobiles was incompatible with old Fordist methods of production. The increased diversity of products threatened the foundation of Fordist mass production—product standardization. As the number of models grew, a specialized plant had to be built to produce each one. Further, the increasing number of options available on each model caused variations in assembly time for cars on the same line. This variation increased workers' discretion and allowed them to slow production in their continuing struggle with management over the effort bargain. The results of increased variety in the context of contentious labor relations were increased unit production costs and decreased unit profits. Automakers during the late 1960s and early 1970s sought to boost sagging profits through their traditional cost-cutting measure, speed-up. But these measures fell on a working class insulated from the threat of firing by strong unions and Keynesian programs like unemployment insurance and social wage programs. So when managers stepped up the work pace, secure Fordist workers revolted, sending rates of absenteeism, turnover, and stoppages skyrocketing. Automakers and other manufacturers realized that they could not offer consumers greater product variety profitably without restructuring not only the production process but also the entire Fordist apparatus of labor relations and social programs (Bowles, Gordon, and Weisskopf 1984).

Automakers began restructuring their production process in the 1970s in order to restore profitability and compete with escalating foreign competition. Foreign automakers gained an even stronger foothold in the American market after the oil embargo of 1973, which sent gasoline prices soaring and placed a premium on the small, fuel-efficient cars that Japan and Germany had been producing for years. Disadvantaged in this competition by rigidly standardized Fordist production processes and bureaucracies, American automakers scrambled to cut costs and find more flexible production methods capable of producing a wide variety of constantly changing products. Taking their cues from Japanese producers, especially Toyota, these corporations began closing plants and shifting parts production to independent contractors, many of which operated in low-wage, third-world countries. And within the remaining plants, attempts were made to render production more flexible and accommodating to variety by using general-purpose machines and workers trained to handle a wide variety of tasks. Sometimes called "lean production" or "flexible specialization," this new organization of production substantially cut the costs of manufacturing and allowed automakers to shift a larger proportion of their capital to the increasingly important nonproduction functions of design and marketing. All of these corporate restructuring measures were facilitated, however, by a neoliberal restructuring of the state, which attacked organized labor, cut social programs, slashed taxes on corporations and the wealthy, and deregulated the financial sector of the economy. These measures not only facilitated the technological restructuring of the workplace but also allowed the capital mobility necessary to cut the high fixed costs of an organized work force with legal protections and shift production to low-wage, casual workers with few rights and protections (Womack, Jones, and Roos 1991; Rubenstein 2001; Milkman 1997; Klein 1999).

During this period of restructuring in the 1970s and early 1980s, the American market for cars was stagnant and sober. The energy crisis and environmental concerns created a practical, no-nonsense attitude toward cars for the first time in decades. Further, the stagnant economy and inflation of these years eroded consumer buying power. But beginning in the mid-1980s, the restructured economy began to grow, creating a bifurcated economic boom in which the wealth and income of the bourgeoisie and professional classes grew rapidly while that of the working class stagnated or fell. It was the consumption of the former that revived the automobile market in the late 1980s and 1990s. Seeking to display not mainly their wealth but their lifestyles, the newly enriched yuppies crowded into the auto market demanding some symbol of their individuality and difference from an older generation of business professionals. American automakers rapidly responded to this demand with their new flexibility. An explosion of diverse auto types, each testifying to a "lifestyle choice," emerged on the market—minivans, retro cars, sports-utility vehicles, eco-cars, mulitpurpose vehicles, hybrid cars. Each appealed not to the masses with varying quantities of what everyone wanted, but to a small niche market based on a specific leisure interest or identity. These lifestyle cars were considered not "better" or "worse" than one another, but just different, in a market no longer hierarchical but fragmented and tolerant. In such a market, automakers did not merely sell cars, they sold a "brand," an entire identity, meaning, or image of life (Klein 1999; Sparke 2002: 198–243; Rubenstein 2001: 217–50, 287–306).

This leveled and pluralized culture of automobility is best explained by postmodern theory. Although there are many theoretical tendencies that fall within the rather elastic boundaries of "postmodernism," I will concentrate on that type elaborated by the Birmingham Center for Contemporary Cultural Studies, within which the work of Stuart Hall and Dick Hebdige is especially useful. Their brand of postmodernism engages directly with the literature on Fordism to argue that postmodern culture coincides with a new form of production called post-Fordism. For these theorists, the new postmodern society emerges in advanced capitalist countries that "are increasingly characterized by diversity, differentiation and fragmentation, rather than homogeneity, standardization and the economics and organization of scale which characterized modern mass society" (Hall and Jacques 1989:11). They argue that during the 1960s the class identities that defined and positioned people in society began to break up, giving rise to a number of new political and cultural groups. The social movements of the 1960s are generally credited with this fragmentation, for they pioneered nonclass political identities around a number of noneconomic issues like gender, sexuality, age, and counterculture. Along with this disruption of class identities came a challenge to the hierarchical culture that expressed them. Postmodern culture is defined above all by a collapse of the distinction between elite and mass culture. For many young artists of the 1960s, high modern art had become discredited by its integration into the administered society of corporate capitalism. They began to embrace aspects of mass culture, blending high and low in new, diverse forms that expressed the proliferating nonclass identities of society (Hebdige 1989).

At this point, mass-production industries began to fall into crisis due to the diversification and fragmentation of cultural identities. Fordist production depended upon a mass market for the production of standardized goods by unchanging machines and assembly lines. These standardized goods could be artificially differentiated in quantitative attributes to sell to different income classes, but the system assumed that everyone wanted basically the same things. The rise of a diversity of nonhierarchical, nonclass subgroups fragmented the mass market, for each group demanded different goods to express its unique identity. The new nature of consumer demand stimulated, according to the postmodern theorists, a new post-Fordist production method based on economies of scope rather than economies of scale. Employing the new technologies of computers and other microelectronic innovations, manufacturers replaced mass production with flexible specialization, a manufacturing system that produces small runs of a large variety of products on machines that can be quickly changed (Mort 1989; Murray 1989). Under the escalating demand for product diversity in a leveled and fragmented consumer culture, more and more manufacturers in all advanced capitalist countries were forced to eschew outmoded Fordism for this new production system of post-Fordism (Amin 1994).

Some postmodern theorists, such as Jean Baudrillard, draw dreadfully bleak political implications from this collapse of class identities and the rise of a culture dominated by an ever-changing array of consumer spectacles expressing the identities of a populace fragmented by lifestyle concerns. The Birmingham School, however, is optimistic about the political configuration of postmodernism/post-Fordist society. Dick Hebdige, in particular, argues for the subversive potential of subcultures defined by consumer style. He welcomes the collapse of class identities and the bifurcated culture that accompanies them. Both are based on hierarchical models that reproduce the passivity of the masses at the bottom, who await deliverance by the experts at the top. The fragmentation and leveling of class identity and culture create, Hebdige (1989) asserts, a plethora of subcultures that transcend class and nation and have the potential to subvert the totality of capitalist society. In his landmark study, *Subculture* (1979), he analyses the consumption-based subcultures of British working-class youth, arguing that their cobbled-together styles represent a serious disruption of the cultural codes that underlie a hierarchical society.

Hebdige also applies his model of lifestyle subcultures as subversive to motor vehicles in his collection entitled *Hiding in the Light* (1988). Here he argues that cars, like other consumer objects, have a multitude of meanings assigned by different groups that appropriate them for their own purposes. There are no essential relations of production to reveal or conceal, only a multitude of competing, surface meanings that can cancel and undermine an oppressive, totalizing hierarchy (1988: 77–80). In his essay on the British reception of American mass-produced cars in the 1950s, he argues that these cars were perceived as and actually were a threat to the established hierarchy of tastes that legitimated class differences. Many upper-class Britons saw in the popular consumer affluence of the postwar period a pernicious "leveling down process," in which elite moral and aesthetic standards were eroded. Large, superfluously decorated American cars like the Cadillac El Dorado were considered particularly decadent and offensive, for they catered to the vulgarity of the masses and destroyed true elegance and refinement in design. For workers, however, these cars were symbols of progress, i.e., the improvement in their standard of living and the advances in science that this made possible. Hebdige argues that these mass-produced American cars did hasten the liquidation of the distinctive cultural heritage on which the authority of the elite rested. But he asserts that the conservatives were wrong about the homogenizing effect of this leveled consumer culture. "Rather, American popular culture . . . offers a rich iconography or set of symbols, objects and artifacts which can be assembled and reassembled by different groups in a literally limitless number of combinations. And the meaning of each selection is transformed as individual objects . . . are taken out of their original historical and cultural contexts and juxtaposed against other signs from other sources" (Hebdige 1988: 74). This multiplicity of meanings freely constructed by different groups to express their own identities makes this leveled consumer culture "a new language of dissent" (1988: 71).

A similar but more recent postmodern analysis of automobiles as the expression of fragmented and subversive subcultural identities is offered in Daniel Miller's collection entitled *Car Cultures*. Miller asserts that people see and express themselves through the car, which thus assumes a "different cultural form or experience among different groups" (Miller 2001: 12). Since these subcultural expressions are intimate and diverse, "the car has become more a means to resist alienation than a sign of alienation" (2001: 3). The volume contains a number of ethnographic studies of autos that seek to validate this postmodern approach, including one of young, working-class Swedish males called *ragarre* or greasers. This subculture is centered on the restoration and driving of big, chromed-up American cars of the 1950s and 1960s. The author of the study, Tom O'Dell (2001), argues that working-class youth adopted these cars specifically to mark their differences from and contempt for the standards of "good taste" enforced by the Swedish middle class, which defined American cars as vulgar, pretentious, and hedonistic. He holds that this automotive subculture was nationally specific, since it was defined against the peculiar values of the Swedish middle class—practicality, rationality, and reserve. O'Dell also sees the *ragarre* as subversive, since the middle class saw them and their cars as symbols of danger and moral decline.

But in his rush to assert the uniqueness of this subculture, O'Dell curiously omits any reference to American hot rodders, who appeared at about the same time. As Moorhouse (1991) makes clear, these American youth also were largely working class and sought to assert their difference from mainstream Americans' cars. And they too were the subject of moral panics and fears. Hot rodders' highly modified and altered cars were different from *ragarre* vehicles, which were mainly stock restorations of American cars. But American hot rodders had to modify their cars to differentiate them from the large, decorated sedans that were common in the United States; the *ragarre's* unmodified American cars achieved the same difference against sober and efficient Swedish cars. So the cultural expression may have been different, but the meanings were the same—freedom, escape, difference. Neither does O'Dell explore in any depth the real impact of this subculture on society. Just because these youth were *perceived* as a threat to bourgeois society does not mean that they were. In the United States many of these "subversive" automotive differences pioneered by hot rodders were incorporated into the models of the mainstream automakers. Thus, this subculture became just another source of individuality and difference for the more pluralized and leveled automotive market.

Similar questions about the automotive expression of subcultural difference can be raised with respect to gender. Pauline Garvey's contribution to *Car Cultures* argues that the automobile provides young Norwegian women with means to transgress established gender roles. Through reckless and illegal driving these women achieve freedom and escape from their restricted routine of domestic chores and social isolation. Such behavior also has the meaning in Norway of defying state authority, since the government in this country has from the beginning of automobility sought to regulate car ownership, by first restricting and then facilitating it. But Garvey also seems to realize that these women use the car just as often to facilitate, not challenge, established gender roles. The daring drive on the wrong side of the road provides merely a temporary relief from domestic chores that makes them a bit more tolerable. And at least for one woman interviewed, driving does not create social relations to alleviate domestic isolation but "occasionally substitutes for absent social relationships . . .," act[ing] as a pressure valve to release the oppressive isolation of long periods inside the home" (Garvey 2001: 140).

Cindy Donatelli has argued, in fact, that one niche-market car aimed specifically at women does not facilitate their freedom but more securely entraps them in traditional gender roles. She sees the minivan, one of the first and most successful lifestyle vehicles, "as a material shell for the retrograde conservative agenda of 'family values' which became one of the dominant themes in political discourse when Ronald Reagan was elected at the beginning of the 1980s" (Donatelli, 2001: 85). This suburban home on wheels reasserts the ascendancy of heterosexual marriage and procreation in this age of backlash against feminism. The very structure of the vehicle is tailored to gender stereotypes. It is large enough to accommodate lots of children, whose production and care defines woman's traditional role. Yet it is close to the ground and handles easily, for women are considered too delicate and weak to drive a traditional truck, a clearly masculine vehicle. Loaded with all the feminine comforts of home, the minivan allows women to efficiently perform their traditional domestic roles while at the same time squeezing in eight or more hours in their newly found "freedom" as wage-earners.

Paul Gilroy similarly argues that autos associated with the subculture of American blacks do not serve to break racial stereotypes but merely to maintain and bind them to mainstream consumer culture. He recognizes that the history of African-Americans' enslavement and coerced labor makes them receptive to the auto as a means of mobility, often allowing blacks to escape racism and move to employment opportunities. Further, their material deprivation and lack of property has inclined African-Americans toward products like luxury cars, which publicly display the wealth and consequent status generally denied them. Despite these recognitions, however, Gilroy sees the African-American auto subculture of expensive cars, chrome rims, and elaborate car stereos as corporate race-branding that maintains stereotypes while simultaneously salving African-Americans' chronic injuries. And more importantly, black automobility diverts energy from collective, political struggles against racism into individualistic, consumerist assertions. Consequently, cars "have helped to deliver us to a historic point where blackness can easily become less an index of hurt, resistance or solidarity in the face of persistent and systematic inequality than one more faintly exotic life-style 'option' conferred by the multi-cultural alchemy of heavily branded commodities and the pre-sealed, 'ethnic' identities that apparently match them" (Gilroy 2001: 86).

The postmodernists have identified a distinct age of automobility, in which the car is produced, purchased, and used not as an expression of class distinction or mass individuality, but as the mark of identity in one of a multitude of lifestyle groups, none of which is necessarily superior to another. But their assertion that this leveled and fragmented cultural logic somehow liberates people from the confining roles of class, race, and gender is questionable. As the polarization of wealth and income proceeds rapidly, affirmative action is dismantled, and women's reproductive rights are whittled away, the appearance of consumer difference may merely provide a smokescreen of freedom and diversity (Jameson 1991). Thus, this age of automobility is best seen not as a replacement of the reification postulated by the Frankfurt School in the age of mass individuality, but its transcendence into a higher form. The basic need addressed by postmodern difference is the same as that found in the Fordist age of mass individuality—that of compensatory individuality in a society that deprives people of economic autonomy. However, with the collapse of Fordist restraints on the economic market over the last two decades, people need an intensified dose of consumer individuality to overcome the loss of autonomy in the production sphere. The quantitative differentiation within a mass of similar consumers no longer suffices, and is replaced by a qualitative differentiation between infinitely divisible lifestyle groups. But once again, this intensified individuality of things serves to obscure the real human relations of class, gender, and race, which have become more homogenized and polarized than ever.

This does not mean, however, that automobility has now stabilized into a balanced system. On the contrary, the transcendence of the cultural logic of mass individuality into that of subcultural difference also generates contradictions, both within and between its constituent parts. First, there are signs that the proliferation of models to differentiate a plethora of lifestyle subcultures is contradicting the demands of even the flexible production system of post-Fordism. As automakers in the 1990s produced more models to please consumers demanding difference, the profit per vehicle dropped, especially among Japanese producers, due to shorter runs and lower economies of scale. Their response was to move toward a system of "optimum lean production," in which productivity and economies of scale were reemphasized as goals. To achieve these, however, corporations had to sacrifice model diversity and innovation. Thus, for example, to cut costs and achieve longer runs of parts, producers under optimum lean production began to design new models to use more and more components from the old ones. Further economies of scale were achieved by reducing the number of different platforms (the structural foundation of a car) and the trim levels and option packages available on each model. Finally, in search of greater scale, companies began to consolidate through mergers or joint ventures, so that the same platform could be used by more nameplates. For example, due to its acquisition of other brands, Ford used the same luxury platform to produce Lincolns, Jaguars, and Volvos. These measures, however, threaten to reduce the real differences between cars that drive the niche markets of postmodernism (Rubenstein 2001: 42–55).

A second contradiction of the current age of automobility has emerged between the culture of difference and the use of cars. When every individual driver demands a car expressing his or her unique identity, the number of cars on the road grows and creates frustrating impediments to automotive expressionism. This problem is further exacerbated if, as the postmodernists claim, each individual has a number of identities that cry out for expression at different times. So, for example, the yuppie software executive may express his high-tech corporate persona by driving a BMW to work, but on the weekends he wants an off-road vehicle to express his back-to-nature leisure persona. Consequently, in the United States there are already more automobiles than licensed drivers. So the car takes over more and more of the environment, and the roads become so jammed that driving becomes an experience of frustration, not liberation and individuality. It is hard to feel like a free individual in a massive gridlock of cars. The roads of advanced capitalist countries become battlegrounds for limited space, where tensions flair in ugly incidents of road rage. When the culture promises drivers effortless speed and escape, any impediment becomes intolerable (Michael 2001: 72). To secure individual advantage in the Darwinian struggle for space, some drivers up the ante by buying large, powerful, military-like sport-utility vehicles, lording it over the lower species of the road in an aggressive grandeur that only makes driving more competitive and dangerous.

This decline of civility on the roads may also reflect a third contradiction of postmodern automobility, one internal to the realm of culture itself. When individuals withdraw from public life into a multitude of lifestyle enclaves, associating only with others exactly like themselves, it becomes difficult to identify with the other driver. He or she is seen not as a fellow human with commonly shared rights and obligations but as an alien other with a different lifestyle competing for scarce space and recognition. Robert Bellah and colleagues have argued in *Habits of the Heart* (1996) that the United States is becoming a collection of "lifestyle enclaves" and losing that sense of shared fate and culture that makes collective effort and identification possible. Such cultural atomization, not environmental exhaustion or unprofitable production, may provide the ultimate limit to the age of postmodern automobility.

CONCLUSION

My research on the cultural logics of the car reveals that disruptions to the culture of automobility have occurred twice before in the history of the car. Both the logics of class distinction and mass individuality were undermined by their own extension and iteration, forcing a restructuring between the elements of automobility. But the three ages of the automobile that I identify all evidence an underlying dynamic that drives the system of automobility and its cultural logic. This dynamic is the confrontation of potentially autonomous human beings with an economic market system that thwarts their self-determination with an alien logic all its own. The development of the laws of the market over the last century has forced humans into the realm of consumption to satisfy their needs for identity, autonomy, and individuality. And the ultimate expression of this compensatory consumption has been the automobile, the individualized means of mobility that has become synonymous with freedom. Each stage of the automobile has ultimately foundered due to the inability of this thing to satisfy human needs, to provide identity in sheet metal and autonomy in movement. So the contradictions pile up from one stage to the next, intensified and exacerbated but not solved. This automotive folly will end only through the actions of humans to reclaim their fate from their own machines.

5 Why Modern Architecture Emerged in Europe, Not America
The New Class and the Aesthetics of Technocracy

In Chapter 4 I argued that the explanatory power of different theories of culture varies by historical period. While Bourdieu's theory of culture as class symbolization seems to well explain the structure of capitalist culture in the early period, cultural dynamics gave rise to changes that undermined the efficacy of the theory and led to a period of mass individuality explained by the Frankfurt School's theory of cultural reification. But the efficacy of cultural theories varies not only by historical period but also by type of culture. In Chapter 3 I suggested that the Frankfurt School's theory of the leveling and reification of culture is more empirically valid for material culture, while Bourdieu's theory of class symbolization is more valid for nonmaterial culture. This is because the consumption of the artifacts of material culture—e.g. automobiles, food, furniture—is more dependent on economic capital (money) than cultural capital (knowledge). Consequently, when the distribution of income becomes more equal, as it did in most advanced capitalist countries after World War II, there is a tendency for the material culture to become leveled and homogeneous. This was the case with American automobiles in the 1950s and 1960s, as I revealed in Chapter 4.

However, the consumption of nonmaterial culture—music, literature, paintings—is more dependent on cultural capital than economic capital. For example, admission to an art museum or a symphony concert costs no more—in many cases it costs less—than admission to a NASCAR race or a country music or rap concert. What prevents working-class NASCAR fans from attending the Richard Serra retrospective at the Museum of Modern Art, for example, is not lack of money but lack of knowledge of the history and issues of modern sculpture. In most capitalist countries, the distribution of knowledge is more unequal that the distribution of money, and much less susceptible to class conflict. So nonmaterial culture is less susceptible to leveling, and usually marked by greater class divisions. But the existence of a high, art-for-art's-sake nonmaterial culture aimed at an audience defined by knowledge, not money, raises a fundamental question, especially in capitalist society. How do the cultural producers in this subfield support themselves, if not from market income? The high arts are notorious money-losers in modern society, because aimed at a very restricted market.

How do producers forego the temptation to generate income by "dumbing down" offerings to reach a larger but less knowledgeable mass market? In other words, how do these high arts maintain their autonomy from the market and thus uphold purely aesthetic standards?

Both Bourdieu and the Frankfurt School are concerned with this question of the autonomy of culture, but for different reasons. Bourdieu must address this issue because his culture-as-class-symbolization model assumes the continued existence of such an autonomous high culture, whose distinctions from the mass culture of the lower classes symbolizes and legitimates class differences. By contrast, the Frankfurt School's theory of culture-as-mass-reification argues that such an autonomous high culture is severely threatened by the leveling forces of the market. But these theorists, especially Adorno, also hold that the continued existence of this cultural subfield is possible and desirable, since only this type of autonomous culture can provide the criticism of class society necessary to change it. Despite these different functions of autonomous culture, both theories postulate that the major sources of its support in modern society are the state and a large subfield of cultural producers with an interest in enforcing aesthetic standards.

This chapter explores the issue of cultural autonomy by focusing on architecture, which, unlike the automobile, does not become leveled and reified in the manner suggested by the Frankfurt School. One of the main reasons for the continued existence of an autonomous, high-art subfield in architecture is its quality as a nonmaterial artifact. Architecture certainly has a material component, which distinguishes it from purely ideal cultural artifacts like musical compositions. A building is an expensive physical product that requires economic resources to consume, whether consumption is defined as ownership, occupation through rent, or even occasional use, as in amusement parks and shopping malls. Yet, in its restricted subfield, architecture is also an art, which requires for proper appreciation knowledge of history and cultivated dispositions to detect subtle distinctions. This hybrid nature of architecture explains the only partial leveling of this field, which occurred in the 1960s and 1970s through the movement of postmodernism. Both the details and the general causal principles of this postmodern leveling are discussed in Chapter 6.

Here, however, I focus on explaining the differential development of high-art modern architecture in Europe and the United States during the early twentieth century. My main argument is that modernism emerged in Europe because there the class whose interests it expressed, the professional-managerial class, remained autonomous from the economic market, due largely to state support for its work. Consequently, it was able to symbolically express through modern architecture its class interest in the rationalization of industry, which in Europe during the early twentieth century was unpopular with both capitalists and the working class. In the United States, by contrast, the professional-managerial class, which includes architects and designers, was integrated early on into industry by modernizing capitalists anxious to employ its services in the mass-production process. But once integrated into mass-production, this class was forced to subordinate its modernist aesthetic to the tastes of the masses, who demanded decorative kitsch to cover over the rationalization of the workplace. As a consequence of losing autonomy from the market, American architects did not express but obscured class differences in an Art Deco style. This case clearly demonstrates that the leveling and reification of culture theorized by the Frankfurt School depends on both the class structure of society, especially the position of cultural producers, and the type of culture, material or nonmaterial, that they produce.

ART AND CLASS STRUGGLE: THE MISPLACED
DEVELOPMENT OF MODERN ARCHITECTURE

Why did modern architecture emerge mainly in interwar Europe, not the United States? Modern architecture was a celebration of the machines of mass production and its mechanical products, which were idealized and abstracted to form a machine aesthetic. America pioneered these machines in the early twentieth century, yet in this land of mass production modern architecture was attenuated and undeveloped. America did have its prescient pioneers of modern architecture, like Louis Sullivan and Frank Lloyd Wright. But only in interwar central Europe, an industrially backward and economically devastated region, did the machine aesthetic of modern architecture emerge in it pure form in the work of architects such as Le Corbusier, Mies van der Rohe, and Walter Gropius. This disjuncture between economic and aesthetic development reminds us that cultural works do not passively and directly reflect the structure of society, but are better understood as active, though often unconscious, interventions in social struggles.

Marxist literary critic Fredric Jameson (1971, 1981) formulates a useful theory of aesthetic form as unconscious class struggle. He argues that art is shaped by the contradictions of a society, which artists seek to resolve in forms. The nature and type of these formal resolutions depend upon the class positions of the producers and the relation of their class to others in history. The artist's class and its struggles provide the conceptual limits to her forms, rendering unthinkable imaginary resolutions that contradict its interests. All artistic productions thus intervene symbolically in the social struggles of the day, but these political interventions are most often unintentional and unconscious.

Pierre Bourdieu (1996a) offers a theory of aesthetics similar to Jameson's, arguing that the class position of the artist unconsciously influences the forms of art by providing both the contradictions that must be solved and the limits of solutions. He calls the unconscious structure that shapes an artist's productions a habitus, a set of durable, embodied dispositions inculcated by early socialization in a particular position in the class structure. These class-specific habitus give rise to specific cultural tastes, which influence the forms of art that people produce and consume (Bourdieu 1984: 169–225). With Jameson, Bourdieu conceives of these artistic forms as strategic interventions in struggles, political moves to accumulate power and "symbolic profits" in competition with opponents.

The theories of Bourdieu and Jameson differ, however, on the directness of the link between class background and aesthetic form. Jameson (1981) postulates a direct link, with the bourgeois background of the vast majority of artists shaping the way they symbolically resolve the problems generated by this class's confrontations with the working class. By contrast, Bourdieu sees class habitus always mediated through the structure and positions of artistic fields. He recognizes that the dominant class is divided between those who possess mainly economic capital, the dominant fraction or economic bourgeoisie, and those who possess mainly cultural capital, the dominated fraction or cultural bourgeoisie. This division parallels that made by Alvin Gouldner (1979) between the "old class" of moneyed capitalists and the "new class" of managers, professionals, intellectuals, and artists. Both Gouldner and Bourdieu argue that most of the class conflict in modern societies is not interclass conflict between the working class and the bourgeoisie but intraclass conflict between intellectuals and moneyed capitalists, with each seeking to make its form of capital the legitimate grounds for the distribution of income and power (Bourdieu 1984: 114–25).

Bourdieu also argues that the cultural fraction of the dominant class is itself divided by relative closeness to the economic pole of the dominant class and the economic market which defines it. Those producers in the cultural field who cater to the large-scale or mass market and are focused on economic profits are in the heteronomous subfield, while those producers who cater to the restricted or small-scale market and are focused on symbolic profits (recognition) are located in the autonomous subfield, which is insulated from the demands of the economic market by state subsidies or sales to other cultural producers. Consequently, the influence of class background or habitus on artistic forms is mediated by the artist's current position within this field of cultural production itself. Class habitus determines where the artist is initially positioned in the field, but then the interests and conflicts of this position determine artistic form (Bourdieu 1993b: 37–44; 1996a: 113–40).

Theorists of the Frankfurt School, like Max Horkheimer and Theodor Adorno (1972) recognize a similar division of art into two types defined by closeness to the capitalist marketplace: the culture industry and autonomous art. In the former, culture is mass-produced in the pursuit of profits and thus must cater to mass tastes. In doing so, it abandons the critical or utopian function found in autonomous art—holding out the promise of a better world, while simultaneously revealing the antagonisms of the existing society that prevent this world from being realized. But unlike Bourdieu (1984: 372–96), who argues that commercial art is shaped by the inherent taste of the working class for immediate pleasure, Frankfurt theorists see mass culture as driven by the contingent demand for compensation originating in alienating conditions of labor. Working-class consumers seek in consumption the freedom and sociality denied them in capitalist production, so they do not want to be reminded of the alienating and rationalized characteristics of capitalism that autonomous art is obliged to reveal (Adorno 1994: 5–28; 1984: 320–69).

The ambivalent position of architecture relative to these two subfields of art is crucial to understanding the emergence of the modernist aesthetic. As Magali Sarfatti Larson (1993: 12–20) recognizes, architecture in the twentieth century has aspired to be an autonomous art, governed by internal aesthetic standards, but it is inevitably heteronomous in part, because dependent upon economic capital controlled by those outside the field to be built.

Bourdieu's insights about the struggles between the cultural and economic fractions of the dominant class, as well as the struggles between autonomous and heteronomous producers in the field of culture, are indispensable in understanding modern architecture. But his theory ignores the importance of the working class, which Bourdieu sees as passive and irrelevant to the struggles in the dominant-class "field of power." Jameson's model, which follows Lukács in conceiving the dominated class as an active force in society, provides a corrective to Bourdieu's one-sided reproduction. We can fully understand the intraclass struggle between the fractions of the dominant class and its effects in the field of art only when we conceive of the working class as a potential ally or enemy of one of these dominant fractions.

Using this model, I argue below that modern architecture emerged in the interwar countries of central Europe, especially Germany, as opposed to the U.S., because of the different class structures and struggles of the two regions and their effects on artistic fields. Modern architecture was part of a broader technocratic ideology that emerged around the turn of the twentieth century to assert the interests of the cultural bourgeoisie against the economic bourgeoisie or capitalists. This ideological art form was undeveloped in the U.S. because there the struggles of the cultural bourgeoisie for power resulted in an early alliance with capitalists. America's strong capitalist class pursued economic modernization via Fordist mass production, and consequently incorporated those parts of the cultural bourgeoisie whose knowledge and skills furthered this innovation. Because Fordism was legitimated to the masses by market-based mass consumption, capitalists were forced to cater to the mass demand for an aesthetic that obscured rather than exposed the forms of machine production.

In central European countries like Germany, however, the persistent power of the aristocracy weakened the capitalist class and made it an enemy of industrial modernization. The professionals, managers, and intellectuals who stood to gain from modernization were forced to look for allies elsewhere, namely, the interwar social-democratic state. State managers teamed up with parts of the cultural bourgeoisie, including architects, to advocate a state-led rationalization program legitimated by a strong technocratic ideology, of which modern architecture was a vital part. Because the important consumer good of housing was delivered by state command, and not subject to market demand, working-class consumers had little choice but to accept the machine aesthetic favored by the architectural elite.

AMERICA: THE SOCIAL FOUNDATIONS
OF A COMPROMISED MODERNISM

From its beginning, America was the land of unadulterated, uninhibited capitalism, where no feudal past stood in the way of the pursuit of profits, and new methods of production were invented incessantly. Unlike Europe, where the remnants of feudal stratification encouraged the waste of plentiful labor in embellishing goods, in capitalist America labor was a scarce commodity, and the lack of an aristocratic leisure class discouraged the costly embellishment of goods. American products were produced with utilitarian simplicity and sold to a broad market (Ewen and Ewen 1982: 117–28; Giedion 1967: 336–52).

Early American architecture similarly reflected this imperative to use scarce labor efficiently in a budding capitalism. Structures of residence and commerce were built simply to accommodate new labor-saving machines and methods. In the 1830s Americans pioneered balloon-frame construction, which eliminated the need for skilled carpenters through the use of standardized, machine-cut lumber assembled quickly with manufactured nails. Around the middle of the nineteenth century, the use of cast-iron fronts and frames assembled from factory-made parts on commercial buildings asserted a similar influence toward flat, rectilinear, undecorated forms (Pulos 1983: 107; Giedion 1967: 195–204, 347–63).

It was not long, however, before these architectural forms dictated by commercial efficiency touched off a cultural reaction among the very classes that they were enriching. Around the middle of the nineteenth century the nouveau riche industrial capitalists began to flee the aesthetic consequences of the capitalist cities they created, moving their residences away from the rigid grids of urban centers to the winding lanes of suburbia. Here they sought to escape the demands of industrial commerce in an insulated world of leisure, constructing mansions designed by Beaux-Arts architects in a variety of historic styles that spoke of preindustrial craftwork. As Bourdieu (1984: 176–77, 292–94) argues, this ostentatious ornament displayed the distinctive distance of the economic bourgeoisie from the practical concerns of other classes (Brain 1989; Jackson 1985: 20–32; Pulos 1983: 190–97; Ewen 1988: 116–20).

This obscuring aesthetic of historicism was soon challenged, however, by an emerging class that had an interest in glorifying the simple, rationalized forms that the economic bourgeoisie hid. This was the new class of professionals, managers, and technicians, who sought to use their education and intellectual skills to solve the emerging contradictions of America's uncontrolled capitalism. An economic downturn beginning in 1874 touched off vicious competition and popular discontent, causing capitalists to seek new methods of wielding power and doing business. The growing class of educated professionals and specialists stepped forward to offer solutions. Leading a reform movement known as Progressivism, this class promised to reconcile conflicting class interests and restore order through the intervention of neutral, scientific knowledge (Wiebe 1967; Weinstein 1968).

The ideology that legitimated this movement of the new class was technocracy. Vigorously contesting the distribution of power and wealth based on economic capital, aspiring technocrats argued for the rule of knowledge, education, and reason (Gouldner 1979: 19–20). The most vociferous advocate of the technocratic ideology in the U.S. was Thorstein Veblen, whose seminal *Theory of the Leisure Class*, published in 1899, denounced the holders of private property as wasteful drones and championed the useful, "industrious classes" as humanity's saviors. Part of his technocratic ideology was a direct attack on the tastes of the nouveau riche industrialists, who, he argued, validated an object as beautiful in direct proportion to its uselessness and conspicuous waste of labor and materials. Veblen argued that the appropriate aesthetic for industrialism was an unadorned functionalism, which expressed the object's efficiency of production. This aesthetic, which Bourdieu (1984: 214) calls "aristocratic aestheticism," also glorified the rational intelligence and technique of the cultural bourgeoisie (Veblen 1934: 115–66).

The technocratic aesthetic of efficiency and functionalism was developed in the Progressive era by Chicago School architects Louis Sullivan and Frank Lloyd Wright. Both men were upstarts, attacking from the periphery an architectural field that was consolidating around an elite of high-class Beaux-Arts architects. Both came from petite bourgeois backgrounds, so their class habitus inclined them to take up the cause of the emerging new class, which was asserting the importance of intelligence and technology over the money of capitalists and the high culture that legitimated it (Frampton 1992: 51–56; Blake 1976: 287–94; Paul 1962: 1–23).

In justification of a practical, ascetic aesthetic that countered bourgeois ostentation, Sullivan coined the slogan "form follows function," making it clear that the function to be served and symbolized was "the organized commercial spirit" (Sullivan 1947: 30). He loved commerce and invention but, like Veblen, vigorously condemned wealth, which stood in the way of technical progress. "For of what use is money alone," he asked rhetorically, "without a chastened guiding spirit . . . when not impelled by carefully selected brains [?]" (Sullivan 1947: 28, 21). Without intelligence, capitalists regressed to "feudalism" and wrapped themselves in "aristocratic" styles. The virile, efficient democracy of America must express itself through simple, open, utilitarian architecture, Sullivan argued (Giedion 1967: 368–93; Frampton 1992: 51–56).

The execution of Sullivan's technocratic aesthetic was, however, not as bold as its rhetorical statement. Although he disparaged historical decoration, his buildings were always enriched by a rather florid, vegetative ornamentation tacked onto the surface. For example, the upper floors of Sullivan's Carson, Pirie, Scott department store in Chicago clearly expressed the rectilinear steel frame of the building, but the first two floors were covered with cast-iron panels decorated with ornate Art Nouveau motifs. Sullivan was reluctant to expose the severe standardization of the new rationalized capitalism because it created "psychic discords whose disturbing influences we must resolve" (Sullivan 1947: 115). Rationalized, bureaucratic capitalism created a contradiction between the objective heteronomy and standardization of office and factory, and the subjective autonomy and individuality promised by traditional capitalist ideology. Sullivan was forced to address this contradiction by the rudimentary beginnings in this period of the mass market, through which middle-class and increasing numbers of working-class consumers registered their demands for escape from rationalized work through leisure. He believed that art could satisfy these demands and reconcile human subjects to the alien objectivity of the new order through the application of "organic ornamentation," in which the harmonious look of nature obscured the rationalized, technological framework of the tall building.

So the necessity of accommodating the mass market led to the compromise of the new class's autonomous aesthetic, but not because of an inherent taste for kitsch among the popular classes, as Bourdieu postulates. It was the desire of all classes to escape rationalized work in compensating leisure, as argued by the Frankfurt School, that conditioned this compromise. And this emerging aesthetic of compensation was even more visible in the growing suburbs, where the insular realm of consumption was increasingly located.

By the late nineteenth century the petite bourgeoisie, along with the emerging professional-managerial class, began to follow the rich industrialists out to the suburbs. There emerged here a new therapeutic ethos of self-fulfillment through leisure and consumption, which compensated these classes for the rationalized bureaucracies that most faced at work (Lears 1983). Like suburbanizing capitalists, they wanted their homes to symbolize distance and insulation from the industrial city. But the historical opulence of capitalists was beyond the financial reach of members of the new class, as well as offensive to their ideology of efficiency and functionality. So they searched for a simpler style, and found it in Frank Lloyd Wright's compromised suburban modernism.

Wright had worked in Louis Sullivan's office and absorbed his concept of organic architecture. However, while Sullivan used the look of nature to merely relieve the alienation of the rationalized city, Wright's architecture sought to destroy the city and create a decentralized suburban utopia. While working with Sullivan, Wright developed a lucrative sideline designing suburban houses for the fleeing new class of professionals and managers, to whose interests he was ideologically inclined by his class habitus and peripheral position in the architectural field (Wright 1932). In his suburban Chicago homes, Wright developed an "organic architecture" of ahistorical simplicity and machine-like rectilinearity. But he relieved these mechanical forms and countered urban artificiality by blending them into the natural landscape. Wright's Prairie Style houses hunkered down close to the ground with long, low lines that stressed horizontality, in contrast to urban verticality. He integrated nature into his houses with open spaces and large areas of glass. Broad, overhanging eaves also created a sense of protection, and his interiors were full of rich decoration, often derived from preindustrial societies. These and other features rendered his suburban houses refuges against a world of growing bureaucratic uniformity and factory standardization. Wright's Prairie Style was popularized in plans he published in magazines, and before long the new-class suburbs were covered with homes incorporating his pioneering elements (Blake 1976: 301–22).

THE SOCIAL SOURCES OF MODERNISM'S DEMISE: NEW CLASS INCORPORATION AND WORKING-CLASS CONFLICT

Although Wright's nature-loving suburban architecture continued in popularity, the functionalist urban style of Sullivan and Wright suffered defeat around the turn of the century. Despite some decorative relief, this style still paid homage to the stark, angular forms of the rationalized capitalism emerging in the cities. Chicago's Columbia Exposition of 1893 offered a more popular vision of the industrial city, one that hid this testimony to rigid rationality under the historic pretense of classical symmetry and order. Here, Beaux-Arts architecture completely obscured industrial building materials beneath layers of tacked-on ornament in historical styles. The Exposition spawned a resurgence of neoclassical architecture that sought to bring visual unity to America's increasingly tumultuous industrial cities (Giedion 1967: 393–96; Pulos 1983: 2–4–10; Ewen 1988: 204–6).

This early defeat of modern architecture in America is explained by the position and struggles of both the new professional-managerial class and the working class in American society. First, American modernism was stillborn because the independence of the new class, which it ideologically represented, was short-lived. As Robert Wiebe (1967) argues, the Progressive movement of educated professionals and managers in the U.S. found a ready ally for its aims of rationalization and bureaucratization in big capital. Struggling to effectively respond to heightened competition and class conflict, capitalists embraced the advice of management, engineering, and social work professionals to divide labor, professionalize management, and rationalize all operations (Weinstein 1968; Noble 1977). Thus, a large part of the new class was securely and lucratively integrated into the corporations controlled by the economic bourgeoisie. Consequently, they no longer needed a separate ideology to justify their project of technocracy. As the new class accumulated wealth and power, it dropped the ideological distinction between idle wealth and productive knowledge and based its legitimacy on the traditional capitalist ideology of the marketplace—wealth testifies to a superior contribution to the market and, hence, individual superiority.

This alliance of parts of the cultural bourgeoisie with industrial capitalists undermined the market for modern architecture. Protomodernists like Sullivan and Wright looked to the technical professions of the new class as patrons of their architecture, because they had money and occupied a position in the field of power homologous to these protomodernists' position in the architectural field—that is, outsiders challenging an established elite. (For an analysis of Wright's architectural clients, see Eaton 1969.) But when engineers, managers, and scientists were accepted into an alliance with corporate capitalists, they lost their autonomy from the market and consequently their interest in the technocratic ideology. These professions forsook the aesthetic of asceticism and rationality, and adopted an aesthetic of bourgeois luxury and historicism similar to their capitalist allies. So around the turn of the century the new class and their capitalist allies converged on Beaux-Arts classicism, at least for large-scale urban projects (Pulos 1983: 204–10; Ewen 1988: 204–6).

This shift is understandable within Bourdieu's theory, which holds that the fraction of the cultural bourgeoisie highest in economic capital adopts tastes similar to the economic bourgeoisie. His theory is not equipped, however, to explain why American architecture ultimately moved beyond this Beaux-Arts historicism to an aesthetic of entertainment and obfuscation, for Bourdieu ignores the major motivating force of this change, working-class conflict, which is better theorized by Jameson and the Frankfurt School. In response to the economic crises of the late nineteenth and early twentieth centuries, large American corporations moved toward mass production, which lowered prices and began to incorporate the working masses into expanding consumer markets. Working-class struggle against emerging mass-production methods also forced capitalists to raise wages, further expanding mass markets. This coupling of mass production with mass consumption produced a social formation called Fordism (Aglietta 1979), which entailed an expanded role for artists and designers themselves within American corporations. There they too lost their aesthetic autonomy from the market and were forced to cater to working-class demands in the mass market.

Initially, new-class Progressive reformers sought to steer this emerging mass market toward simple, ascetic designs, which symbolized and validated their sober rationality. They encouraged workers to buy simple, unupholstered wood furniture and "antiseptic" iron bedsteads, and to dispense with dust-collecting carpets, rugs, and draperies in favor of wooden floors and light window treatments. But for the most part, American workers rejected this new-class asceticism, embracing instead a domestic aesthetic of decorative surfeits. Drawing upon the mass market of cheap, machine-made furnishings, they covered floors with carpets and walls with wallpaper, and acquired plush, upholstered chairs and sofas in kitschy Victorian style (Cohen 1982; Pulos 1983:215–19).

This preference of American workers for elaborately decorated but cheap goods contradicts Bourdieu's assertion (1984: 372–96) that working-class habitus determines a "taste for necessity"—that is, for simple, functional goods that immediately display their use and make no attempts to show distance from economic necessity. He does at one point (1984: 379) acknowledge workers' "taste for trinkets and knick-knacks which adorn mantelpieces and hallways," and explains it by this class's practical attempt to obtain maximum "effect" at minimum cost. But such a calculus of aesthetic effects is surely meant to symbolically display distance from necessity and cannot be subsumed under mere functionality. Yet, although Bourdieu misses this symbolic component of working-class consumption, I believe he is ultimately right in stating that workers are not competing for distinction, not seeking to show themselves to be better than others. Rather, as the Frankfurt School's theory of mass culture contends, the intent of workers' consumption is to create an escape and respite from the increasingly heteronomous workplace produced by Fordist rationalization, just like the suburbanizing new class. Yet, unlike the latter, which exerted some discretion within this new workplace, workers were subjected to its full alienating force. Further, most still lived in the city near factories, being economically unable to seek refuge in the rural idyll of suburbia. The working class, consequently, needed more symbolic insulation and distance from the new workplace than did the new cultural bourgeoisie, and they could not find it in the simple unadorned styles pressed on them by the latter. Refuge from work could only be found in a domestic world of objects that covered over standardization and fragmentation with unified, varied decoration (Forty 1986: 101).

The dynamics of the mass market ensured that this popular aesthetic of obfuscation and entertainment would ultimately win out over the fading functionalism of the cultural bourgeoisie as well as Beaux-Arts historicism. As the 1920s progressed, the wages of working Americans rose at the same time as competition for consumer dollars escalated. In order to sell goods to this expanding mass market, mass-production corporations were forced to eschew standardized, utilitarian goods in favor of goods with the look of diversity and decoration. To supply this demand for aesthetic obfuscation, mass producers hired artistically trained designers, many of whom came from working-class and petty-bourgeois backgrounds, and the profession of industrial designer was born (Meikle 1979; Gartman 1994).

Slowly the majority of American artists and designers were drawn into large, mass-production corporations, where they were compelled to abandon any remaining class allegiance to a functionalist aesthetic and meet the popular demand for obscuring ornamentation. The integration of the cultural bourgeoisie and the working class into the capitalist project of mass production/mass consumption thus resulted in the eclipse of the class-distinctive aesthetics postulated by Bourdieu and the rise of a broadly shared mass aesthetic of entertainment and ornamentation, at least with respect to material artifacts. This result is more consistent with the culture-industry thesis of the Frankfurt School (Horkheimer and Adorno 1972).

THE ARCHITECTURE OF MASS CONSUMPTION

During this period the emerging consumer culture of insulation, obfuscation, and decoration also infiltrated the built environment, a cultural field with a substantial material component. The order and symmetry of the Beaux-Arts historicism that had displaced America's incipient modernism did not meet the demands of the dynamic economic growth of the post-World War I period, nor did its high-class pretensions appeal to America's populist consumer culture. More expressive of the consumer culture's exuberant escapism and obscurantism were the mass entertainment venues such as amusement parks, built by cultural entrepreneurs on the edges of cities to capture the rising income of working Americans. New York's Coney Island, for example, offered working-class refugees from urban grids of standardized, empty spaces a fantastically full landscape of dreams, in which a dizzy mélange of exotic architecture momentarily obscured the reality of urban capitalism (Rosenzweig 1983; Koolhaas 1994: 29–79).

By the 1920s this peripheral architecture began to infiltrate the centers of many American cities through migrating places of mass entertainment. Corporate office buildings also began to adopt aspects of this style, for in this age of advertising, companies realized that they too needed to project an enticing image to the consuming masses. Thus, architects commissioned to design buildings for producers of mass consumer goods were, like the artists and designers directly employed by them, also exposed to the demands of the mass market.

The architectural style that rose to dominance in this age of mass consumption was known variously as moderne, modernisitic, or Art Deco. Its underlying objective, determined by the imperatives of the mass market, was to create an aesthetic unity that obscured the fragments of production. In urban skyscrapers the visibility of standardized, mass-produced floors was an unwelcome reminder of the rationalized production process, so architects designed building exteriors in a unifying and decorative aesthetic that obscured these fragmented parts (Koolhaas 1994: 100–4). For example, Ralph Walker's pioneering design for the Barclay-Vesey building of 1926 disguised the separate floors with a series of continuous piers, separated by recessed spandrels, which ran up the entire height of the building. Then he added simplified Gothic decoration on the exterior, along with naturalistic Art Noveau embellishments on the interior, to relieve the rectilinearity. Lewis Mumford wrote that this "decoration is an audacious compensation for the rigor and mechanical fidelity of the rest of the building: like jazz, it interrupts and relieves the tedium of too strenuous mechanical activity" (quoted in Tafuri 1990: 183). Another skyscraper-cum-advertisement, the Chrysler building, sported an elaborately ornamental, six-story, stainless-steel spire whose arches were reminiscent of car radiators, in order to catch consumers' attention and advertise the corporation's products (Wilson et al. 1986: 150–65).

The saga of New York's Rockefeller Center, completed in 1932, reveals the extent to which and the reasons why urban architecture during this period was transformed from Beaux-Arts historicism appealing to the upper classes to Art Deco entertainment aimed at the working masses. This project was initially planned as the new home for the Metropolitan Opera, a high-art venue obviously appealing to the city's bourgeois elite. But supporters quickly discovered that this elite program could not attract enough consumers to pay for itself on Manhattan's expensive real estate. So the architect, Benjamin Wistar Morris, expanded his original design into a three-block Beaux-Arts composition that included commercial space to pay for the money-losing opera house. But it soon became apparent that even this cultural mongrel was not financially viable in Manhattan's ruthlessly pecuniary grid, forcing John D. Rockefeller to step in and reformulate the project into a mecca for the emerging mass culture of entertainment. The serene Beaux-Arts symmetry of the original design was rudely irrupted by the insertion of a huge office shaft, to be leased to the corporate giant of mass communication, Radio Corporation of America (RCA), as well as a theater for popular entertainment, Radio City Music Hall, which became the home of The Rockettes dance company. The design of this new plan was entrusted to a master of Art Deco, Raymond Hood, who gave his clients a jazzy, jagged composition that turned the erstwhile program of an impoverished high-culture into a cash machine of enriching mass culture (Koolhaas 1994: 162–207).

This mass-consumption aesthetic of obfuscation and entertainment soon inundated the American landscape, engulfing both upstart modernist and established Beaux-Arts architecture. Under the pressure of this new mass market, which integrated the working class into capitalism through consumption, the economic bourgeoisie gave the masses what they wanted in order to make money. Because much of the cultural bourgeoisie was also integrated into these mass-production industries, either through employment or sale of professional services, it abandoned its own ideologically motivated preference for modernism and followed the money as well. Neither class fraction put up much cultural resistance to this aesthetic of mass consumption in material culture, for neither faced much of a challenge to its legitimacy. Economic capitalists faced no pre-existing aristocracy and its traditional culture, and mass consumption undermined the cultural basis of working-class resistance. The cultural bourgeoisie of professionals, managers, and artists faced no entrenched opposition to its rationalizing project, but was embraced by modernizing capitalists. The peculiar American class structure and struggles thus created a convergence on an aesthetic of mass consumption in the material culture.

This does not mean, however, that American culture as a whole was leveled and homogenized. By most accounts, in the United States there continued to be an exclusive high culture in the less public and visible fields of nonmaterial culture. The higher classes continued to disproportionately consume opera, for example, because this art form required of consumers a substantial endowment of cultural capital. And the consumption of this exclusive nonmaterial culture continued to provide a mechanism for the recognition, selection, and solidarity of the dominant class in American society (DiMaggio 1987). But it was the material and visible mass culture of Art Deco buildings, streamlined automobiles, and stylish appliances that provided the public face of American culture as an inclusive, egalitarian society, in which the only stratifying mechanism seemed to be market income determined by an individual's work abilities.

BLOCKED MODERNIZATION AND THE RISE
OF EUROPE'S TECHNOCRATIC PROJECT

The class structure was different in central Europe, giving rise to the paradox that these technologically backward countries pioneered a technocratic aesthetic that adulated a mass-production process that they had yet to achieve. Unlike the U.S., where the absence of an aristocratic order gave the modernizing industrial bourgeoisie a free rein, in Europe capitalists confronted an entrenched Old Regime of feudal interests, which blocked the modernization of industry toward large-scale mass production. The aristocracy also maintained a tight control over culture, using traditional historical styles entrenched in state-sponsored institutions to legitimate its continuing power. The class of industrial capitalists was consequently weak, and most sought power and prestige by integration into aristocracy-controlled state bureaucracies and by embracing their culture (Mayer 1981).

This class of capitalists reluctant to modernize left the emerging cultural bourgeoisie of professionals, managers, scientists, and artists not only with little demand for their services, but also subordinate in power and prestige. Artists were in a particularly vulnerable position. In the late nineteenth and

early twentieth centuries the ranks of artists grew rapidly due to expanding education, drawing new recruits from petite bourgeois and working-
class backgrounds. But the sources of artistic support narrowed, with the
prosperous bourgeoisie and the state purchasing classical art dispensed by
established institutions. Industry provided a glimmer of hope for struggling
artists, but the small, craft-based nature of most businesses precluded the
need for design services (Mayer 1981: 253–72; Jackson 1995: 20–34).

Blocked from a livelihood by regressive economic and aesthetic policies,
artists and other members of the cultural bourgeoisie began to articulate
an autonomous technocratic ideology, which reached its zenith at the end
of World War I. Then the Old Regimes fell, only to be replaced by more
liberal governments racked by continuing class conflict, especially in Germany. The cultural bourgeoisie inserted its technocratic project into this
conjuncture, promising a reconciliation of class interests through a neutral
program of economic rationalization that would guarantee prosperity for
all. The model for rationalization in Germany and elsewhere was America's Fordist combination of mass production and mass consumption (Maier
1970; Nolan 1994).

Modern architecture was the aesthetic wing of this growing technocratic movement in interwar Europe. The architectural designs of modernists reflected their attempts to reconcile the social contradictions of this
era in favor of the class of educated professionals, managers, and artists.
This analysis goes against the frequent characterization of modern architecture as inherently socialist and anticapitalist. Although often allied with
socialists, modern architecture was mainly an ideology of the intelligentsia,
which opportunistically sought allies across the political spectrum to further its interests (Maier 1970; Gouldner 1979: 11). This opportunism of
technocracy is revealed by the political vicissitudes of modern architects
after World War I in Germany.

Immediately after the 1918 Revolution that toppled the Old Regime,
most German modernists were enthusiastic supporters of the Social Democratic government of the Weimar Republic, which they saw as an ally in
their assault on established artistic elites. To consolidate such a political/
cultural coalition, modernist leader and director of the Bauhaus school,
Walter Gropius, called for breaking down class barriers between artists
and workers and unifying both into feudal-like guilds of craftsmen (Gropius 1938a; Lane 1985: 41–49). By 1922, however, socialist enthusiasm
in German was waning, and the government shifted to the right, causing the cultural bourgeoisie to shift its political hopes from workers to
industrialists. Gropius and other modern architects advocated a scheme
of economic rationalization, which included integrating art into the factories of the machine age. Guilds of egalitarian cooperation between workers
and artists were jettisoned in favor a hierarchical order of Fordist mass
production, in which architects and engineers would be the benevolent rul-
ers of deskilled proletarians. Following the increasingly conservative Social

Democratic Party line, Gropius insisted that workers would be compensated for any losses in skill by the increased consumption of beautiful and bountiful mass-produced goods. For their part of the technocratic bargain, capitalists were promised more efficient production, more aesthetically pleasing goods, and a working class placated by increased consumption (Gropius 1938b; Lane 1985: 65–68).

Thus, modern artists in Germany moved away from revolutionary fervor toward a sober resignation to the harsh material facts of the age, a trend known as *Neue Sachlichkeit* (new objectivity or facticity). They now believed problems could only be solved by material progress through rationalized production, ignoring the fact that these rationalized industrial methods were not neutral "facts" but moves in a class struggle that placed power in the hands of a coalition of capitalists and technical intellectuals. The new objectivity swept across Europe in the mid-1920s, and no one captured the chilling mood of matter-of-factness better than the ideological founder of the movement of modern architecture, Le Corbusier. His modernist manifesto of 1923, *Vers une architecture*, deftly captured this new ideological move of technocracy by promising to overcome social conflicts with a program of industrialized building. "Architecture or Revolution," Le Corbusier threatened the dominant class of the day. Industrialization had thrown society "out of gear" and had left people powerless before their own tools. The only way society could reconcile people to this alien reality and avoid revolution was to offer them diversion and recuperation in homes designed by architects and manufactured efficiently and cheaply with mass-production methods. To accomplish this rationalization of production and consumption and reconcile class interests, Le Corbusier advocated turning over broad bureaucratic power to the new class of professionals, whose rule would be despotic but disinterested (Le Corbusier 1967; 1986).

THE IDEOLOGY OF THE MODERNIST MACHINE AESTHETIC

In the 1920s modern architects such as Walter Gropius, Mies van der Rohe, and Le Corbusier pioneered a new architectural aesthetic to support and testify to this technocratic project to rationalize production and consumption and place professionals in power. Known as the "new objectivity" or "machine aesthetic," their style was generally characterized by simple, undecorated, geometric forms, usually of severe rectilinearity and constructed of industrially produced building materials like steel, glass, and concrete. Open, free-flowing space also replaced traditional architectural space enclosed by barriers and walls.

Some of these aesthetic forms could be explained by practical functionalism—that is, attempts to adapt buildings to quick and efficient mass production. But modern architects acknowledged that their architecture went beyond utilitarian determinants to embody a new concept of beauty. This aesthetic dimension of the machine style promoted the technocratic project by ideologically symbolizing with orderly, beautiful forms the domination of abstract, instrumental reason over humans and nature. To integrate people into rationalized mass production, their housing had to glorify its instrumental reason while simultaneously alleviating some of its worst human consequences. The ugly exigencies of mass-produced houses and furnishings had to be purified; technique had to be spiritualized to facilitate its acceptance. Modern architecture idealized technology by expressing it in purified form, creating a visual order out of its sometimes disorderly and confusing material appearance (Frampton 1996: 205–7).

The Frankfurt School of critical theory (Horkheimer and Adorno 1972; Horkheimer 1974; Marcuse 1964) long ago exposed the fallacies of such thinking. This instrumental reason, as they label it, fetishizes the technological means to human ends, conceiving them as developing according to a determinate logic beyond human control. The precise, efficient application of neutral means alone is rational, it claims, and must be separated from the choice of ends, which is an arbitrary and irrational process. Frankfurt theorists hold that instrumental reason is not neutral but oppressive, an instrument of domination, for it allows those in control of the technological means to ignore the inherent ends of humans and nature and turn them into means for an alien purpose. Adorno (1997: 17) specifically criticizes functionalist architecture for its instrumental reason, arguing that its "rational functions" are not neutral but determined by the irrational end of profit in capitalist society. Its concept of function provides a disguise for human domination and exploitation.

The aesthetics of modern architecture symbolized and glorified instrumental reason in several ways. First, modernists exalted technological means by simply borrowing the forms of machines for their buildings. They used simple, elementary shapes in the belief that these resulted from the standardization and mechanization of mass-production technology. And the straight line was preferred to the curve, because of its labor-saving predominance in mass-produced machines like automobiles, and also because it symbolized the precise, instrumental reason underlying mass-production technology (Le Corbusier 1987: 5–12).

Second, the modernist aesthetic symbolized the rule of instrumental reason with its open, flowing space, which erased the distinction between the inside and outside. Modern architecture obliterated the traditional wall, which protected the private interior from the public exterior, by tearing down internal walls and opening up exterior walls with extensive use of glass. Fredric Jameson (1997: 263–65) argues that this "free-plan" arrangement of space was anti-capitalist in its assault on the bourgeois ideology of individualism and its integration of the person into a collective or public space. While it is true that the modernist aesthetic celebrated a new collectivity, this was not Jameson's egalitarian socialism but Ford's hierarchical and rationalized capitalist production process, in which the educated and credentialed ruled benevolently over all others. "Openness" eliminated workers' privacy and facilitated their constant surveillance by the gaze of technocratic reason. As Mies van der Rohe (1970: 74) wrote of his design for an office building with large, wall-less work areas: "The office building is a house of work of organization of clarity of economy. Bright, wide workrooms, easy to oversee, undivided except as the organism of the undertaking is divided." In modernist residential complexes the scarcity of internal dividing walls and extensive glazing submitted individuals to the same sort of collective surveillance in the realm of consumption, battering down the bulwarks of privacy and allowing the invasion of technocratic reason into their homes.

Another reason for opening up the exterior of the building was to expose the technological framework supporting the structure. The modernists demanded that industrial materials doing the work of support be revealed on the outside, thus celebrating the technology and the instrumental reason of the technocrats who created it. In residential buildings modernists also believed that the exposed technological structure served "to impose discipline on the inhabitants" by creating an orderly realm of consumption to complement the rationalized process of mass production (Le Corbusier 1986: 242–43).

The space created by the technological grid of modernist architecture was not merely open but also abstract and mobile, symbolizing the rationalized space of the commodity. While the grid of supports captured and commodified space, it did not fix it for a specific use but merely opened it up for the movement of capital. This abstract, flexible space facilitated the mobility of business tenants in and out of office buildings in the fast-paced urban real estate market (Blake 1976: 236–38). Modernists created residential spaces that were also universal and nonspecialized to allow the rapid turnover of workers, for as Le Corbusier (1987: 231) argued, "labor will shift about as needed, and must be ready to move, bag and baggage." To symbolically express such mobility, modernists created space that was never at rest but flowed and moved constantly. This movement was often achieved by the asymmetrical placement of volumes, as at the Bauhaus complex in Dessau, where Gropius placed the three main buildings at right angles to one another, creating a pinwheel composition that seemed to rotate (Giedion 1967: 491–97).

The abstract, homogeneous, mobile space of modernist architecture was really a metaphor for the commodity in the age of technocracy, a vessel emptied by new technologies of any qualitative uses to become a mere holder of quantitative exchange value. But modern architects understood that their forms could not directly express the imperatives of technocratic capitalism, for they knew that the system of mass production was frightening and alienating to the classes who stood to lose from it: workers, tradesmen, petite bourgeois. To facilitate their acceptance, this technology had to be purified, striped of its fragmented and alien appearance and given the look of order and unity. For example, Mies revealed the steel frameworks of his buildings but at the same time concealed their assembly, specifying that the welds on exposed beams be ground flat and painted. He and other modernists also suppressed the work of support. Mies's Barcelona Pavilion employed steel columns so thin that they denied the work of bearing the structure. The technology that was visible in these buildings was dematerialized—it was the abstract idea of work, not its physical reality (Frampton 1996: 175–78, 203–7).

UTOPIA REALIZED? THE MODERNIST HOUSING ESTATES

The technocratic program symbolized by modern architecture faced opposition, however, from the economic bourgeoisie, especially in Germany. This class was reluctant to undertake full-scale Fordist modernization due to cost considerations and cartel arrangements. So unlike the technocratic professionals in the U.S., who were embraced by a strong capitalist class, the European technocrats were rejected by a still weak private sector. In Germany, the Netherlands, and other central European countries, however, they did find support in states dominated by social democrats, which provided modern architects with the autonomy from the marketplace that was crucial in realizing their aesthetic (Nolan 1994: 73–41). For example, in Germany during the mid-1920s Weimar state managers, many of whom were from the Social Democratic Party, instituted programs to encourage industrial rationalization. One of these was an aggressive housing program, which used government funds to support the mass production of large housing estates on the outskirts of major cities. With this program, Social Democratic politicians hoped not only to demonstrate the fruitfulness of their strategic compromise with capitalism, but also to construct a realm of disciplined and individualistic mass consumption that facilitated workers' acquiescence to technocratic domination in politics and industry. Progressive reformers in the U.S. promoted similar goals, but their efforts were channeled largely through the private sector. In Germany the main vehicle of cultural rationalization was the state-sponsored housing program (Lane 1985: 87–90; Nolan 1994: 119–20, 206–7; Von Saldern 1990).

Between 1919 and 1932, various public and semi-public authorities in Germany built 2.5 million apartments, many of them designed by modern architects. Unencumbered by the marketplace demands of common consumers encountered by American aesthetic reformers employed in or selling services to corporations, German modernists employed by the state realized their machine aesthetic of simple, undecorated, rectilinear forms. Concerns for efficiency and standardization dominated not only the industrialized building methods but also the design of space. In an attempt to rationalize working-class consumption, modern architects designed for a niggardly "existence minimum"—the minimum space required for efficient human existence. The kitchen received the most attention, since the large kitchen was the traditional center of working-class life. Modern architects broke up the "unhealthy" communality of the kitchen by designing tiny, one-woman kitchens, where housewives undertook their lonely, Taylorized tasks. Space for eating was provided in a small dining room, and for socializing, the middle-class parlor was installed in diminutive form (Tafuri 1990: 200–202; Nolan 1994: 206–26; Heskett 1980: 81–84; Giedion 1967: 522–27; Teige 2002).

At the same time that the housing estates sought to Taylorize workers' consumption, they also sought to provide them with relief and escape from Taylorized production. Residents were supplied with ample "nature" in the form of parks and green spaces, where they could recuperate from the tensions of their mechanized work. Escape was also provided by creating privacy within each apartment, which was isolated from its neighbors both visually and socially. Outside of these privatized dwellings, there were few public meeting rooms or community centers, for Social Democratic Party leaders feared that any worker activism would benefit the more radical Communist Party, not themselves (Von Saldern 1990: 342–46).

The German case gives us greater insight than the American one into the reactions of the various classes to the modernist machine aesthetic. While in the U.S. modernism was cut short by an emerging mass marketplace, in Germany the modernists who designed housing estates for the state were unconstrained by consumer preferences. For all Germans this aesthetic symbolized the rapid industrialization and economic rationalization of the period. But the specific responses to these associations varied by class position. While the technocratic new class generally supported modern architecture, the reactions of the economic bourgeoisie were mixed. Some large industrialists supported this aesthetic as a symbol of the industrial rationalization they favored, but small capitalists were economically threatened by rationalization and attacked the modern architecture associated with it. But modern architecture posed a greater threat to the bourgeoisie's cultural capital than its economic capital. The modernist cult of rationality and efficiency undermined the high culture on which capitalists had hitherto based their legitimacy and threatened to expose their naked economic interests. Consequently, most bourgeois attacks on modern architecture denounced its leveling effect on the cultural differences of German society (Lane 1985: 69–86, 125–45; Nolan 1994: 108–26).

Unlike the bourgeoisie, the working class had no high-culture legitimation or small businesses to protect, but it too was threatened by economic rationalization and suspicious of the modern architecture that symbolized it (Fromm 1984: 98–104). Residents of German housing estates, however, expressed surprisingly few objections to their new lodgings, probably because, due to high rents, most were middle class. A better gauge of working-class reactions to modern architecture is found in Le Corbusier's Pessac housing project near Bordeaux, France, where heavy state subsidies made it possible for most of its working-class residents to purchase, not merely rent, their units. Thus, unlike like the renters in most German estates, the owner-residents at Pessac were able to undertake alterations to their housing, in which we can detect the true reactions of the working class to modernist architecture.

Many Pessac residents rearranged the living spaces in Le Corbusier's concrete boxes. One popular alteration was the expansion of the tiny Taylorized kitchen into the parlor, thus asserting the working-class preference for the informal sociality of the kitchen over the bourgeois formality of the parlor. Other alterations were motivated by objections to his machine aesthetic. Workers covered over symbolic references to the factory, which were reminders of the rationalized work they hoped to escape, and filled his austere spaces with symbols of cozy domesticity. The factory-like ribbon windows were divided into traditionally narrow windows with wooden frames. Pessac residents also sought in their alterations to restore the barrier between inside and outside, the modernist eradication of which deprived them of the symbols of privacy and protection embodied in traditional architecture. Wide ribbon windows were narrowed and given awnings, shutters, and curtains to close the inside to public view. The open terraces on top of the units were covered by peaked roofs with overhanging eaves. And visually open chain-link fencing was replaced by opaque hedges and wooden fencing. Through these and other alterations, the working-class residents of Pessac resisted the intrusion of the instrumental commodity logic into their lives, and turned Le Corbusier's standardized concrete spaces into cozy domestic bunkers in which reminders of the invading social forces outside were carefully eradicated (Boudon 1972).

THE DIALECTICAL PROGRESSIVISM OF MODERN ARCHITECTURE

The modern architecture that arose in Europe in the interwar period was part of a technocratic ideology that justified the intervention of the new cultural bourgeoisie into capitalism in order to rationalize and stabilize its operation. For Bourdieu, whose early work cynically holds that all culture is inevitably tainted by class interests, this aesthetic can be judged as no better or worse than the American aesthetic of mass consumption, which was more attuned to the mass market dominated by the popular classes. Frankfurt School theorists, however, hold that there are universal standards whereby the progressive nature of socially influenced art may be judged. Theodor Adorno (1984, 1994), in particular, argues that authentic art holds out the promise of a better, more rational world, while at the same time criticizing the oppressive irrationality of the existing society. Such art refuses to conform to the capitalist market's demand for comforting illusions that reconcile people to the contradictions of the existing society.

But neither does it cynically reify or eternalize these contradictions. Art performs a delicate balancing act between promising utopia and denying its current existence through a dialectic of beauty and ugliness. The beauty of art's forms, which evokes happiness, is disrupted by the intrusion of the ugliness of the existing world, which prevents this happiness from being realized. In faithfully reflecting on its surface the scars and lacerations inflicted on beauty by social antagonisms, art keeps faith with utopia and prevents its own immediate use as a comforting illusion for the masses.

Adorno makes it clear that in order to realize this authentic aesthetic, art must be totally autonomous from the capitalist marketplace, whose demand for mass illusion turns art into kitsch. But he does not identify the social basis for such cultural autonomy. Adorno has lost the traditional Marxist faith in the ability of the industrial proletariat to ideologically transcend capitalist reification, and seems to deny a class basis for any transcendence. For him, artists seem to constitute a class unto themselves, capable of willing themselves free of determinations of the market. Bourdieu's sophisticated class analysis provides a more satisfactory method of sociologically grounding artistic autonomy and the resulting aesthetic. He shows that support from the state or from other cultural producers can free a fraction of the cultural bourgeoisie from the practical demands of the market, and allow them to pursue in a disinterested manner cultural standards for their own sake. The problematic grounds for the autonomy of cultural producers will be explored in more depth in Chapter 7.

The art of these early modern architects of Europe meets Adorno's criteria for authenticity, especially in comparison to the consumer-responsive architecture of the U.S. In the latter, the progressive part of the technocratic project—the demand for the rational organization of society—was compromised by the closeness of the new class and its artists to the capitalist market. Confined largely within capitalist corporations designing commodities that would sell, American artists offered consumers comforting illusions that covered over the ugliness of a rationalized capitalism. Disguising the rectilinearity, standardization, and heteronomy of the Fordist factory, these American buildings and goods ideologically announced that the utopia of individuality, autonomy, and reconciliation was to be found in this society, through the capitalist marketplace.

In Europe, by contrast, modern architects found autonomy from the market through state commissions. Consequently, they were free to express the logic of technocracy in its veritable form, revealing both the beauty and the ugliness of their project and denying immediate reconciliation with the existing society. Although Adorno (1997: 15, 19) is critical of modern architecture, he also recognizes its authenticity as art, for it displays the social antagonisms between people and technology rather than seeking to cover them over. The buildings of the best modernists possessed beauty, for they took the often fragmented forms of machines and industrial products and shaped them into harmonious proportions, reflecting the unifying potential of human reason. But at the same time these modernists unconsciously reflected the ugliness of the machine age and the instrumental form of rationality that underlay it. The unbending rectilinearity of their architecture testified to the unforgiving discipline of the specialized machines that absorbed workers' skills and subjected them to mind-numbing routine. The standardized similarity of their designs proclaimed the mass-production factory's destruction of the individual. The plain, unadorned surfaces of modernist boxes, as well as their stingy internal accommodations, symbolized the niggardly economy of effort and material imposed on capitalists and workers alike by the market. The empty, open spaces reminded occupants that they were just interchangeable commodities to be stored temporarily until the market again mandated their movement.

By faithfully reflecting the damage done to people within the rigidly authoritarian and dehumanized mass-production process, modern architects undermined their own intentions to reconcile workers to this society with a beautiful world of home consumption. Workers had difficulty finding peace and comfort in domestic surroundings disrupted by the ugliness of the instrumental rationality of work. By boldly bringing this ugliness into the domestic refuge, modernists prevented consumption from becoming a substitute and sublimation for human needs denied in the workplace. Despite their intentions, they did not provide a palliative for revolution but kept revolutionary hopes alive through their uncompromisingly alienated aesthetic.

6 Bourdieu's Theory of Cultural Change

Explication, Application, Critique

In this chapter I seek to systematize, formalize, and compare Bourdieu's early theory of culture. In Chapters 3 and 4 I argued that the explanatory power of Bourdieu's theory of class distinction is limited by both historical time and type of culture. Although in the early stage of modern capitalist society much of culture seems to conform to Bourdieu's model, in late modern capitalism many cultural fields, especially those comprised by materialistic products, undergo the leveling and homogenization postulated by the Frankfurt School's theory of mass reification. Below I seek to specify and formalize these insights into precise, predictive propositions. After a systematic exposition of Bourdieu's theory, I draw on my two empirical cases—the automobile and architecture—to reveal its limits.

For automobiles, I review the dynamic forces that propelled the field from a class-symbolizing hierarchy, through homogenized and reified mass individuality, toward a pluralized diversity of distinctive subcultures that are considered merely different from, not better than, one another. Then I develop the case of modern architecture, whose beginnings I treated in Chapter 5. Following this cultural artifact on into the late twentieth century reveals that the field of architecture was only partially leveled. In the post-World-War-II United States architecture was divided between a high-art modernism in urban areas, which celebrated mass production, and a mass-cultural populism in the suburbs, which hid all reminders of production. But in the 1960s increased competition and the changed habitus of producers and consumers created the leveling trend of postmodernism, which brought the glitz and decoration of mass culture to high architecture. But unlike automobiles, the field of architecture did not become completely leveled but retained a hierarchical and distinctive nature. This was due to the ideal nature of architecture, which even in its postmodern form required substantial cultural capital (knowledge) to consume, not merely economic capital (money). I conclude by using these cases to construct a series of propositions on cultural change for further debate and testing.

DIMENSIONS OF CULTURAL CHANGE: INTERNAL
VS. EXTERNAL, SUPPLY VS. DEMAND

There is a tendency among recent sociologists of culture to assert the radical autonomy of the cultural realm from other institutional spheres, especially the economy and politics. In his *Sociology of Philosophies*, for example, Randall Collins (1998) argues that the intellectual world, like economics and politics, is a conflict for scarce resources among groups and individuals in different social positions. But he adamantly asserts that the intellectual game is autonomous, with its own rewards, strategies, and resources, which show little overlap with the political and economic games. "Economic and political macrostructures do not explain much about abstract ideas because such ideas exist only where there is a network of intellectuals focused on their own arguments and accumulating their own conceptual baggage train. It is the inner structure of these intellectual networks which shape ideas . . ." (Collins 1998: 2). Consequently, he explains thousands of years of philosophical change with very few references to economic or political changes. Collins focuses on the internal structure of intellectual networks and laws specific to them, like the law of small numbers, to account for all philosophical changes.

Another recent sociological contribution on cultural change, Stanley Lieberson's (2000) *A Matter of Taste*, is similarly focused almost exclusively on mechanisms of change internal to cultural markets. Using a sophisticated analysis of the frequency of first names, he argues that most changes can be explained by a few simple mechanisms specific to taste and fashion, such as class imitation, the ratchet effect, and incremental replacement. Lieberson does recognize the influence of some external factors on name frequency, such as the Civil Rights movement, feminism, and the names of presidents and actors. However, these external influences are not conceptually incorporated into his theory, but conceived merely as arbitrary inputs into his internal taste mechanisms. In general, he sees their impact as less important than the latter, which operate with law-like, formal regularity despite their contents.

The recent emphasis of sociologists like Collins and Lieberson on mechanisms of change internal to cultural markets is surely a welcome corrective to the often simplistic and unmediated use of external factors like politics and economics to explain cultural change. But to substitute a unilateral internalist approach for a unilateral externalist approach is not helpful. Both internal and external factors must be incorporated into a theoretical framework that precisely conceptualizes the nature and types of their interactions in the process of cultural change.

Some internalist approaches to cultural change ignore not only the importance of external factors but also the influence of one or the other side of the cultural market itself. Markets have both a demand or consumption side and a supply or production side. In capitalist society, in which much of culture has become a commodity, the production and consumption of cultural goods are separate and have independent dynamics. In his study Lieberson is concerned only with internal taste mechanisms specific to the demand side of the market. This is largely because his chosen empirical case, first names, has no separation of supply and demand. Those producing and consuming first names are the same people—parents of the children named. Thus he simplistically assumes that demand directly and problematically creates its own supply. But this is an unrealistic assumption for most cultural goods, in which producers and consumers are separate. Unlike names, automobiles, for example, are manufactured by people different from their consumers, under a set of production costs and constraints that exert an effect on the product independent of consumer demand.

The production of culture school of cultural analysis focuses specifically on these internal market mechanisms of supply. Pioneered largely by Richard Peterson (1976, 1994), this school reveals that the structure of organizations producing culture exerts important influences on the type of artifacts produced and their propensity to change. One of the important findings of the school is that in markets for large-scale, commercial products, the number of producers and their competitive relations are important influences on both the rate of change and the diversity of cultural goods. Although not acknowledging the Frankfurt School's analysis of culture and economics, the production of culture perspective agrees with its assertion that oligopolistic firms, which emerge in markets with few producers and little competition, tend to produce homogeneous goods that change slowly, if at all, in order to save on production costs. Peterson and Berger (1975: 159) argue that this is because oligarchs compete for the largest share of a single mass market. Thus they seek to find the one product that pleases the most people and offends the least. Innovative and heterogeneous goods emerge mainly when markets are more competitive, that is, when a larger number of firms compete with one another for consumers. Such competition forces firms to meet consumer demand for a variety of cultural goods that change often.

Yet, in its emphasis on the production side of cultural markets, the production of culture school neglects the demand side. It has no good explanation for the observed fact that, when forced by competition to cater closely to consumer demand, firms produce a greater variety of changing products. Why do consumers generally want variety and change in cultural goods?

There is one account, however, that weaves together all these dimensions of cultural markets in a powerful and sophisticated theory of culture. This is the theory of Pierre Bourdieu. Elaborated in a series of empirical studies and theoretical works, Bourdieu's theory details the intricate interweaving of mechanisms of cultural production with the vicissitudes of consumer demand for cultural goods. And he reveals that although these internal mechanisms render it relatively autonomous, culture is also intricately interconnected to the organization and struggles of the rest of society, which provide external resources and demands that impact both the production and consumption of cultural goods. In the next section I offer an explanation of the basic points of Bourdieu's theory of cultural change, as well as a few of its intricacies. Then I will demonstrate its explanatory power by applying it to two cases of aesthetic change—the disappearance of the automobile tail fin in the 1950s and the decline of modern architecture in the 1960s. These two cases drawn from American culture are not, however, unconnected illustrations. The demise of the tail fin within popular culture is an index of a larger trend that in the next decade brought down the modern style in the high art of architecture. This trend is the leveling and pluralization of American culture. Although the internal and external dynamics postulated by Bourdieu help to account for this large-scale cultural change, it ultimately points to a cultural structure at odds with his model of class distinction.

BOURDIEU'S THEORY OF THE DYNAMICS OF CULTURAL DISTINCTION

Bourdieu founds his theory on the assumption that culture is a field of contest like the economic world, in which interested actors compete to accumulate various types of resources or "capital." While in the economy actors struggle over economic capital, in culture they compete to appropriate cultural capital, goods and practices that are socially defined as distinctive and hence lend individuals an aura of superiority. But Bourdieu makes it clear that the cultural struggle for distinction is intricately connected to the economic distribution of material goods, which it both legitimates and reproduces. An individual's material conditions of existence, determined by her economic capital, ingrain a habitus or set of dispositions, which in turn generates cultural tastes. The legitimate tastes facilitate the accumulation of cultural capital, which makes the individual look distinctive and hence justifies the economic capital that determined her cultural tastes to begin with. So closely intertwined is culture with the economy that Bourdieu conceives society as a social field or space formed by the intersection of the economic and cultural fields. The positions in the social field are classes, each determined by its relative proportions of economic and cultural capital and its overall volume of the two kinds of capital combined (Bourdieu 1984: 169–75).

The cultural field is the site of production of the cultural goods that the different classes appropriate and employ in their struggles for legitimating distinction. There is "something for everyone" here, that is, each class is able to find a supply of goods (literature, art, movies, newspapers, food, furniture, etc.) that precisely matches its demands. This is not just because cultural producers are attuned by their habitus, engendered by position in the social field, to the needs of consumers with similar habitus. The affinity between producers and consumers also exists because these producers have interests engendered by their position in the field of cultural production. Bourdieu divides the cultural field into two subfields, each with its distinct, structurally defined producers and consumers. The subfield of small-scale or restricted production is composed of the high arts, or art for art's sake. Here the stakes are not economic profits but symbolic profits, that is, recognition by other artists on the basis of the internal, autonomous standards of art. These cultural producers have more cultural capital (taste, knowledge, education) than economic capital (money). Consequently, their works match the dispositions of consumers in the social field who similarly have more culture than money. Bourdieu calls these consumers of high art the dominated fraction of the dominant class, or the cultural bourgeoisie, which includes all professions that rely on knowledge and education for a living. Lacking the money of the dominant fraction or economic bourgeoisie, these people prefer culture that is more cerebral than expensive, more ascetic than self-indulgent—just the kind of art that innovative, avant-garde artists struggling for symbolic profits in the restricted subfield are motivated to produce. The subfield of restricted production itself is split between those artists who have successfully accumulated symbolic profits and those who have yet to do so. Successful high artists, or the consecrated avant-garde, gain recognition outside of the restricted subfield as well, cashing in some of their symbolic profits for economic profits. This stimulates the less successful high artists, or the bohemian avant-garde, to vehemently reject the consecrated artists as "sell-outs" and to pioneer art that is pure and free of monetary taint in order to distinguish themselves (Bourdieu 1996a; 1993b; 1993c).

The other subfield of the cultural field is that of large-scale or mass production. Here are located the producers motivated by the heteronomous logic of the marketplace, that is, the accumulation of economic profits. They have more economic capital than cultural capital, so consequently their works match the dispositions of consumers in the social field who also have more money than culture. These consumers are the economic bourgeoisie, composed of professions and occupations that rely more on their wealth than their knowledge and education for a living. This class prefers culture that is more luxurious and sedately hedonistic, which conspicuously but tastefully displays its economic resources—just the kind of goods that cultural producers struggling for economic profits in the large-scale subfield are motivated to produce. Yet, like the restricted subfield, this subfield is also divided into two parts: bourgeois art and commercial art. Producers of the former cater to the high economic bourgeoisie and, like their consumers, have considerable cultural capital, although it is outweighed by their wealth. Because they are in the same position in the cultural field that their consumers are in the social field, they intuitively understand that their well-heeled customers want cultural goods that are tasteful and formal, and that conspicuously display their cultural knowledge as well as their wealth. In fact, this high economic bourgeoisie needs this cultural distinction to legitimate its economic resources. To satisfy this need of their clients, as well as distinguish themselves from their competitors in the subfield of large-scale production, bourgeois-art producers borrow and distribute the work of the consecrated artists in the restricted subfield, leading the latter to "sell out." The producers of commercial art in the large-scale subfield have less cultural capital, and thus cater to consumers who are similarly "culturally deprived," that is, the petite bourgeoisie and the working class. Their goods are mass-produced "kitsch," profitable but crass, catering to unmitigated self-indulgence and simple hedonism (Bourdieu 1984; 1996a).

Into this rather static, structuralist model of the cultural field and its class consumers, Bourdieu introduces the dynamic element of class imitation, which is also found in Thorstein Veblen (1934) and Georg Simmel (1957). It begins with the idea that the dominant class or bourgeoisie attempts to distinguish itself and legitimate its economic capital by borrowing the pure, disinterested aura of art from the restricted subfield. By demonstrating a taste for pure culture, members of this class prove their personal superiority against the crass and materialistic lower classes. However, members of the petite bourgeoisie, seeking to distinguish themselves from the working class, consume imitations of the goods of the bourgeoisie, since they lack the economic and cultural capital to appropriate them in their authentic form. For Bourdieu, however, class imitation stops here, for there is no element of pretension or distinction in the consumption of the working class, which due to economic deprivation is driven simply by material necessity and function. However, petite-bourgeois imitation is sufficient to taint the specific goods of the bourgeoisie with commonality and commercial greed, undermining the rarity and purity that lend them distinction. Then the dominant class must adopt from the restricted subfield new cultural goods, more distinctive and unsullied by the taint of widespread commercialism. Thus, Bourdieu writes (1984: 251–52), imitation "helps to maintain constant tension in the symbolic goods market, forcing the possessors of distinctive properties threatened with popularization to engage in an endless pursuit of new properties through which to assert their rarity. The demand which is generalized by this dialectic is by definition inexhaustible since the dominated needs which constitute it must endlessly redefine themselves in terms of a distinction which always defines itself negatively in relation to them."

This petite-bourgeois imitation of the cultural goods of the dominant class, however, disrupts and changes the contest for distinction within the dominant class between the cultural and economic fractions. These dominant class fractions compete for power, each working to define its specific form of capital as the "principle of hierarchicalization" (Bourdieu 1993b: 37–43), that is, the basis on which power and wealth are distributed. The cultural bourgeoisie displays its pure, disinterested taste and knowledge though the high arts, which are governed by rules removed from the crass logic of the marketplace. The economic bourgeoisie borrows some of this cultural capital by adopting the works of the consecrated avant-garde from the restricted subfield dominated by the cultural bourgeoisie. Yet, petite-bourgeois imitation of these bourgeois-art works lowers them to the status of commercial art in the large-scale subfield. The economic bourgeoisie must then go back to the restricted subfield to select more distinctive forms of high art from those exclusively consumed by the cultural bourgeoisie. This, in turn, leaves the latter to scramble to adopt new cultural goods from less recognized or bohemian avant-garde artists that set them off from the now redefined bourgeois art. In effect, then, cultural innovations follow the path of an inverted U-curve. They start at the bottom of the restricted subfield among unknown avant-garde artists, rise to the top of this subfield as works of the consecrated avant-garde, and then migrate laterally to the top of the large-scale subfield as bourgeois art, until imitation by the petite bourgeoisie lowers them to the status of commercial art (Bourdieu 1996a: 121–28, 146–61, 253–56).

For Bourdieu, however, it is not this struggle of *consumers* for distinctive goods that is responsible for the constant generation of new cultural goods within the subfield of restricted production. Rather, it is the struggle among *producers* for distinction in this subfield that creates the supply for this demand.

> Thus, the case of fashion, which might seem to justify a model which locates the motor of changing sartorial styles in the intentional pursuit of distinction (the "trickle-down effect") is an almost perfect example of the meeting of two spaces and two relatively autonomous histories. The endless changes in fashion result from the objective orchestration between, on the one hand, the logic of the struggles internal to the field of production, which are organized in terms of the opposition old/new . . . and on the other hand, the logic of struggles internal to the field of the dominant class, which, as we have seen, oppose the dominant and the dominated fractions, or, more precisely, the established and the challengers . . . (Bourdieu 1984: 232–33)

The constant stream of new and different cultural products is generated by the struggle for symbolic profits between the old or consecrated artists and the new or bohemian artists in the restricted subfield of production. New entrants to the subfield must struggle for distinction or recognition against those already recognized. But they usually do so within the logic of the subfield, producing innovations that are pure and disinterested, and that stand out among the older forms that have been tainted with the commercial profits of the subfield of large-scale production. Inevitably the consecrated are overthrown by the upstarts, creating a cycle of innovation that generates the new products to meet the demand for distinction of the battling fractions of the dominant class (Bourdieu 1996a: 126–61, 253–56).

Bourdieu argues, however, that these cycles of artistic innovation endemic to the cultural field do not produce deep and lasting changes in its structure unless they draw upon and incorporate external changes in the larger social field. The most important of these external changes is the growth in the educated population, which increases the number of both cultural producers and cultural consumers. A more educated populace allows more producers to enter the cultural field, thus heightening the competition between them and stimulating greater innovation to stand out in a crowded field. At the same time, increases in general levels of education also provide more consumers for cultural goods, since more people possess the cultural capital necessary to appreciate them (Bourdieu 1996a: 127, 225). New cultural producers not only stimulate the quantity of distinctive innovations but also determine the qualitative directions of the changes. The newcomers, who often come from different class positions due to broadening opportunities, bring with them habitus that are new to the field and thus incline them to new cultural forms. For example, in his study of the French literary field of the nineteenth century, Bourdieu argues that the growth in the number of educated readers created opportunities for upwardly mobile writers from petite-bourgeois and working-class backgrounds. These newcomers, the most prominent of which was Émile Zola, distinguished themselves from the established bourgeois literature in the field by pioneering realism or social art, whose aesthetic was determined by their lower-class disposition for the functional and the politically engaged (Bourdieu 1996a: 71–76, 85–86). The aesthetic upstarts in the cultural field very often draw support for their internal struggles against the established producers from those externally struggling in the social field against established classes. This external support is due not only to the fact that these new artists often come from the same class as those struggling in the social field. Even when they come from different classes, external support is often forthcoming because the struggling artists occupy a position in the cultural field homologous to that occupied by the struggling classes in the social field; that is, both are outsiders seeking to depose an established power. Thus, in his analysis of the French academic field in *Homo Academicus* (1988: 165–66), Bourdieu argues that the radical students and teachers of the May 1968 revolt, struggling against established authority in an increasingly crowded and competitive academic field, found sympathetic support among young industrial workers, who were subordinated by this academic authority in the social field by their exclusion from the university.

Pierre Bourdieu's theory of cultural dynamics is more sophisticated and multidimensional than that of sociologists who recognize competition on only one side of cultural markets. It reveals that cultural change results from the struggle for distinction by both cultural producers and consumers. And the theory also conceptualizes the external social forces that intervene *through* these internal competitive struggles to fundamentally transform the cultural field. To illustrate the power of Bourdieu's multidimensional theory of cultural distinction I will use two empirical cases: automobile design and modern architecture. The automobile market is part of Bourdieu's subfield of large-scale production, in which producers are motivated by economic profits. In this cultural good there is no subfield of restricted production, in which production is strictly for other cultural producers and motivated by symbolic profits defined by autonomous rules. Consequently, the major dynamic driving cultural change in automobiles is competition for distinction among producers and consumers at the high end of the mass market (bourgeois art) with producers and consumers at the low end of the same market (commercial art). The art of architecture, however, is the restricted subfield of the larger building market, which also contains a subfield of large-scale production. In contrast to the strictly pecuniary motives of commercial builders in the later subfield, architects in the restricted subfield are artists struggling for symbolic profits in a game of relatively autonomous rules. Consequently, the major dynamic driving cultural change in architecture is competition of producers and consumers of the consecrated avant-garde with those of the bohemian avant-garde in the restricted subfield, as well as the competition of this entire subfield with the subfield of large-scale or mass building.

Both cases reveal the limited applicability of Bourdieu's model of cultural change through class imitation within a clearly marked cultural hierarchy. Under specific social conditions revealed by both autos and architecture, hierarchies of cultural tastes and products that testify to class position break down, producing a leveled and pluralized culture that obscures rather than reveals class differences in power and wealth. But as a comparison of the two cases demonstrates, this cultural leveling seems to impact cultural fields differently, depending on the relative proportions of materiality and ideality embodied in their artifacts. Consequently, within the cultures of most modern societies leveled and pluralized cultural fields exist alongside cultural hierarchies that symbolize class position. These cases thus demonstrate that the dynamics of Bourdieu's theory of cultural change often point beyond his specific conclusions about the configurations of modern cultures.

THE RISE AND FALL OF THE AUTOMOTIVE TAIL FIN

The meteoric rise and precipitous fall of the automotive tail fin in the 1950s reveal both the strengths and weaknesses of Bourdieu's model of imitation in a hierarchy of popular culture testifying to class position. As I recounted in Chapters 2 and 4, the automobile entered American culture in the late nineteenth century and quickly came to symbolize the increasingly contentious conflicts of the period. The high prices of the first automobiles put ownership beyond the reach of all but the wealthiest Americans. This upper class used the vehicle not as a practical machine of transportation but as an instrument of leisure, employed mainly for racing, touring, and parading. These early cars thus fit Bourdieu's model of the conspicuous symbols of the grand bourgeoisie, communicating the removal from practical necessities bought only with great wealth (Bourdieu 1984: 270, 293). The reactions of the lower classes to this symbolism were marked by hostility and resentment.

By the middle of the first decade of the twentieth century, however, the saturation of the high-bourgeois luxury market motivated many manufacturers to target upper-middle class professionals and managers with less expensive cars. This class was anxious to mark its own prosperity by borrowing from the high bourgeoisie a symbol of prosperity, leisure, and freedom. So, as Bourdieu predicts, this symbol spread down the class hierarchy through imitation, as rising incomes combined with the falling auto prices due to mass production to bring ownership within the reach of the petite bourgeoisie and even the upper reaches of the working class. However, within this broadened field of mass production, there remained differences that correspond to Bourdieu's distinction between bourgeois art and commercial art. At the top of the market were the grand luxury makes like Cadillac and Lincoln, which were distinguished from the low-end Fords and Chevrolets by both price and aesthetics. The luxury cars were produced in small numbers by a time-consuming process of craft production. Consequently, these cars were distinctive not only in their greater size and power but also in their appearance. The different components of the car were integrated by careful hand-fitting into an aesthetic whole. The bodies were works of art in themselves, crafted by coachbuilders into sleek, unified forms based on centuries-old traditions. The elegant appearance of these luxury cars testified to hundreds of hours of unhurried skilled labor commanded by great wealth and, consequently, to their owner's distance from the hurried concerns of costs and efficiency. On the other hand, the mass-produced cars of the commercial market symbolized the lower-class position of their owners with obvious concerns for cost-cutting efficiency. They were not only smaller and less powerful but also possessed an aesthetic of functionality determined by quick production. The speed and unskilled nature of labor on production lines prevented careful assembly, so these cars had a fragmented, unintegrated appearance. They were also rigidly rectilinear, because curved body panels presented problems for machines. Everything about these cars communicated efficiency, standardization, and cost-cutting, thus symbolizing the conditions and concerns of the lower classes, as Bourdieu argues.

By the mid-1920s, however, a development emerged that defies Bourdieu's model of differential class taste. All consumers, even those of the working class, began to demand mass-produced cars that imitated the style of the grand-bourgeois luxury makes. Bourdieu (1984: 372–84) argues that the lack of economic resources prevents workers from entering the market for symbolically marked goods and inclines their tastes to simple and functional goods, with no cultural pretensions. This is clearly mistaken, especially with respect to products of material culture like the automobile. Although the members of the working class may be prevented from imitating the nonmaterial culture of the higher classes (music, painting, literature) by the lack of the necessary cultural capital (especially education) to appropriate it, they are able to emulate the material culture of the higher classes as soon as their incomes rise to the necessary level. Mass-produced cars like the Model T embodied an unpretentious, functional aesthetic, the type that Bourdieu argues appeals to the working-class habitus. Yet they were increasingly rejected during the 1920s by workers with rising incomes, who demanded in their cheaper cars the look of the expensive, craft-built cars. But why?

One could argue, only minimally altering Bourdieu's general theory, that workers were, like the petite bourgeoisie, merely imitating the aesthetics of the grand bourgeoisie, motivated by a similar desire to appear distinctive or superior to others. I argue, however, following the Frankfurt School (Horkheimer and Adorno 1972; Adorno 1978) that another motive may be more salient for the working class, a desire not for superiority but for individuality, in compensation for their standardized work. In this model, members of the working class seek in their consumer goods compensation for the needs denied them in the mass-production process, especially a sense of efficacy and individuality in the face of its standardized and fragmented work. Mass-produced autos, with their standardized, fragmented, thrown-together look, were constant reminders in workers' leisure time of the characteristics of their work. Consequently, they preferred and demanded in mass-produced cars the unified and individual *look* of the craft-built cars, since this aesthetic obscured the degraded work process that produced them. Bourdieu comes close to recognizing this motive of consumption in his assertion that the bourgeoisie seeks in its aesthetic of temperate hedonism and restrained luxury to display its distance from economic necessity and practical urgencies, its freedom from the practical concerns of making a living and staying alive (Bourdieu 1984: 53–56). He does not recognize, however, the inherent appeal of this same aesthetic for workers, not because it displays their superior economic position, but because it allows them to forget at leisure their inferior position at work. It was this working-class demand for compensation, not merely class imitation, which combined with competitive pressure on the supply side of the market to cause a transfer of the aesthetic features of luxury cars to the lower-priced, mass-produced cars.

In the mid-1920s General Motors was in desperate competition with Ford, whose cheap, functional Model T dominated half of the automotive market. Instead of engaging Ford in direct price competition, GM's Alfred Sloan decided to offer consumers more aesthetically refined cars, which borrowed styling features from the luxury classics. The success of this strategy led GM to institutionalize a trickle-down styling policy that manipulated the consumer desire for individuality. The head of its styling department, Harley Earl, first introduced a style feature, often borrowed from the craft-built cars, in the top make of GM's product hierarchy, Cadillac. In the following year, he transferred it to the next lower make, thus lending it some of Cadillac's aura. He continued this trickle-down styling in successive model years until the feature reached the cheapest make, Chevrolet, and became commonplace, at which time he introduced a new feature at the top.

This successful styling strategy was determined in part by the consumer demand for individuality among all classes in an increasingly prosperous mass-production society. But it was the production requirements and the market structure of the large-scale firms that determined the type of individuality that consumers got. Here the insights of the production of culture perspective can be a useful supplement to Bourdieu's model, which overlooks the detailed constraints on the production side of large-scale markets. Mass-production firms like these automakers require long runs of standardized goods to justify investments in specialized machinery and processes. Thus, they tend to avoid product innovations. Further, these large-scale firms are at least partially sheltered from consumer demand by the lack of competition. Large capital investment in machinery drives small competitors out of business and leaves an oligopolistic industry structure. In the American auto industry, the top three firms in 1927 accounted for 72% of auto output. This type of market control allowed firms to avoid costly and risky competition through price cuts and technological innovations. Yet, there was still competition between the large automakers, especially in this period of the mid-1920s, when the market of first-time buyers became saturated. The oligopolistic firms used superficial styling to compete in an increasingly tight market without jeopardizing either the price structure or product standardization (Baran and Sweezy 1966:112–41). The appearance of the auto body and accessories were differentiated and changed slightly every year in the annual model change, while the major technical components remained unchanged for decades, allowing long runs on specialized machines. Even the costs of body changes were minimized by merely changing the inexpensive components, such as headlights and grilles, on standardized, mass-produced shells. So consumers got the individualized cars they demanded, but in superficial forms dictated by the production constraints of the supply side of the oligopolistic auto market.

These style policies pioneered by GM were slowly adopted by other mass producers, but no other company challenged GM's preeminence in style until the 1950s. Due to lower production volumes, other companies could not afford as large a design staff as GM. So they did not try to innovate but merely followed the aesthetic lead of Earl, who could dictate style for the entire industry through the sheer volume of GM's production. This lack of real competition in style combined with the industry's oligarchical structure to produce a stable, predictable cycle of incremental changes, providing consumers with small but steady doses of trickle-down individuality. The style structure was altered slightly by the Great Depression of the 1930s, which largely eliminated the craft-built luxury cars at the top of the market. The grand luxury makes either went out of business or moved down to compete in the larger middle-priced market, so the only style differences remaining were those between the makes in the hierarchies of mass producers. But the unique developments of the postwar era in the United States reduced even these differences and revolutionized the stable system of style changes created previously.

As Bourdieu suggests, this revolutionary change in the culture of auto design was the result of a conjuncture of forces both external and internal to the field. The most important of the external changes was a sharp increase in and more equal sharing of family income, which brought millions of new consumers—most of them working-class—into the market for new cars (Harrison and Bluestone 1988). By 1953, however, this new demand had been met, and the seller's auto market of the immediate postwar years turned into a highly competitive buyer's market. But this market was still a highly concentrated oligarchy, which steered renewed competition largely into superficial styling and away from disruptive and risky price-cutting and technological innovation. To capture a larger share of consumer income in this market in which unit demand was falling but discretionary income was rising, automakers followed a two-pronged strategy focused on styling and quantitative dimensions. First, to raise the unit price they increased the size, power, and accessories on each car. These developments were more pronounced in the lower-priced models in each corporate hierarchy, for the more equitable income distribution made this the largest market. As a result, corporations concentrated their upgrading efforts there, where the biggest gains were to be had. The result was a decrease in ostensible quantitative differences between lower- and higher-priced models, which had served as class markers.

The qualitative aesthetic differences between models also lessened as a result of the second prong of the automakers' strategy. They sought to stimulate consumers to buy a new car more often by accelerating the cycle of novelty focused on style. In the mid-1950s the usual three-year interval between major body changes was shortened to two on many models, and the off-year cosmetic changes became more drastic. The accelerated style cycle might still have been controlled and orderly if GM had maintained its style leadership. But in the 1950s increasing style competition between the Big Three prevented this, and the accelerated style cycle quickly spun out of control. It was this internal competition for distinction on the supply side among automobile stylists that combined with the growth on the demand side to cause the incredible rise and spectacular fall of the tail fin within a few years.

The tail fin began its short life in 1948 as another of Harley Earl's carefully controlled, trickle-down style devices. Inspired by the vertical stabilizers of the P-38 fighter plane, Earl placed little bumps of sheet metal on the rear fenders of the first postwar Cadillac, hoping to borrow for the car the national pride and technological superiority the public associated with wartime aviation. Over the next several years he spread this prestige marker down GM's model hierarchy, in his usual trickle-down, class-imitation manner. As in the past, Ford and Chrysler slavishly followed Earl's lead, incorporating small fins in 1952 models. Starting in 1953, however, internal supply competition converged with external demand competition to propel the game out of control. Increased competition for sales compelled Ford and Chrysler, both now flush with postwar profits, to greatly increase their styling staffs and give them more power and resources. As a result, auto styling became really competitive for the first time. To stimulate trailing sales, Chrysler decided in 1955 to make a bold styling move, introducing tail fins on all its cars. Then in 1957 the company raised the fins dramatically, introducing in one year a change that Earl would have trickled out over three or four. At this point, the stylists abandoned incremental changes and, driven by desperate efforts to make their cars stand out in a competitive market, vied with one another to make the boldest changes. Tail fins soared, bodies lengthened, and chassis lowered in an unprecedented succession of automotive change. All semblance of aesthetic differences between the makes in automakers' hierarchies was lost.

Thus, increased producer competition in a relatively oligarchic market constrained by mass-production costs led to an aesthetic convergence of automobile models, undermining the individuality that consumers sought in their cultural goods. During this period *Business Week* (1959) argued that there was not enough newness and difference in Detroit cars to fuel the program of planned obsolescence. The aesthetic and structural convergence of American automobiles provided consumers so little individuality that a growing number began to buy imported cars, opening the oligarchical market to real competition for the first time in decades. This move seems to have begun with the cultural bourgeoisie, which Bourdieu argues is often the instigator of cultural change. The late 1940s and the early 1950s saw a rising chorus of complaints from artists and design professionals in the restricted subfield of cultural production, who seemed to resent the fact that middle- and working-class consumers were encroaching on their automotive distinction (Ehrenreich 1989: 37–38). *Fortune* magazine (1947) called American cars "jukeboxes," and argued that their "balloon-like chromium-encrusted bodies are designed so that middle-class wives may impress each other with their opulence." Thus did the cultural bourgeoisie criticize the masses for imitating the economic bourgeoisie's taste for ostentation and luxury. To distinguish themselves, these people with an excess of cultural capital asserted their taste for "aristocratic asceticism" (Bourdieu 1984: 214), which in the automotive field translated into lithe little foreign makes like the MG roadster and the Volkswagen. By 1959 this rejection of Detroit's homogenized opulence had increased sales of imported cars to 700,000, 10% of the American market. Many of these buyers were more concerned with distinction than economy, as revealed by one study that found that two-thirds of Volkswagen owners had incomes at least 40% higher than average new-car buyers (Cray 1980: 402). The cultural bourgeois were not the only car buyers, however, to seek greater distinction and individuality outside the increasingly homogenized market of American-made autos. To distinguish themselves from the middle and working classes, many members of the economic bourgeoisie turned to luxurious and ostentatious European makes like Jaguar and Mercedes-Benz. Even working-class youth, whom prosperity had brought into the auto market, rejected homogenized American cars and sought difference and individuality by modifying stock cars, touching off the hot-rod and customizing subcultures.

By the early 1960s, consumer demand for greater automotive distinction had combined with genuine competition from foreign producers to force American automakers to abandon their long-established policies of superficial styling symbolized by the tail fin. After reaching their outrageous zenith in 1959, fins declined precipitously in subsequent years and were gone from most models by 1962. In the place of such superficially distinctive style features, automakers offered consumers an increasing variety of cars that differed not merely in aesthetics but also in structure and engineering. Between 1960 and 1970 the number of models offered by American automakers increased 50%, to 370. During this decade the Big Three introduced a vast variety of new vehicle types: compacts, subcompacts, intermediate-sized cars, muscle cars (powerful performance cars), pony cars (sporty, youth-oriented vehicles), sports cars, and personal luxury cars. Each type was targeted not, as previously, to a broad income class but to a smaller, more specific market niche, with no hierarchical connotations. Further, to meet consumer demands for individuality, each model was offered with an array of optional components that buyers could order to individualize their cars. Consequently, Bourdieu's hierarchical distinction model collapsed in the automotive field, under the pressure of a prosperous society in which all consumers demanded individuality and difference, and style innovations spread too rapidly to maintain an orderly class trickle-down. What succeeded the hierarchical market was a pluralistic automotive culture, in which aesthetic differences proliferated on a flattened playing field, spreading not from high to low, but from periphery to center.

Randall Collins (1975: 270–99; 2000) presents an analysis of American society that validates this collapse of the hierarchical structure (or deference culture, as he calls it) postulated by Bourdieu. He argues that the growth in absolute incomes of the working and lower-middle classes in the postwar period allowed them to emulate the culture of the traditional upper class, with big, luxurious cars, respectable clothing, tea parties, piano lessons, and concert attendance spreading down the class hierarchy. But, he holds, this cultural leveling was caused not only by higher incomes but also by greater class segregation, which made the cultural differences in the classes less visible. The working class moved to the low-priced suburbs in the 1950s, allowing its members to create their own worlds of private leisure and removing them from the constant surveillance of their class betters, who supervised them at work. Consequently, the different classes directly encountered each other less often, reducing their chances to study and distinguish one another. Further, the commercialization of more and more cultural fields in this period eroded the monopoly of the upper class over culture, as profit-making corporations lowered offerings to cater to the biggest market. When so many could attain at least the external trappings of the old elite culture, it ceased being distinctive, and a new, more pluralistic and segmented culture emerged, especially among the youth of the 1960s.

Collins recognizes, of course, that differences in power and income between the classes persist, as do differences in private beliefs and attitudes, as Michele Lamont (1992, 2000) has documented. His argument is merely that these differences are not expressed in visible, commonly recognized cultural demarcations between classes. This does not mean, however, that the legitimacy of class stratification breaks down, as Bourdieu's analysis might imply. This new, leveled and pluralized culture continues to legitimate class inequalities, but in a different way than Bourdieu's model of class cultures. Instead of clearly marking out class differences and asserting the superiority of some over others, the new pluralized culture legitimates class inequalities by hiding them behind a superficial equality of consumption. It is this latter model of a mass culture obscuring real class power that is extensively developed by the Frankfurt School (Horkheimer and Adorno 1972; Marcuse 1964; Adorno 1978).

Both Collins and the Frankfurt School fail to address directly, however, the sources of difference in this new, leveled and pluralistic culture. The automotive case seems to recommend that people continue to be motivated in cultural competition by attempts to achieve the individuality that is often denied them at work. But where does individuating difference come from when the visible markings of upper-class culture have become widely dispersed in a homogenized culture? I contend that cultural difference increasingly comes not from above but from outside, from marginal groups and subcultures not fully integrated into mass culture. The auto industry in the 1960s, for example, drew on the emerging youth subculture, in both its working-class and middle-class variants. The popular music of the 1960s drew its innovations from marginalized ethnic minorities, in the cases of rock and roll, blues, and rhythm and blues, and from the rural poor, in the cases of folk and country music. There continues to exist a cultural cycle of innovation and imitation, whereby rare culture spreads until it becomes so popular as to lose its individuality. But now the cycle moves from the margins of society to the center, not from higher to lower classes. It is just this cycle of marginality and popularity within a fragmented and leveled culture that the postmodernists seek to capture in their theories (Jameson 1991; Featherstone 1991). This epochal cultural transition, along with its requisite internal and external determinants, is also evident in my second case study, the architectural field, which gave rise to the concept of postmodernism.

THE CONTENTIOUS COLLAPSE OF MODERN ARCHITECTURE IN THE UNITED STATES

During the 1950s, while the popular art of automobile design was soaring to heights of self-indulgent decoration and hedonistic luxury, American high-art architecture was dominated by the severe, antidecorative, ascetic style of modernism. Pioneered mainly in central Europe in the interwar period, modern architecture was adopted relatively late in the United States, after World War II. Modernism was geographically segregated in the corporate, government, and institutional buildings of urban cores, while a commercial aesthetic of entertainment reminiscent of automobile styling reigned in the suburban buildings dedicated to mass consumer culture. By the 1960s, however, modernism was coming under criticism from outside the architecture field for reasons directly related to the late 1950s crisis in consumer culture exemplified by automobiles. But these external forces alone would not have caused the rapid downfall of this widespread style in the architectural subfield of restricted production had they not converged with changes internal to architecture itself, especially the increased competition between producers during this period. The combination of these forces caused the high-art subfield of architecture to be transformed in a way similar to the large-scale field of auto design, that is, a leveling of class-based aesthetic differences and a proliferation of a plurality of popular forms. But due to architecture's status as a hybrid art, combining elements of both material and ideal culture, this leveling was not as severe as in automobiles, and hierarchical distinctions continued to exist. This coexistence of ostensible democratic leveling alongside more clandestine elite distinctions was the hallmark of the new architectural aesthetic known as postmodernism.

In Chapter 5 I argued that the modern style in architecture expressed the interests and ideology of the cultural bourgeoisie, those who have more cultural capital than economic capital. The simple machine forms, smooth surfaces, exposed structural supports, and industrial materials used by this style testified to the importance of the technical knowledge and skills of the engineers, managers, and technicians who were central to the new process of mass production. Modern architecture arose mainly in central Europe, not America, because of the differential strengths of the technocratic movement of this cultural bourgeoisie in each region. In the United States the independent technocratic movement was relatively weak, for in the first years of the twentieth century modernizing capitalists incorporated these technical professions into the new production process. Consequently, they had no need for a separate ideological justification of their ambitions. Further, employed by the mass-production corporations catering to the working masses, these professions, which included industrial designers and architects, were forced to abandon their preferred aesthetic of functionalism or "aristocratic asceticism" and yield to the masses' demand for hedonistic decoration and entertainment. In interwar central Europe, however, the technocratic movement was stronger and more independent. Blocked in their ambitions by an industrial class that was reluctant to modernize, the technical professions, including architects and designers, launched an independent movement for modernization and mass production, the wonders of which modern architecture exalted. They eventually entered an alliance with social-democratic state managers, not capitalists, to deliver state-subsidized housing to the masses in the modern style.

Ironically, however, after World War II the modern architecture that was designed for workers' housing in central Europe was adopted as the preferred aesthetic for prosperous American corporations and government bureaucracies headquartered in the core of major cities. This sudden aesthetic transformation of American architecture in the 1950s is explained in large part by the external changes in the American economy and society. World War II fundamentally changed the governance of the economy. The planning and control of the war economy shifted the balance of corporate power from the old-line entrepreneurs/owners to the new technocratic elite of educated managers, engineers, and professionals (Galbraith 1972; Whyte 1956). Government technocrats cooperated with their corporate counterparts to regularize and stabilize both production and consumer demand in the postwar economy. This newly empowered technocratic elite symbolized its triumph with modern architecture, which testified to its instrumental rationality, technology, and bureaucratic power. The government and corporate skyscrapers in the modern style symbolized an efficient and rational administration of society's resources (Gartman 2009: 191–208).

Even though the technocrats now controlling major corporations preferred modern architecture, it would not have triumphed had it not been for a general tolerance among the working public for this style. What had changed since earlier in the century, when public disdain for modernism had forced mass-production corporations to adopt a more decorative Art Deco style for their headquarter buildings? The answer is found in the increasing segregation of work and consumption during this period. In the early period American workers lived in the urban centers where they worked, and the modern style testifying to rationalized production was constantly visible in their leisure time as a symbol of the class subordination they experienced at work. So they demanded through the marketplace, and got from consumer-sensitive corporations, an architectural style that concealed the rigors of mass-production work under exciting and decorative surfaces, just like the newly styled, mass-produced autos of the day. But as Randall Collins (2000; 1975: 210–16) argues, the postwar period brought the geographic segregation of work and consumption, as the working class moved to the new suburban developments. There, in their leisure hours workers constructed lives and identities based on private consumption, free of reminders of their subordinate class status at work. Consequently, they were more tolerant of technocracy-symbolizing modernism in their workplaces, since they could escape this symbolism into an ostensibly egalitarian consumerism in leisure hours. Such escape was assisted by the aesthetics that dominated the large-scale subfield of building, which was located mainly in the suburban realm of consumption. Here decorative and diverse housing, often in pseudohistorical styles nostalgically invoking preindustrial America, obscured the uniformity and standardization of mass-produced work. So the two architectural styles entered into an ideological symbiosis. The pleasure of consumption, symbolized by suburban architecture, was the justification and motivation for rationalized, bureaucratic production, symbolized by modernism. And rationalized work was the price one had to pay for self-indulgent consumption.

But this ideological trade-off began to come apart in the 1960s due to changes in the popular consumer culture explored in the automobile case, changes that ultimately impacted the high art of architecture. As we saw above, the increasing homogenization of goods in the subfield of large-scale cultural production forced producers to offer a greater variety of fundamentally differentiated goods to satisfy consumers' demand for greater individuality. But such product diversity began to undermine the requirements of mass production, especially product standardization. This is especially clear in the automobile industry, in which the number of models and equipment options exploded during the 1960s. Product diversity lowered production runs, and equipment options slowed assembly lines. Consequently, this consumer-driven diversity increased unit production costs. To contain costs, automakers and other manufacturers increased the speed of machines and lines, forcing workers to work faster. But these new production demands fell upon a workforce well-insulated from the threat of firing by Keynesian methods of demand management, such as unemployment insurance and social wage programs. Thus protected, workers revolted against new demands, sending rates of absenteeism, turnover, and work stoppages soaring by the late 1960s (Rothschild 1974; Bowles, Gordon, and Weisskopf 1984: 84–91). Other signs of discontent with the postwar bargain appeared in the realm of mass consumption, as consumers began to question the real benefits of a society built on ever escalating levels of consumption. The environmental movement arose to question the impact of consumerism on the landscape. The emerging consumer movement questioned the safety of products engineered for quick production and planned obsolescence. Among the young, the Vietnam War raised deeper questions about the costs of America's privileged access to third-world raw materials sustained by military dominance. And among inner-city black Americans, discontent arose against the discrimination that excluded them from the mass prosperity of the period. Put briefly, in the eyes of many Americans the pleasures of mass consumption declined and the hardships of mass production rose to the point where the former no longer seemed an adequate legitimation for the latter (Gartman 1994: 203–11).

These external social forces impacted the restricted subfield of architecture directly, since it was dominated for over a decade by a modernist aesthetic that symbolized and celebrated the system of standardized mass production and its technocratic elite, both of which an increasing number of Americans were questioning (Ehrenreich 1989: 121–43). Young architects in particular began to attack the modernist establishment in the profession as complicit with the technocratic corporate and government elite, especially in the controversial program of urban renewal. In this program modern architects helped developers and government bureaucrats "renew" urban areas by replacing low-cost housing and its poor residents with profitable, upscale housing and amenities for the upper classes (Green and Cheney 1968). Modern architecture came to symbolize for many this undemocratic system imposed on the majority by an insulated and venal elite unconcerned with the interests and needs of average citizens. But the impact of these external forces on architecture was heightened by being filtered through internal forces which exacerbated the usual competition between artistic generations. This convergence of internal and external forces explains the ultimate demise of modern architecture.

In the high art of architecture, just as in the commercial art of automobile design, the major internal force responsible for revolutionizing the subfield was increased competition among producers. During the 1950s and 1960s there was a general increase in enrollments in higher education due largely to government subsidy of educational costs through programs such as the GI Bill. As Diana Crane (1987: 4–9) has argued, this increase in education, combined with growing government and corporate support of the arts during this period, led to a rapid increase in the number of artists competing in the restricted subfield of cultural production, or high art. This was also true of the high-art subfield of architecture. The number of architects in the United States rose from 25,000 in 1950 to 31,000 in 1960, a 24% increase, then to 57,000 in 1970, an 84% increase over 1960 (U.S. Bureau of the Census 1975: 140). Most of these new architects were trained in modern architecture, especially those attending the more prestigious schools of architecture, where European modernist émigrés were in great demand as teachers and directors. Although the general prosperity caused a building boom in the postwar period, several peculiarities of the architectural market prevented it from fully absorbing all of the new architects being trained.

First, in most states the law required licensed architects only on large buildings and public structures, allowing many builders, especially suburban developers, to hire less expensive engineers and designers to lay out houses and communities (Crawford 1991: 30). Second, modern architects excluded themselves from the design of suburban housing with their aesthetic and ethical convictions. They were convinced that the most efficient method to house people was multifamily apartment buildings, and believed single-family houses to be enormously wasteful (Blake 1964). Further, modernists knew that most people preferred housing in more decorative styles, which they refused to design. For these reasons, American modern architects generally confined their efforts to large-scale urban buildings for corporations and government agencies, where their services and aesthetic were welcome.

A peculiarity of modern architecture, however, ensured that a small number of firms were able to meet this expanding demand. From the beginning, modernists had promoted the industrialization and standardization of building, using in their designs materials manufactured to standard dimensions and assembled into repeated units. But this standardization of design and construction made it possible for large, bureaucratic firms, employing a few name designers and hundreds of specialized architects, to design a large portion of all buildings demanded by the market. Younger architects with small firms were left with little business, and many were forced to work for the big firms in specialized and subordinate positions. Such positions, however, frustrated their aspirations of artistic creativity, which were cultivated in architecture schools of the day (Blau 1984: 49–50).

The crowding of young architects in a subfield where a few established modernists dominated design heightened the normal competition that Bourdieu postulates between the consecrated and newcomers in artistic fields. Hostility between the architectural generations increased substantially, and one of the major charges of youth against their elders was, as Bourdieu anticipates, venality or "selling out." In the postwar period modernism was transferred from the consecrated avant-garde in the restricted subfield to bourgeois art in the large-scale subfield of architecture, as large corporations adopted it as the distinctive legitimation of their growing economic capital. When this transfer greatly enriched a few famous modernists, the young denounced them for compromising pure art for the sake of money. As early as 1962 Philip Johnson, an older architect who identified with the youthful outsiders due to his own outsider status, condemned the association of modernism with the business world. Money and profits, he argued, "have precious little to do with the Art of Building. . . . Eating is not as important as art" (Johnson 1979: 146). Peter Blake (1977: 9) similarly wrote: "The Modern Movement—once dedicated to the ideals of an egalitarian democracy—had suddenly become the symbol of American capitalism at its most exploitative."

One particularly contentious area of confrontation of the young and the old in architecture was urban renewal. Throughout the 1950s and early 1960s modern architecture was directly associated with the ground-clearing renewal of urban centers that displaced the poor and working class for the benefit of developers and their upper-class clients. Young architects harshly criticized this type of renewal, motivated largely by their own interests within the field of architecture. In nearly all cases, the architecture of renewal projects was controlled by the older modernists, who, in cooperation with their technocratic political allies, froze young architects and their new ideas out of these lucrative architectural commissions. In 1968 Yale architectural historian Vincent Scully, an elder champion of younger upstarts, wrote with anger of the conspiracy between the large, established architectural firms and the "relatively unqualified" architects working on urban renewal and review boards to deny work to creative young architects. "These [problems] call the whole problem of review boards into question, since they seem about to impose upon the nation's capital a pompous rigidity and a jealous authoritarianism which may be appropriate for Lyndon Johnson's Washington but hardly for that of its founders" (Scully 1988: 227, 229). This was a classic case of sour grapes—young architects dismissed as tainted and corrupt the fruit they could not attain due to their peripheral position in the architectural field.

Scully's direct association of young architects' problems with the authoritarianism of the national political establishment, however, reveals the important influence of external social struggles on this internal contest between the old and young in the restricted architectural subfield. Their criticism of modern architecture, especially its role in urban renewal, found allies external to architecture among the poor and working-class people displaced by it. Young, white, upper-middle-class architects and architectural students often teamed with older, often black, poor workers to oppose the destruction of urban neighborhoods by the renewal plans of developers and city politicians. Their cooperative efforts blossomed into a full-blown alternative to technocratic urban renewal called advocacy planning, in which architects worked with neighborhoods targeted for renewal to develop counter-plans that expressed the interests of the current residents (Davidoff 1993).

Young architects also sought to enlist other external allies for their fight within the architectural field by developing a broad critique of the newly empowered technocratic elite that would appeal to other Americans questioning its rule. Perhaps most important for this effort were Robert Venturi and Denise Scott Brown, two architects and professors at Yale University. Scott Brown had been a student of sociologist Herbert Gans at the University of Pennsylvania and was heavily influenced by his populist critique of urban renewal in *The Urban Villagers* (1962). In this study Gans charged the urban planners and politicians who controlled urban renewal with class bigotry, for they judged the lives and aspirations of the working-class people they displaced by the narrow standards of their own upper-middle-class subculture (Gans 1962: 305–35). In 1972 Scott Brown, writing with her architectural partners Robert Venturi and Steven Izenour and representing the younger generation of architectural challengers, extended Gans's class-based critique to the consecrated elite of modern architects in *Learning from Las Vegas* (1977). They accused these architects of "class snobbery" (155) for arrogantly denigrating the popular culture of "middle-class Americans." This culture, represented by the large-scale architectural subfield responsible for commercial strips, Las Vegas casinos, and developers' suburbs, addressed the real needs and desires of the masses, they claimed, not the overblown monuments to technology erected by the modernist experts. "As Experts with Ideals, who pay lip service to the social sciences, they build for Man rather than for men—this means to suit themselves, that is, to suit their own particular upper-middle-class values, which they assign to all mankind" (154).

This militant denunciation of elitism and class snobbery resonated with and was influenced by the growing questioning of the rule of technocratic experts by the "silent majority," as problems with mass production and consumption intensified in the early 1970s (Ehrenreich 1989: 57–143). Developments in popular culture helped to render the general populace less tolerant of this elite and the high-art architecture that symbolized its rule. As we saw above, the competition of mass producers for consumer dollars in an increasingly broad and prosperous mass market had leveled aesthetic differences between products and replaced a hierarchical culture with a pluralistic one. Against this background, the surviving hierarchical differences between elite and popular culture in the 1960s must have been particularly annoying aesthetic reminders of the continued class differences within society. This was especially true in architecture. While the continuing gaps between elite and popular culture in the fields of painting, music, and literature were not very visible due to the more private nature of the consumption of this ideal culture, architecture is a largely public and material artifact, so differences between buildings were visible to all. When modern architects and their technocratic patrons asserted the superiority of their architecture to degraded commercial buildings, this was resented by the classes of Americans who were beginning to question the ability of this elite to rule.

Populist talk about elitism and snobbery may seem puzzling coming from architects such as Scott Brown and Venturi, who were trained at elite universities (University of Pennsylvania and Princeton, respectively) and were themselves certified members of the cultural bourgeoisie of experts. But there were real affinities of interest between young architects and the working masses of America that can be understood with Bourdieu's concept of homologous positions (1996a: 251–52). The architectural challengers stood in a position in the restricted architectural subfield homologous (similar in form) to the position occupied by the poor and working class in the larger social field of classes. Both were peripheral and powerless, and shared a common subordination to the technocratic power structure, whose members were dominant in both fields. This homology of positions also helps to explain the external influences on the new aesthetic that young architects pioneered to combat and ultimately displace modernism.

The highly competitive nature of high-art architecture in the 1960s and 1970s caused the young to make revolutionary innovations, since only the boldest departures from modernism would stand out in the crowded subfield. Thus, Robert Stern wrote of one architectural rebel of the period, Stanley Tigerman, that although he was trained as a modernist, he had to abandon this aesthetic in a search for distinction. "Almost all of Stanley's work has been in Chicago, which is full of the ethos of Mies [van der Rohe, a modern architect]. . . . Stanley had to take the most outrageous counter-position to get even a moment's hearing by the press or public" (Stern interview in Diamonstein 1980: 235; see also Larson 1993: 247–48). When Stern, Tigerman, and others searched the cultural landscape for signs of aesthetic difference in the 1960s, one of the most obvious sources was the invigorated and pluralistic mass culture. Pressured by competition to cater to consumers' demands for difference, mass producers of cars, music, movies, and other forms of amusement created a widening array of innovative products to offer people escape from, and individuality within, the technocratic system they were questioning. This popular aesthetic was imported into high-art architecture by architectural rebels such as Stern, Tigerman, and Charles Moore to distinguish their work and undermine the modernist establishment.

One reason for this aesthetic borrowing was the homology of positions between the working and middle classes and these young architects. Being outsiders in the architectural field, young architects were sympathetic to the culture of outsiders in the social (or class) field of contest. Bourdieu also mentions another external source of aesthetic innovation that may also have been at work here, the changing habitus of producers and consumers. When higher education was expanded in the 1950s and 1960s, more students from working-class and petite-bourgeois backgrounds received the degrees to compete in the restricted subfield of cultural production. They had formal training in arts, but they did not have the deeply ingrained habitus of the upper class, which is acquired in the home and inclines its members to formalization and aestheticization. The larger number of architects competing for distinction in the restricted subfield encompassed many whose habitus were shaped by lower-class positions and hence inclined them toward the more direct and unsublimated forms of pleasure found in popular culture. This was also true in the field of painting, which was revolutionized during this period by Pop artists who similarly drew on the vitality of popular culture to challenge the dominance of modernism. Many of these artists, including Andy Warhol, began their careers in the commercial arts and carried their petite-bourgeois and working-class habitus with them into the restricted subfield of painting (Crane 1987: 32–33).

Even though the populists in architecture protested elitist modernism and mobilized elements of popular culture to combat it, they did not seek to destroy the restricted subfield of architecture and reduce it to a commercial art like automobile design. It is clear that the young populists were making a strategic move *within* the restricted subfield, for they appropriated these new elements within its rules, especially the one privileging form over content. As Bourdieu (1996a: 299–300) argues, the defining characteristic of the restricted subfield of cultural production is its emphasis on the cerebral form of expression, which distinguishes it from the emphasis on the function of inducing immediate pleasure found in popular culture. Venturi and other young populists took the expressions of direct hedonism from popular culture and inserted them into the restricted subfield of architecture as forms, stripped of their content. The authors of *Learning from Las Vegas* made it clear that they were not seeking to lower their art to commercial culture, writing that "learning from popular culture does not remove the architect from his or her status in high culture" (Venturi, Scott Brown, and Izenour 1977: 161). This was still high art, they insisted, because their effort "was a study in method, not content" (6). Venturi and his colleagues brought ordinary commercial symbolism into dialogue with the established traditions of the restricted subfield, in order to speak to the common man on the street as well as the educated aesthetic elite (Jencks 1986: 10). So, for example, in his Guild House apartment building in Philadelphia, Venturi used several elements from popular culture: standard double-hung windows, a commercial-type sign over the entrance, and a fake television antenna crowning the façade. But the educated viewer also noticed that the windows were out-of-scale—too large, like a Claes Oldenburg Pop Art light bulb—and that the overall layout of the building was modeled on a Renaissance palace (Venturi 1977: 116; Venturi, Scott Brown, and Izenour 1977: 91–101).

The explanation for this insertion of external influences into the high-art subfield of architecture must address the changing habitus of consumers as well as producers. This hybrid architecture found a burgeoning market because the same forces that were transforming architectural producers were also transforming consumers. Increasing college attendance meant that upwardly mobile Americans were gaining formal knowledge of the high arts, while simultaneously retaining sympathy for popular culture due to their habitus inculcated informally at home. The architectural populists brought the high arts of architecture down to meet this rising middle class or petite bourgeoisie. The familiar elements of popular culture treated formally made high-art architecture more friendly and familiar to these cultural neophytes, in addition to wiping out the negative technocratic connotations of modernism.

Despite this blending of popular and high art, architecture was not, like automobile design, leveled to a commercial art devoid of hierarchical distinctions. There remained noticeable hierarchical distinctions between buildings designed for the large-scale, commercial market and buildings designed for the restricted, high-art market by trained architects. These different developments of architecture and auto design are explained by the relative proportions of economic and cultural capital required for their appropriation. As Bourdieu recognizes (1996a: 147), in commercial culture the reception of products depends mainly on income and is largely independent of cultural capital, while in high-art culture reception depends vitally on cultural capital. What he does not recognize, however, is the implication of this difference for cultural leveling. As Herbert Gans states (1999: 11), the leveling of a cultural field is inversely proportional to the amount of education (a form of cultural capital) required for appreciation. Where money alone is required to consume a cultural product, leveling is likely to occur as general prosperity grows, for producers are motivated by market size to distribute distinctive characteristics widely until hierarchical differences break down. This is especially true of products of material culture—automobiles, appliances, clothes—that require little knowledge to consume. Where cultural capital figures heavily in consumption, however, hierarchies are likely to remain. (On this point, see also DiMaggio 1987.) Cultural capital—especially as it is defined by Bourdieu to encompass not merely education but also dispositions acquired in the home—is more unequally distributed in advanced capitalist society than income. Further, these cultural differences in disposition and taste are less visible than strictly economic differences, because the former are more likely to manifest themselves in nonmaterial culture (e.g. music, dance, and literature), which is consumed privately in class-segregated society. This lack of visibility makes cultural capital less susceptible to redistributive pressures from below, which routinely affect economic capital and its material manifestations. Consequently, markets for such cultural goods are more differentiated and smaller. The lower classes generally do not demand or seek to imitate the qualities of these goods of the higher classes because they do not perceive them. And even if they did, their lack of cultural capital would prevent them from appropriating or appreciating cultural goods with these distinctive qualities. So the hierarchical differences remain, and in conjunction with the leveling of cultural differences in the realm of material culture, these may be effective in reproducing class inequality. On the visible, material surface of culture society seems to be classless, since there are few ostensible differences in the goods people consume, and those that do exist are matters mainly of quantity, not quality. But beneath the surface, in the more private, nonmaterial realms of culture, upper-class individuals can recognize one another by distinctive cultural traits unnoticeable to others. These cultural cues provide the basis for selective association and advantage, thus serving to reproduce the class.

In the automobile field economic capital clearly outweighs cultural capital, so it shows a tendency to leveling. From the beginning the possession and consumption of this material product depended mainly on economic capital, with few ingrained or acquired cultural dispositions necessary. Price largely separated higher-class from lower-class makes, and the aesthetic differences that did exist as marks of prestige were highly visible in this good consumed in public areas of communication between the classes.

Consequently, the lower classes sought to imitate these distinctions, and as they acquired greater income in the postwar years, these demands became effective in the market. Especially in periods of increased competition, auto producers were pressured to give lower-class consumers the largely superficial high-class markers they sought, and the aesthetic hierarchy was flattened and pluralized.

Architecture, however, is a more hybrid cultural field, in which both economic and cultural capital are important in consumption. A building is an expensive material product that requires substantial economic resources to "consume," whether consumption is defined as ownership, occupation through rent, or even occasional use. Yet in its restricted subfield, architecture is also an art, which requires for proper appreciation knowledge of an extensive history and cultivated dispositions to detect subtle distinctions. This hybrid nature explains the partial leveling of this field and the retention of hierarchical differences. The distinction between severe, ascetic modernism and the hedonistic entertainment aesthetic of popular architecture testified to class differences in cultural as well as economic capital. Yet in the 1950s the lower classes did not demand imitations of modernism in their architecture, despite the fact that the aesthetic differences were very visible in public areas. This was due not merely to their lack of cultural capital or taste to appreciate modernism, but also to its symbolic association with the technocratic system, from which they were trying to escape in their leisure lives. So when internal competition increased in the field, young architects seeking distinction were compelled to bring not high-art architecture to the masses, but mass culture to high-art architecture. They used popular elements within the rules of high art, maintaining the cultural distinctions to cater to a class rising not merely in income but also in cultural capital. This new populist or postmodern architecture presented a public face of egalitarianism and classlessness, appealing to the masses with its popular elements. Yet at the same time, it privately distinguished those privileged in cultural capital with inside references to the subfield of high-art architecture.

CONCLUSION: PROPOSITIONS ON CULTURAL CHANGE

In conclusion I summarize the findings from my comparison of these cases by offering several generalizations about cultural change in propositional form. These propositions modify Bourdieu's' theory of cultural change by specifying the social conditions giving rise to cultural hierarchies that symbolize class position, as well as the social conditions under which hierarchies break down to produce leveled and pluralized cultural fields, as postulated by the Frankfurt School and postmodern theory. Thus, these propositions represent an attempt not to refute Bourdieu's theory, but to go beyond it, using his variables to explain a broader range of cultural configurations than he recognizes.

1.0 The lower the relative equality of and absolute average levels of economic and cultural capital in a society, the more cultural markets are differentiated and hierarchical, with cultural products visibly symbolizing class positions.

1.1 In such highly stratified societies, culture legitimates inequality by marking members of the higher classes as individually superior to members of the lower classes.

1.2 In highly stratified societies, cultural innovations originate in the higher classes and are gradually diffused to the lower classes through imitation.

    1.21 Imitation of the cultural products of the higher classes by the lower classes is motivated by the latter's attempts to achieve both distinction (superiority) and individuality.

    1.22 The greater the competition between producers of cultural products in highly stratified societies, the shorter the cycle of innovation, for producers are motivated to quickly bring distinctive cultural products to the lower classes.

2.0 The higher the relative equality of and absolute levels of economic and cultural capital in a society, the more cultural markets are leveled and pluralized, dissociating cultural products from class position.

    2.01 The greater the competition between producers of cultural products, the greater is the leveling and pluralizing effect of the increase and equalization of economic and cultural capital, due to greater pressure on producers to bring distinctive cultural products to the lower classes.

    2.02 The increase in the equality of and absolute average level of economic capital results in leveling and pluralization mainly in markets of material culture, by increasing the demand for distinctive and individual material products whose consumption requires mainly income.

    2.03 The increase in the equality of and absolute level of cultural capital results in leveling and pluralization mainly in markets of nonmaterial culture, by increasing the demand for distinctive and individual nonmaterial products whose consumption requires mainly cultural knowledge and training, and by increasing the number of suppliers of nonmaterial products and hence the competition between them.

2.1 In less stratified societies, culture legitimates inequality by obscuring the existing inequalities of capital between the higher classes and the lower classes.

2.2 In less stratified societies, cultural innovations originate in marginalized social groups and are gradually diffused to the mass culture.

    2.21 Imitation of the cultural products of the marginalized by consumers of mass culture is motivated by the latter's attempts to achieve individuality alone, not distinction (superiority).

2.22 The greater the competition between producers of cultural products in less stratified societies, the shorter is the cycle of innovation, for producers are motivated to quickly bring the individual products of marginalized groups to the mass market.

3.0 Cultural innovation in both types of societies is accelerated by external struggles in the larger social field that challenge the system of stratification.

    3.1 The stronger the challenge of these external struggles in the social field, the stronger the challenge of cultural producers in peripheral positions in the cultural field to those in established positions.

    3.2 The stronger the challenge of external struggles in the social field, the more likely it is that they will influence the content of cultural innovations by providing both consumers and producers with new habitus.

7   Bourdieu and Adorno
Converging Theories of Culture and Inequality

In the previous chapters of this book I have discussed both the similarities and differences of the theories of culture developed by Bourdieu and the Frankfurt School. Both share a fundamental focus on the way that the myriad manifestations of culture in modern society are inextricably linked with the unequal structure of power and wealth. For both theories the structure of economic domination generates a system of cultural domination that unintentionally legitimates its material inequalities. But as I argue in Chapter 3, Bourdieu and the Frankfurt School postulate widely diverging social mechanisms to explain how culture legitimates and reproduces class inequality. For Bourdieu, modern culture is a class culture, characterized by social ranked symbolic differences that mark classes out and make some seem superior to others. For the Frankfurt thinkers, by contrast, modern culture is a mass culture, characterized by a socially imposed symbolic unity that obscures class differences behind a façade of leveled democracy. In other chapters I have sought to specify the social and historical conditions under which each of the theories is valid.

In the course of researching Bourdieu's theory, however, I discovered that he subtly changes his positions on these issues in the last fifteen years or so of his life. Although he never renounces his earlier theory of culture, this shift is perceptible in both his theoretical work and his political interventions. Like the Frankfurt School, he becomes increasingly critical of mass culture for placing the profits of the market ahead of the independent cultural standards of intellectuals. Bourdieu also begins to privilege the high culture of intellectuals over mass culture, using as a universal standard the former's "disinterestedness," or autonomy from pecuniary interests. So his analysis of mass culture in the 1990s begins to sound surprisingly like the Frankfurt School's writings of the 1930s and 1940s.

In this final chapter I analyze this remarkable convergence of these two critical theories of culture. Although Bourdieu moves closer to the established positions of the Frankfurt School, he never acknowledges their influence on his theory. On the contrary, the vicissitudes of Bourdieu's theory seem to be driven mainly by two other factors: his early theory's internal contradictions and his historically situated political interventions.

Regardless of the impetus of this movement, however, Bourdieu ends up agreeing with the Frankfurt School that there are universal standards by which culture may be judged, and that autonomous high-cultural fields better embody these than mass culture, which is driven by the market. But this theoretical convergence is not total, and differences remain. The most important of these is the origin of the critical component in autonomous culture. Bourdieu grounds this critical culture in the continuing social conflicts of modern society. The Frankfurt School, by contrast, believes that mass culture is successful in suppressing all class conflict, and is thus forced to resort to technology to ground its concept of critical culture.

In the following arguments about the convergence of these two theories, I will narrow my discussion of the Frankfurt School almost exclusively to the work of Theodor Adorno. I do so for several reasons. First, although other members of the Frankfurt School, especially Max Horkheimer, Herbert Marcuse, and Walter Benjamin, treat the topic of culture, Adorno's work on culture is the most developed and extensive among the loose confederation of thinkers falling under this label. Second, there are substantial differences—even contradictions—between the ideas on culture within the group. Consequently, a close, detailed comparison requires choosing among these variants. Finally, I personally believe that Adorno's theory of culture is more powerful, for reasons that I hope will become evident below.

THE INITIAL DIFFERENCES IN CULTURAL CRITIQUES

One way to understand the initial differences between the theories of culture by Bourdieu and Adorno is to compare their evaluations of Kant's theory of aesthetics as presented in *Critique of Judgment*, which both cite. Here Kant argues that beauty is a judgment that the *form* of an object produces in the perceiving subject a feeling of pleasure that is *disinterested*. That is, aesthetic pleasure, unlike other pleasures, is not practical or useful, not based on the subject's need to possess the physical existence of the object. Rather, it is a purely contemplative pleasure, which seeks merely to maintain the subject's harmonious state of mind as it perceives the object (Crawford 1974).

In *Distinction* Bourdieu builds his theory of culture as class legitimation on a strong rejection of Kant's universal standard of disinterestedness, arguing it is neither universal nor disinterested. "Empirical interest enters into the composition of the most disinterested pleasures of pure taste, because the principle of the pleasure derived from these refined games for refined players lies, in the last analysis, in the denied existence of a social relationship of membership and exclusion. . . . Pure taste [is] an internalized social relationship, a social relationship made flesh" (Bourdieu 1984: 499–500). The social relation expressed in the judgment of pure taste is a historical relation of class domination, for it imposes on all the particular taste of the dominant class, which alone has sufficient resources to be uninterested in the practical value of culture. Aesthetic judgments based on disinterestedness thus make all other classes seem inferior, because their lack of resources dictates that they must always be concerned with the pay-off of culture. Thus, the economic resources of the dominant class are legitimated by making it look culturally superior and thus deserving of more resources. So the pure, disinterested taste of the dominant class is in reality interested, because it functions historically to secure its wealth from the challenge of other classes.

Although Theodor Adorno is not uncritical of Kant's theory of aesthetics, he is sympathetic to his universal cultural standard of disinterestedness. In *Aesthetic Theory* Adorno argues that when culture is interested and gives consumers immediate sensual pleasure, it maintains economic inequality by providing a soporific, a superficial satisfaction for needs that prevents people from taking action to create a more just and equal society. This is what mass culture does in modern society, Adorno holds. Capitalism turns culture into another commodity that must make a profit on the market. This commodification of culture forces cultural producers to cater to the largest number of consumers, who demand substitutes for needs denied them in capitalist production, such as individuality and freedom. Thus, an interested, commodified culture legitimates the status quo by accommodating the victims to the inequalities of capitalism.

Adorno holds that only those varieties of high bourgeois culture that remain disinterested or autonomous from the practical demands of the market play a critical or progressive role. Unconcerned with sales, these hold out the promise of human happiness in their beautiful forms, but deny the realization of happiness by simultaneously revealing the ugly antagonisms of the present society. Adorno argues that by revealing life could be happy, but is prevented from being so by an unjust society, disinterested art delegitimates existing inequalities and stimulates social change. Consequently, this disinterested high art stands on the side of the oppressed in history.

> One of the basic human rights possessed by those who pick up the tab for the progress of civilization is the right to be remembered. . . . This right demands that the marks of humiliation be committed to remembrance in the form of *images*. Art must take up the cause of that which is branded ugly. In doing so, art should not try to integrate or mitigate ugliness, or seek to reconcile it with its existence by employing humor, which is more repulsive than all the ugliness there is. Instead, art has to make use of the ugly in order to denounce the world which creates and recreates ugliness in its own image. (Adorno 1984: 72)

Against Bourdieu, then, Adorno holds that Kant's disinterested aesthetic is not the particular taste of the dominant class, historically defined and imposed as a standard on all and thus resulting in the legitimation of social inequalities. Rather, he sees it as the universal criterion of art that is critical of social inequalities. Further, he denies that the interested aesthetic of immediate pleasure is the authentic expression of the relational position of the working class, which is asserted by Bourdieu and others. Instead, Adorno holds that *this* aesthetic is the inauthentic one, for it is imposed on all of society by the market and serves to legitimate inequalities by obscuring real class differences. While Bourdieu sees modern culture as a ranked diversity of subcultures that simultaneously symbolizes class positions and makes some seem superior to others, Adorno sees it as a homogeneous unity of superficial pleasures, imposed on all, that obscures class inequalities altogether. Thus for him what is oppressive about this culture is that it has virtually eliminated the disinterested high culture that provides a standard of criticism, that the pressure of the market has leveled all cultural expression to simplistic gratifications that reconcile the oppressed to their own oppression.

ADORNO ON AUTONOMOUS CULTURE, MASS CULTURE, AND LEVELING

Adorno acknowledges the continued existence of critical art that exposes the gap between potential happiness and existing repression. This is especially true in his specialty field—music. Here he argues that modern music like Arnold Schoenberg's twelve-tone compositions illustrate the critical tension between the ugly reality of instrumental reason and the beautiful potential for a reconciled, rational society (Adorno 1994). Yet, he laments the increasing rarity of critical art in monopoly capitalism, in which all human needs, including cultural ones, are reduced to commodities sold on the market. When culture becomes just another money-making industry, there is an inevitable tendency to reduce cultural expression to products that offer immediate pleasure and eliminate the painful reminders of repression and ugliness.

The rise of monopoly capitalism concentrates power into fewer and fewer hands, thus intensifying the alienation of work and depriving people of their needs for freedom, individuality, and sociality. Under these circumstances, the promise of happiness in authentic art becomes an unbearable reminder of the unhappiness of damaged lives. "The masses want the shameful difference separating art from their lives eliminated, because if art were to have any real effect on them it would be that of instilling a sense of loathing, which is the last thing they want" (Adorno 1984: 24). So they demand pleasure now, in the form of consumer goods that deliver superficial, fetishized substitutes for the real satisfactions denied them by society. This demand provides the basis for a profitable industry that produces cultural commodities that console people for their alienating jobs. The freedom and individuality that monopoly capital takes away from it victims in their work lives is returned to them as ersatz satisfactions in their leisure lives—for a profit. Art thus loses its purposelessness and is reduced to another means of making money.

Adorno argues that the emergence of a profit-making mass culture in monopoly capitalism destroys the erstwhile gap between high and popular culture, to the detriment of both. Authentic high art, which criticizes society, exists only when culture is autonomous, free from consumer demands for immediate usefulness. This autonomy exists, Adorno argues, mainly in the early bourgeois era, the late eighteenth and early nineteenth centuries. Before this period artists were generally feudal retainers directly controlled by aristocratic patrons, who used art to glorify their power and wealth. The early bourgeois era freed artists from feudal dependency by creating a market for their works in the rising bourgeoisie, which had the education and leisure to cultivate the image-consciousness necessary to appreciate disinterested, sublimated artistic forms. The anonymity and dispersion of this bourgeois market demand provided artists with autonomy from the direct control of individual patrons and allowed them to develop independent aesthetic forms. But art in this early era was only partially autonomous, Adorno argues, for artists were still dependent on the general market demand of bourgeois consumers as a group. Bourgeois art thus became purposeless for the purpose of the market (Adorno 1984: 320–21; 1991b: 55; Horkheimer and Adorno 2002: 127–28).

This new, partially autonomous art of the early bourgeois era stood in stark contrast to the popular culture of the masses, which was not without progressive elements. The economic status of the lower classes deprived them of the education and leisure necessary to cultivate the appreciation of sublimated forms. Consequently, their amusements and entertainments were characterized by rebellious physicality and crude mimicry, which testified both to the deprivation of the masses and their refusal to supinely accept it. For Adorno, this gap between high and low culture expressed the truth of an oppressive society.

> The purity of bourgeois art, hypostatized as a realm of freedom contrasting to material praxis, was bought from the outset with the exclusion of the lower class; and art keeps faith with the cause of that class, the true universal, precisely by freeing itself from the purposes of the false. Serious art has denied itself to those for whom the hardship and oppression of life make a mockery of seriousness and who must be glad to use the time not spent at the production line in being simply carried along. Light art has accompanied autonomous art as its shadow. It is the social bad conscience of serious art. The truth which the latter could not apprehend because of its social premises gives the former an appearance of objective justification. The split between them is itself the truth: it expresses at least the negativity of the culture which is the sum of both spheres. The antithesis can be reconciled least of all by absorbing light art into serious or vice versa. That, however, is what the culture industry attempts. (Horkheimer and Adorno 2002: 107–8)

The age of monopoly capitalism, which follows this early bourgeois age of competitive capitalism, conspires to destroy this bifurcated culture's testimony to an unequal society by leveling the difference between high and low culture into a mass culture. During this age capitalists like Henry Ford pioneer methods of mass production that are so expensive and require such a large scale of production that capital becomes concentrated into large, bureaucratic corporations. Due to the planning required by such large firms, Adorno sometimes calls this new stage "administered capitalism," or simply "the administered society." When such large, totally rationalized mass-production corporations seize control of the production of cultural products, the result is the loss of oppositional elements in both high and low culture. The autonomy of high art from the market is destroyed, and it is leveled into a homogeneous, standardized mass culture whose sole purpose is to make money by giving consumers what they want—immediate gratification of desires repressed by the totally administered society. The crude physicality and rebellion of popular culture, which testify to the deprivation of the lower class, is also destroyed, as mass culture sanitizes and "civilizes" the expression of this group to make it acceptable in "polite society."

In various writings, Adorno discusses two interrelated factors that force the corporate mass-producers of culture to abandon the aesthetic diversity that symbolizes social differences and to adopt homogenized goods—the technology utilized by cultural suppliers, and the demand of cultural consumers themselves. On the supply side of the cultural market, the search for profits leads corporations to lower costs by mechanically producing large quantities of the same products. Just as Ford was forced by the high costs of specialized machines to eliminate all car models but one—the standardized, unchanging Model T—so the mass producers of films, music, and radio and television programs are similarly forced by production costs to focus on a few types with standardized formulas. When Adorno speaks of the "technology" of cultural production leading to standardization, he understands this term broadly to include not merely the mechanical apparatus but also, and more importantly, the administrative apparatus that organizes and controls human work. Citing Max Weber, Adorno (1991a: 95–96) argues that bureaucratic corporations reduce the diversity of human tasks in order to impose abstract, standardized rules that allow centralized control. "Technical rationality today is the rationality of domination. It is the compulsive character of a society alienated from itself. . . . For the present the technology of the culture industry confines itself to standardization and mass production and sacrifices what once distinguished the logic of the work from that of society. These adverse effects, however, should not be attributed to the internal laws of technology itself but to its function within the profit economy" (Horkheimer and Adorno 2002: 95). So it is the imperative to dominate alienated labor within the corporation for the sake of profit that leads to the standardization of work and its cultural products alike. A similar relation between the concentration of power in oligopolistic firms and the homogeneity of cultural products has been documented by the production of culture perspective in sociology (see DiMaggio 1977).

Adorno argues, however, that the leveling of cultural diversity is driven not merely by the corporate imperative of technological domination but also by the demand of consumers themselves. The alienated consumers of the administered society *want* what is forced upon them by their corporate masters, because their needs are just as much products of the technological apparatus as the goods they consume. As workers, they have been standardized and homogenized by the same production process that levels and standardizes cultural goods. "The might of industrial society is lodged in men's minds. The entertainments manufacturers know that their products will be consumed with alertness even when the customer is distraught, for each of them is a model of the huge economic machinery which has always sustained the masses, whether at work or at leisure—which is akin to work. . . . The culture industry as a whole has molded men as a type unfailingly reproduced in every product" (Horkheimer and Adorno 1972: 127).

It is not just workers, however, but also the bourgeois who have been molded by the apparatus of technological domination, which controls them as much as they control it. "The mechanism of psychic mutilation upon which present conditions depend for their survival also holds sway over the mutilators themselves, and if these are similar enough to their victims in terms of drive structure, the victims thus can take some solace in the fact that they can also partake of the commodities of the dominant class to the extent that these are intended to appeal to a mutilated instinctual structure" (Adorno 1989–90: 49). From this mass culture consumed by the dominant and dominated alike there emerges an identification between classes, a pseudo-democracy that serves to conceal the continued existence of real differences in power and wealth (Adorno 1993: 22).

Adorno gives numerous examples of this leveling process, which results in the collapse of the class-symbolizing differences between high and low culture. But perhaps his most convincing case for leveling is classical music, the art form he knows best. Although he argues that composers like Schoenberg continue to produce autonomous, critical music that carries the promise of happiness but exposes the ugliness of the existing society, he shows that many classical composers have succumbed to the imperative of the culture industry to offer immediate gratification. In his *Philosophy of Modern Music* (1994), Adorno is highly critical of the compositions of Igor Stravinsky, comparing them unfavorably to Schoenberg's. While the latter's highly technologized serial music realistically reveals the individual struggling in the clutches of the collective domination of instrumental reason, Stravinsky's primitivism, exemplified in *The Rite of Spring*, abandons reason altogether and celebrates the return of humans to an infantile state of nature. In this piece the individual joyously surrenders itself to the primitive collective in an act of self-sacrifice, symbolizing an abandonment of the ego and its rational relation to the world. Here, as in mass music, the negativity of denial and historical suffering is displaced by the positivity of total fulfillment in the eternal now. Seeing parallels with the Nazi destruction of individual freedom by the dominance of the collective *Volk*, Adorno argues that Stravinsky's music models the submission of humans to a totalitarian collective of hysterical obedience.

This leveling of differences between high and low culture occurs not merely in the mass production of new art forms, Adorno argues, but also in the mass distribution of older forms that were progressive in their day. For example, in order to facilitate the consumption of classical music by masses of radio listeners whose aesthetic sensibilities have been dulled and degraded by alienated work, the culture industry condescendingly instructs them in simplistic formulas of "music appreciation." Instead of raising the masses to the level of high culture, such distribution strategies lower culture to a simplified fetish. For example, Adorno (1993: 31–33) cites a popular book of the 1930s that purports to teach listeners to recognize the main themes of famous symphonies by giving them lyrics that can be easily memorized. This focus on the thematic fragment diverts attention from what it essential in music—the structure of the composition, the relation of the parts and their development. This device reduces culture to a set of facts, mere information to be used as a status symbol to display one's superiority over others and compensate for the lack of real power (Adorno 1993: 27–29, 32–33).

The leveling and homogenization of culture under the imperatives of monopoly-capitalist production and distribution creates a dilemma for the culture industry, however. Although Adorno argues that consumers are conditioned by their standardized jobs to accept and even demand these standardized cultural products, he also holds that this conditioning is never complete. Human beings can never be totally reduced to standardized things, because they are inherently thinking subjects with free will (Adorno 1991b: 80). To grasp and dominate these potentially resistance subjects, the culture industry must offer products that promise freedom and individuality while in reality denying both in order to produce a profit. This is accomplished by incorporating superficial symbols of these desired qualities to disguise the underlying sameness, a trait that Adorno labels pseudoindividuality and develops in his infamous analysis of jazz. He argues that mass music must simultaneously conform to established conventions to facilitate production and distribution, but also deviate from them to disguise standardization and give consumers substitutes for denied individuality. Jazz accomplishes this by following standardized forms of rhythm and tonality, but disguising these with superficial deviations that make each piece seem endlessly changing and unique. For example, most jazz pieces incorporate simple melodies that are merely repeated, not developed as in classical music. This simplicity allows it to function as a means to an ulterior end—a musical accompaniment to dancing. Yet, the melody is also departed from in instrumental improvisation, in which players spontaneously create random variations on the theme without altering its basic structure. Adorno concludes that jazz is "a reproduction which respectfully dresses up its bare walls in order to disguise its inhumanity, but which helps to prolong this inhumanity surreptitiously in doing so" (Adorno 1989–90: 56).

Due to these mass-market imperatives of cultural production and distribution, Adorno believes that the existence of a critical of high culture is precarious at best in monopoly-capitalist society. In this society cultural producers lose their autonomy, which rests on a source of economic support that does not interfere with production by demanding practical results like market sales. Adorno holds out only one such source of support for critical high culture in these circumstances—the private wealth of individual intellectuals or their benefactors. In *Minima Moralia,* his book of reflections and aphorisms written during his exile in the United States, Adorno writes that only "the man of independent means" can avoid the increasing instrumentalization and commercialization of culture (Adorno 1974: 21). He recognizes the irony, however, that the individual wealth that confers autonomy on the privileged intellectual most often comes from the commercial world itself, so that "his own distance from business at large is a luxury which only that business confers" (26). So in the end even the independent intellectual or artist remains entangled in the capitalist society that he seeks to escape. The only advantage of this semidetached cultural producer is his "insight into his entanglement" (26), or, to put this in more contemporary terms, his reflexive knowledge of his own social situation.

Adorno also recognizes the shameful behavior often motivated by intellectuals' reliance on private wealth—the vicious competition between supplicants for the benefactors' support. He concludes that the only responsible course of behavior in such a situation is "to deny oneself the ideological misuse of one's own existence, and for the rest to conduct oneself in private as modestly, unobtrusively and unpretentiously as is required, no longer by good upbringing, but by the shame of still having air to breathe, in hell" (27–28). So Adorno seems to assert that the autonomy of critical cultural producers ultimately rests on acts of individual will, fortified by guilty knowledge of their own privilege. But this is a very weak reed on which to rest the continued existence of critical culture, which may explain why he is so unrelentingly pessimistic about it.

Adorno's reliance on private wealth as the foundation for cultural autonomy surely reflects his own biography, as well as the history of the Frankfurt Institute for Social Research, with which he was affiliated for almost his entire career. He grew up the pampered son of a well-to-do wine merchant and a mother of noble pedigree, both of whom economically indulged his musical and intellectual pursuits. He became a *Privatdozent* (an unsalaried lecturer supported by student fees) at the University of Frankfurt, where he became associated with and ultimately employed by the Institute for Social Research, which was funded privately by an endowment from a rich German grain merchant. But the Institute's members were forced to emigrate to the U.S. in 1934 by the Nazi persecution of left-wing and Jewish professors. This experience must have impressed on Adorno the danger of relying on state funding for intellectuals, since the political demands of the state can be every bit as damaging to the autonomy of culture as the economic demands of the marketplace (Jay 1973; Wiggershaus 1994).

In his American exile, Adorno became almost entirely dependent for economic support on the privately endowed Institute. The Depression, however, severely depleted the value of its investments, forcing the director, Max Horkheimer, to look for alternative methods to support the staff and its work. Securing university positions for members in the U.S. was difficult, not only because of the language barrier and shortage of openings but also because of the nature of the Frankfurt School's work. While most American social scientists were dedicated to empirical research on social problems that could yield incremental improvements in capitalist society, the Institute's research was more theoretical and philosophical, and ultimately dedicated to the revolutionary change of society as a whole. The only way to support the Institute's theoretical research was to engage in American-style empirical projects that attracted private funding from foundations like the American Jewish Committee. Although these projects entailed some compromises with respect to methods, they did allow the Institute to keep together its core members, of which Adorno was one, and to test the empirical implications of its theoretical work, which was continued in their spare time (Wheatland 2009). Thus, before he returned after the war to the University of Frankfurt at the invitation of the new German state, Adorno's work as an intellectual was supported almost exclusively by private funds, which surely shaped his ideas on the foundation of cultural autonomy. This presumption made him very pessimistic about the prospects for the continued existence of a critical high culture that could resist accommodation to the imperatives of the market.

BOURDIEU AGAINST ADORNO ON MASS CULTURE, AUTONOMOUS CULTURE, AND LEVELING

Like Adorno, Bourdieu also recognizes the existence of a low culture of immediate gratification that stands in contrast to a high culture of ascetic contemplation. But Adorno's theory of "mass culture" differs from Bourdieu's analysis of "popular culture" in important ways. Bourdieu argues that this culture is the authentic expression of the working class's socially conditioned desires. Being raised in families in which material resources are scarce, workers have to be constantly concerned with acquiring the necessities of life. They thus internalize a habitus, a set of unconscious dispositions, that privileges the functions of things over their forms or appearances. This habitus motivates them to consume functional goods that assert their solidarity with the collective class, not formalized goods that assert their distinction as individuals. Only the bourgeoisie has sufficient economic capital to instill a habitus conditioning a taste for freedom, that is, cultural goods that show a distance from necessity by a concern for aesthetic form or appearance. By consuming such aestheticized goods, members of this class unintentionally distinguish themselves as individuals and set themselves apart from the mass of humanity. Thus, for Bourdieu popular culture must be judged relative to workers' social position, and cannot be compared to high culture on some universal criterion of worthiness, as Adorno seeks to do. He holds that it is not inferior to, but relationally opposed to, the high culture of ascetic disinterest, in ways dictated by the class position of its consumers.

Bourdieu's position of socially relative differences in class tastes contrasts with Adorno's assertion of a universalism of human needs across classes. The latter attributes to workers the same need as the bourgeoisie to assert themselves as free, self-determining individuals, and thus presumes that they ultimately cannot be content with standardized goods, which are imposed on them by monopolistic corporations, not chosen freely to match their desires. Consequently, even the homogeneous mass culture must provide the illusion of individuality in goods to appeal to this need. But Adorno's universalistic concept of individuality, unlike Bourdieu's relational concept, is not achieved in opposition to others, by asserting an invidious *superiority* over them. For him, individuality is merely the right to be *different* from others, which can be achieved only in collective solidarity with other free individuals. Only the cooperation of a society of individuals can provide the security that is the foundation for the freedom of each to be different from others. Adorno argues, however, that the emergence of the totalitarian society of administered capitalism denies this need for individuality and destroys the high culture that keeps its promise alive (Witkin 2003: 6–12).

This brings us to the second, and arguably the most important, of Bourdieu's differences from Adorno. For the latter, the sin of modern culture is its collapsed sameness, which accommodates all of humanity to society's denial of freedom by its standardized and superficial pleasures. The mass culture of monopoly capitalism levels the differences between high and popular culture, and legitimates social inequalities by obscuring the real social differences between the classes. Because all classes consume the same standardized cultural goods, class distinctions are hidden behind the appearance of a democratic culture shared by all. For Bourdieu, by contrast, the problem with modern culture is not its collapsed and standardized sameness, but its hierarchical and differentiated nature, which makes some seem superior to others. Because the dominant class has the economic resources to "throw away" on cultural products that have no immediate benefit, they seem individually gifted and selfless, above the base struggle for survival. So culture legitimates class inequalities not by hiding them, but by symbolically displaying them in such a way as to make some seem deserving of their unequal rewards.

Bourdieu's early works—those before about 1988—contradict Adorno's idea of cultural leveling by demonstrating that differences between high and low culture persist into contemporary society. He labels these two halves of the cultural field, respectively, the subfield of restricted or small-scale production and the subfield of mass or large-scale production. Bourdieu agrees with Adorno that the defining difference between the two cultural subfields is the former's relative autonomy from the marketplace or economic field. But he conceives the chronology of and social conditions for the emergence of the autonomous realm of high culture differently from Adorno. As we saw above, Adorno places the emergence of a partially autonomous high culture in the late eighteenth and early nineteenth century, when the rise of a bourgeois class of industrialists and businessmen provides a market for art, thus freeing artists from the direct control of feudal patrons. The anonymity and dispersion of market demand provides artists freedom from the control of particular individuals and allows them to develop independent, critical aesthetic forms, even though they are still dependent on the general demand of bourgeois consumers as a group. But Adorno argues that this partial autonomy is revoked in the early twentieth century by the rise of the large, monopolistic corporations of the culture industry, whose concentrated power allows them to directly manipulate all culture, high and low, in order to capture the largest markets and highest profits.

By contrast, Bourdieu (1996a: 47–112) argues that an autonomous high culture of restricted production emerges in a later period—the middle of the nineteenth century—and sees its autonomy resting on a different foundation. He holds that in France before this period the literary field was divided largely into two markets, both of which were dependent on a particular class for sales. Writers from bourgeois backgrounds produced works in the style of formal Romanticism, which appealed to the aestheticizing habitus of other bourgeois. Writers from the popular classes produced works in the realist style, which appealed to their functional habitus. Bourdieu argues that the autonomy of literature from a specific class market was pioneered by writers from a class position between these extremes, the intellectual professions, whose habitus inclined them to precision and impartiality. These writers created a neutral, art-for-art's-sake style that stripped writing of social content and emphasized form itself. This style was supported not by classes external to the field, but by artists and writers within it, especially the expanding ranks of the great bohemian reserve army of underemployed cultural producers. This group, imbued with the autonomous aesthetic standards by the high-art subfield to which they aspired, could appreciate and support an art of pure form that did not cater to the immediate tastes and interests of classes in the economic field.

Bourdieu argues, however, that this hard-won autonomy of the cultural subfield of high culture ultimately binds it back to the field of economic classes through a legitimation function. Even though the newly autonomous works of art no longer reflect the immediate interests of the economic bourgeoisie, members of this class purchase the works of the most successful and conservative artists from the autonomous art subfield, because their habitus privilege the form of things over their function. And because such works are concerned with autonomous aesthetic forms and not with immediate economic gain, they seem more prestigious for being above the selfish, crass materiality of everyday life. Consequently, the wealthy bourgeois who "throw away" their money on this autonomous high art with no immediate pay-off seem superior to the masses who consume culture from the mass producers, who are obviously out to make money. The very autonomy or disinterestedness of art thus unintentionally legitimates and reproduces the economic interests of the bourgeoisie.

BOURDIEU'S VICISSITUDES: MOVING TOWARD ADORNO'S POSITION ON CRITICAL, AUTONOMOUS CULTURE

Before about 1988, Bourdieu's criticism of autonomous high culture as an unintentional yet powerful legitimation of class inequality is unconditional and unwavering. But beginning around this date he begins to backpedal, and by the end of his life in 2002 he is denouncing the debasement of autonomous culture by the mass market as if channeling the ghost of Adorno. Incontrovertible evidence of Bourdieu's changing analysis of culture comes in a 1989 address, in which he declares: "I am ready to concede that Kant's aesthetics is true." Here he recognizes that Kant's concept of the beautiful as pure, disinterested pleasure is a "(theoretical) universal possibility," which is both possible and desirable for all humanity (Bourdieu 1998c: 135). Bourdieu thus modifies his relational position, which sees the different class cultures as equally valid historical products, for a more universalistic position like that of Adorno, which privileges autonomous high culture over interested mass culture.

One factor responsible for this change is surely Bourdieu's difficulty in reflexively accounting for his own theory of culture. The inescapable conclusion of the relational cultural theory he presents in *Distinction* is that all knowledge, without exception, is interested. Even the high culture that portrays itself as autonomous and disinterested has an interest in domination, since its consumption by the dominant class serves as ideological proof of the personal superiority of its members, and thus leads others to misrecognize the economic foundation of its privilege. Despite this assertion, however, Bourdieu argues that scientific objectivity is possible, and claims such a status for his own work. As a participant in the subfield of high intellectual culture, how does he claim to escape the ubiquitous bias postulated by his own theory? He does so in several ways.

First, Bourdieu seeks to base intellectual objectivity on a reflexive sociological knowledge of the way that factors like habitus and cultural capital operate in intellectual fields to determine perceptions and preferences. With knowledge of these factors, he claims that he and other scientists can consciously neutralize their effects and ensure the autonomy of scientific knowledge from interests (Bourdieu and Wacquant 1992: 36–46). This is similar to Adorno's claim, discussed above, that intellectuals semidetached from the business world through private wealth have the advantage of insight into their own entanglement in this world. In both thinkers, however, this claim has a distinctly hollow ring. Any beginning student in the sociology of knowledge can immediately identify the problem here. What ensures that the intellectual's knowledge of the social factors that bias knowledge is not itself biased? And thus we begin an infinite regress that can find no ultimate grounds for knowledge claims.

Bourdieu's second basis for objectivity or disinterested knowledge is stronger but also problematic. He argues that, unlike the rest of the social world, the intellectual fields comprising the subfield of restricted cultural production can produce objective knowledge because they are insulated from the bias of economic interests by independent sources of economic support. The main sources of such support that he mentions are the internal markets of intellectual fields (i.e. intellectuals purchasing the work of each other) and the state. Both sources of support give scholars, artists, and scientists sufficient economic security that they can be unconcerned with the economic practicality of their ideas, and thus establish strictly intellectual standards against which to judge each other's work. There is, of course, competition between participants in these fields, but not for economic capital (material resources). Participants compete for symbolic capital, that is, recognition of their work by other intellectuals in the field. Thus, the actions of participants in intellectual fields are governed by "interests" that are fundamentally different from the economic interests. Socialization into these fields imbues intellectuals with an "interest in disinterestedness;" that is, they are taught that recognition is achieved by showing a concern for universal ideas, and a concomitant unconcern for practical applications or pecuniary rewards (1998c: 75–123).

Thus, in his later works Bourdieu sets up a sharp opposition between the interested knowledge of those in the economic field and the disinterested knowledge of participants in the autonomous cultural subfield of restricted production. The standard of knowledge is now universalistic, not relational and historical; all humanity has the potential to grasp the beautiful and the true. But only those in the subfield of autonomous or high culture have access to the independent economic resources that turns this potential into reality. Others are "deprived of the adequate categories of aesthetic perception and appreciation" by the unequal distribution of the economic resources that are the necessary condition of this realization (Bourdieu 1998c: 135).

At the same time that Bourdieu's changed theory praises the superiority of high culture, it also judges the practical aesthetic of the working class as degraded and inferior. He writes in *Practical Reason* (1998c: 137) that intellectual praise for working-class culture is a form of radical chic, *ressentiment*, and class racism. Although such praise seems to politically and ethically validate "the masses" or "the people," it really serves to enforce their domination by transforming "a sociologically mutilated being . . . into a model of human excellence" (Bourdieu and Wacquant 1992: 212). Now Bourdieu holds that the simplistic validation of working-class culture as equal to or better than the autonomous high culture of the upper class serves to enforce class inequality by accepting or obscuring the inequality of economic resources that gives rise to class differences in culture to begin with. This "radical" inversion of the hierarchy of class cultures prevents the mobilization of what he calls a *"Realpolitik* of the universal." By this he means a struggle by intellectuals and their allies that defends the institutional autonomy of intellectual activity, but simultaneously fights for the more equitable distribution of material resources in order to ensure access to disinterested intellectual activity for everyone (Bourdieu 2000: 80).

Bourdieu's new position thus asserts the universal superiority of the disinterested high culture of intellectuals and artists. But this assertion raises more fundamental questions. What about this high culture makes it universally desirable for all human beings, regardless of society or social position? Bourdieu states in *Practical Reason* (1998c: 135) that there are universal "anthropological possibilities" inherent in humanity that are developed by this culture, and that Kant sketches an analysis of them. One of these universals is ascesis, or self-discipline. Bourdieu asks himself: "Is there not something universal about culture? Yes, ascesis. Everywhere culture is constructed against nature, that is, through effort, exercise, suffering: all human societies put culture above nature. . . . It is in this sense that we can say that 'high' art is more universal. But, as I noted, the conditions of appropriation of this universal art are not universally allocated" (Bourdieu and Wacquant 1992: 87).

The later Bourdieu thus argues that authentic culture is the product of effort and labor, the endless series of refusals and transcendences of mere animal pleasures through which humans lift themselves above the heteronomy of nature. Culture is thus the realm of autonomous, self-conscious efforts, chosen by humans for *their* purposes, not forced on them by material interests or necessities. It is the useless, disinterested efforts humans impose on themselves through the self-made rules of their games. Consequently, any practices or productions that are forced on people by the economic necessities of earning a living are not really culture, because not freely chosen. It is precisely because working-class culture is focused on such practical interests that Bourdieu now describes it as "mutilated" and "devoid of any social value." The ultimate pay-off of truly human culture is not anything practical, such as money or power, but the pleasure of free play itself. Bourdieu's new conception of the universality of culture's ascesis corresponds with Adorno's insistence on the autonomy of culture from the economy's purposefulness. In both thinkers, autonomous high culture stands as a token of potential freedom in a world of human subjection to material production. By providing a model of activity beyond the inequality and oppression of the economy, autonomous art provides an implicit critique of these injustices, bringing them to consciousness and thereby making possible their subjection to willful action.

Bourdieu goes on to suggest another universal possibility of human beings that also characterizes autonomous high art—one that seems compatible with Adorno's analysis but is not explicitly addressed by him. This is the inherently social nature of humans, their selfless elevation of group interests over individual interests. It is this universal, which is another variant of "disinterestedness," that Bourdieu develops extensively in his later works. He argues in *Practical Reason* (1998c: 90) that the disinterested cultural practices of the dominant class "can fulfill their symbolic function of legitimation precisely because they benefit in principle from universal recognition—people cannot openly deny them without denying their own humanity." What people universally recognize in these practices is the imperative of the universal, that is, the demand that the interests of the group take precedence over those of particular individuals. "There is nothing that groups recognize and reward more unconditionally and demand more imperatively than the unconditional manifestation of respect for the group as a group . . . , and they give recognition even to the recognition (even if feigned and hypocritical) of the rule that is implied in strategies of universalization" (Bourdieu 2000: 125). Bourdieu does not specify exactly why sociality is a human universal, but he would presumably agree with the argument that because humans have little behavior genetically programmed into their bodies, they must rely on the group to nurture and protect the young until socialization is complete. Since the survival of each new generation depends on the group, humans universally recognize and reward actions that negate the individual in favor of the collective, that deny egoism and particular interests in favor of generosity and disinterestedness.

Bourdieu argues that in modern society this universal of sociality is advanced by the fields comprising the subfield of restricted cultural production (art, science, academics, etc.). Because these fields are autonomous from the economic field, due to the control of independent economic resources, participants can afford to be unconcerned with earning a living and concentrate on following the consensual rules of the game laid down by the group as a whole. Of course, the scientists, artists, scholars, and others in these fields pursue their self-interests, but their primary interest is not economic profits but symbolic profits—that is, recognition from the group as a whole. And this recognition is awarded to those who play by the rules, one of which is to ignore economic profits in one's work. So ironically, these autonomous cultural fields institutionalize an "interest in disinterestedness," as Bourdieu calls it. That is, participants receive recognition only when they produce work aimed not at making money but at advancing the entire field by playing by the rules. Thus, the rules of the field itself force actors to sublimate self-interest into universal interest, or the good of the group as a whole (1998c: 83–91).

One of the main reasons that Bourdieu begins to recognize the potential universality of culture during the late 1980s is to defend the autonomy of intellectual fields from the threat of external political forces. During this period in France the administration of Socialist Party President François Mitterand begins to withdraw public funding from the arts, sciences, and other intellectual fields in pursuit of a neoliberal policy of privatization. The disinterested knowledge of intellectuals is thus threatened by the competition of commercial media and publishers, which subjects knowledge to the pecuniary demands of the market and thus undermines the ability of intellectuals to criticize the structures of authority. Consequently, Bourdieu calls in 1989 for an "Internationale of intellectuals," a collective organization to fight for the autonomy of reason against the encroachment of economic and political power. And to start building such an organization, he founds in the same year *Liber: Revue Européenne des Livres*, a journal designed to provide a forum for cross-disciplinary and cross-national exchanges between intellectuals (Bourdieu 1996a: 337–48; Swartz 1997: 247–69).

Bourdieu's initial conception of human universals, as well as his emerging politics based on it, seem flawed, however. His universals are accessible only to the privileged few in autonomous cultural fields, which have sufficient resources to free their participants from economic concerns. So in the name of the universal interests of all humanity, he seems to defend the particular interests of already privileged intellectuals, with little concern for members of the unprivileged classes, whose chances of entering these fields are, as his research reveals, slight. Bourdieu's universals seem particular in another sense as well. Since there are several autonomous intellectual fields—art, literature, science, scholastics, etc.—each with its own rules and type of cultural capital, the "universal" appears plural and fragmented, with each field advancing its own particular group good, contradicting the very definition of the universal. Bourdieu solves these problems of the privilege and plurality of the universal, however, in his work of the 1990s, in which he postulates the institution of the state as the repository of the common interest of society as a whole.

As with his shifting position on the universality of culture, Bourdieu's changing conception of the state is driven as much by political contingencies as by theoretical contradictions. His earlier work on the state (Bourdieu 1998c: 35–63; Bourdieu and Wacquant 1992: 111–15) is marked by a conception typical of Marxists and other conflict theorists—the state institutionalizes the particular interests of the dominant class. But as Mitterand's government, heavily influenced by American-style neoliberal economic policies, begins to cut state support not only for intellectuals but for social welfare programs as well, Bourdieu's portrayal of the state becomes more complex. He divides state functions into two parts or "hands," and argues that only one of these, the right hand, favors the dominant class. This hand of the state, comprised of the technocrats of the Ministry of Finance, public and private banks, and the ministerial cabinets, engineers and enforces the economic policies that further the interests of the propertied. But in order to legitimate these interested policies to the rest of society, the state is forced to disguise them as neutral, as furthering the public good.

By using the universal good to cynically legitimate its particular interests, however, the dominant class unwittingly creates a standard that its state representatives are forced to live up to by the dominated. Consequently, a site is created for a struggle over the definition of the public good, giving the dominated the power to force the state to actually adopt policies benefitting the universal interest. As a consequence, the left hand of the state, or the social state, is created, which encompasses all the social services that actually benefit the entire public, but disproportionately the working masses, such as health, education, welfare, and housing (1998a: 1–10). Thus, the state becomes the institutional site of rationality and universality, which "is capable of acting as a kind of umpire, no doubt always somewhat biased, but ultimately less unfavorable to the interests of the dominated, and to what can be called justice, than what is exalted, under the false colors of liberty and liberalism, by the advocates of 'laisser-faire,' in other words the brutal and tyrannical exercise of economic force" (Bourdieu 2000: 127).

This reconceptualization of the state as the potential foundation of universal human interests solves another problem in Bourdieu's sociology of culture—that of finding a source of material support independent of the economic field for the autonomous cultural fields. This problem also plagues Adorno, who falls back on private wealth for supporting the impractical arts. But Adorno does not explain why private benefactors of the arts and sciences would not make their own interested demands on cultural producers, thus undermining the autonomy of the field. Bourdieu's early work relies on the economic demand of other cultural producers to provide an independent source of support for artists and others in autonomous fields. While such an internal market seems feasible in certain fields, such as film or literature, it seems infeasible for basic research in the sciences, in which the costs of production are so large and the audience for products so small that purchases by participants could not possibly provide adequate funds.

By the early 1990s, Bourdieu's theory of culture increasingly relies on the state, now seen as the institutional repository of universal interests, as the source of economic support for autonomous cultural production dedicated to human universals. Science and art need the state to exist, he declares, because the value of works in these fields is inversely correlated to the size of their markets. "Cultural radio stations or television channels, museums, all the institutions that offer 'high culture,' as the neocons say, exist only by virtue of public funds—that is, as exceptions to the law of the market made possible by the action of the state, which is alone in a position to assure the existence of a culture without a market" (Bourdieu and Haacke 1995: 69). Bourdieu argues that the support of such culture cannot be left to individual or corporate patrons because they dictate what artists and scientists produce in order to stifle criticism and further private gain. And more generally, these private sponsors reap symbolic profits, that is, the good will of the public that comes with "disinterested" generosity. Thus, these cultural fields can no longer serve the universal good, of which the state is the official guarantor, but become the tools of private interests (Bourdieu and Haacke 1995: 72).

Two years after his general attack on the decline of state support for the arts and sciences, Bourdieu writes an essay detailing its effects on French television, which is part of what he calls the journalistic field. He asserts that this field's responsibility is to provide access to disinterested, universal knowledge for the dominated classes, which do not have the economic resources to engage in the pursuit of such knowledge themselves (Bourdieu 1998b: 1). This knowledge is especially important in politics, in which the popular classes need accurate information and informed analysis of issues to exercise influence over state policy. Note that Bourdieu's main criticism of the culture of modern society is no longer, as in his early work, that the dominant class uses its power to impose its particular culture as a universal standard on the dominated class. The criticism is now that the dominated are deprived of the resources necessary to appropriate high culture, which is the universal knowledge of humanity but is monopolized by the dominant due to their superior resources. The only institution that can break this unequal access is the state, which protects the general interest by subsidizing not only the costs of producing and disseminating universal culture but also the cost of educating people in the skills necessary for appropriation.

The neoliberal project, Bourdieu argues, deprives the popular classes of this universal knowledge by motivating journalists to deliver information in ways that foster depoliticization and fatalism. He states that the journalistic field in France is divided into two subfields: the mass-circulation subfield, governed by the external incentive of market sales; and the limited-circulation or intellectual subfield, governed by internal standards of peer recognition. Only the latter is autonomous, and thus largely dependent on the state for economic support. But the neoliberal slashing of state support for culture undermines the autonomy of the intellectual subfield of journalism and subjects it to the market imperatives of the mass-circulation subfield, which is increasingly dominated by television. Consequently, intellectuals who want to deliver their universal knowledge to a larger public are forced to tailor their communications to the mass media's market-driven model of appealing to the largest possible audience. This is done, Bourdieu asserts, by avoiding the deeper issues of policy debates and focusing instead on entertaining confrontations and scandals. "Because they're so afraid of being boring, they [journalists] opt for confrontations over debates, prefer polemics over rigorous argument, and in general, do whatever they can to promote conflict" (Bourdieu1998b: 3–4). Sensationalism attracts a big market, but detracts attention from the important issues about which people need information and analysis.

Bourdieu also argues that competition between media conglomerates for the biggest audience at the lowest cost produces homogeneity—all compete to break the latest scandal or conflict, while the differences on real issues are ignored. The ultimate result is a general cynicism and fatalism about politics that favors the status quo. All politicians are seen as selfish and greedy. And the world in general is depicted as "an absurd series of disasters which can be neither understood nor influenced. . . . a world full of incomprehensible and unsettling dangers from which we must withdraw for our own protection" (Bourdieu 1998b: 8). Bourdieu's analysis of mass media is now very close to Adorno's, for both recognize that the domination of culture by large, profit-driven corporations has a leveling effect, as these businesses seek to capture the largest market for the least costs. And both Bourdieu and Adorno argue that the culture industry produces fatalistic and conformist consumers, whose individuality and efficacy are drowned in a sea of standardized, deterministic images.

Despite their similarities, there is one major difference that separates these two theorists of the market-driven culture industry—their analysis of the demand side of the market. Bourdieu's newly critical analysis of mass culture pays little attention to consumers' needs or demands. He focuses almost exclusively on the dispositions of producers, arguing that the dominance of the market has led to a common set of mental categories among journalists, a shared vision of the world that they impose on all (Bourdieu 1998b: 22, 47). But in Bourdieu's general theory of culture, he holds that producers do not *impose* their habitus or dispositions on consumers. Rather, consumers are attracted to particular products because they *share* the same dispositions as their producers, who occupy in the cultural field a position homologous to that of consumers in the economic field. Bourdieu's new work does assert that media conglomerates favor topics that interest everybody in order to reach the largest market, but he never discusses the mental structures of consumers that determine these preferences (Bourdieu 1998b: 44–45). He implies that the sensational subfield of journalism corresponds mainly to the habitus of working-class people. But he does not offer a structural explanation of the growth of this subfield relative to the "serious press" or intellectual subfield.

Adorno does provide a structural analysis of the changing consumer demand behind cultural leveling or homogenization. Contrary to Bourdieu, he argues that the working class does not have a structurally determined taste for kitsch and diversion, ingrained by its relative lack of economic resources. Adorno holds that the cultural demands of workers are conditioned by their position at work. The alienating nature of this class's labor—its lack of freedom and individuality—leads its members to demand superficial diversion and difference that can be easily consumed. By contrast, the greater economic freedom of the early bourgeoisie leads its members to demand culture that is difficult, not diverting, and requires a sustained exercise of intellectual abilities cultivated in substantial leisure time. But Adorno argues that the rise of monopolistic corporations degrades the position of the bourgeoisie to mere employees as well. No longer independent entrepreneurs and professionals, as in the liberal phase of capitalism, the bourgeois are reduced in the monopoly phase to mere functionaries of a bureaucratic apparatus that is just as alien to those who administer it as it is to those who are administered by it. Being similarly mutilated by the apparatus, the bourgeoisie needs simple, commodified substitutes for freedom and individuality as much as the working class. So the demand for mass culture is nearly universal, and autonomous art shrinks to a paltry, embattled outpost in the land of commodity culture.

If we use Adorno's theory of homogenized cultural demand to supplement Bourdieu's theory of homogenized supply, then we have a powerful theory of the displacement of autonomous culture by mass culture. But one problem remains for both theories—that of explaining the source of culture's critical social content. Both Bourdieu and Adorno demand that autonomous culture be critical of an oppressive society and provide an impetus for social change. What ensures that autonomous intellectuals free of economic interests will produce such a culture?

ADORNO'S TECHNOLOGICAL SOURCE OF CRITICAL CONTENT IN AUTONOMOUS CULTURE

I first examine Adorno's method of introducing critical content into autonomous cultural fields, which I believe to be questionable because it relies almost exclusively on technology. But one benefit of Adorno's argument is that it highlights the social basis of Bourdieu's solution to the puzzle of a critical culture that contradicts the society that produces it.

From its inception the Frankfurt School paid more attention than most Marxist-inspired theories to the importance of the natural world. Often instrumentalized by orthodox Marxists as merely a material means to human ends, nature becomes, in the hands of Horkheimer, Adorno, and Marcuse, both a victim of human oppression and a crucial part of its transcendence. In *Dialectic of Enlightenment*, Horkheimer and Adorno (1972: 3–42) argue that the emergence of class domination in society inevitably gives rise to an abstract, instrumental reason that is used to dominate nature as well. In this form of reason the natural world is emptied of any ends of its own and conceptualized as a mere means to achieve externally imposed human ends. But in order to dominate nature for their own ends, humans must also dominate themselves, by renouncing their own natural needs so as to muster the self-denying labor to appropriate nature. So the Enlightenment reason that is supposed to free humans from natural necessity ultimately enslaves nature and humans to a logic alien to both.

This instrumental logic of domination reaches its apotheosis in the totally administrated society of monopolistic capitalism, in which even the working class benefits from the rationalized system of mass production, although to a lesser extent than those in command of the bureaucracies. Marx's biting criticism of capitalist society for its exploitation and impoverishment of the working class is rendered toothless by general consumer prosperity, and consequently no foothold can be found for opposition *within* this one-dimensional society. The same system that eliminates the material basis for opposition also eliminates its cultural basis by producing a perverted consciousness that reduces human needs for individuality and freedom to the consumption of superficially differentiated, standardized goods that ultimately reproduce the system. In these circumstances, it is not surprising that Adorno looks for opposition to this omnipotent social system in a source that is removed from the human subjectivity produced by it. This source is technology, which is a natural force beyond human subjectivity or consciousness but nonetheless involved in the historical development of society.

Adorno's anti-subjective philosophy will not allow him to base aesthetics on subjective needs. He believes the cause of most repression in history to be instrumental reason, in which the grasping, greedy subject attempts to reduce the object to a mere instrument of *it's* needs, with no regard for the object's own requirements or purposes. Reversing this repressive logic requires recognizing the preponderance of the object or thing (1973: 183–86), which Adorno does by offering technology, or the forces of production, as the source of the critical social content for art in modern society. He does not argue that in all societies art must express social contradiction through technological form. In earlier societies, presumably those with more overt class conflict, Adorno sees it possible for art to be critical by directly expressing the contradictory social relations within it. "The fact that form *per se* [based on the forces of production] is a subversive protest is peculiar to the present situation, where social structure has become total and completely melted together" (Adorno 1984: 362).

In this totally administered society class conflict is suppressed by a common interest in the repressive apparatus of mass consumerism, and the only critical leverage against the system lies outside it, in the technological forces of production. The existing technology of a society reveals the contradiction not between one social class and another, but between the potential for a nonrepressive society and the existence of the present repressive one. Technology contains potentials for human liberation that cannot be developed within the repressive social relations of domination. The most advanced art of a society borrows these techniques from the realm of production and expresses their true potentials in its forms. "The development of aesthetic forces of production . . . is tied up with the progress of material forces of production outside. There are times when aesthetic forces of production are given completely free rein because the material ones, hemmed in as they are by existing relations of production, cannot be unleashed" (Adorno 1984: 48).

Adorno recognizes that these production techniques borrowed by art are deeply involved in the historical domination of nature for instrumental ends outside of it. How, then, can art transform these forces of domination into an anticipation of freedom? He argues that even though the intent of a society's productive forces is to exploit nature, in order to do so they must conform to and express the needs of nature itself, apart from human will. So technology combines a language of the subjective will to dominate with a language of objective things in and for themselves. But because autonomous art is free of the world of economic production, it is able to eliminate the repressive intent from society's technological forms, leaving behind only the needs of objective things themselves. "In the latter [the world outside of art] the prevailing forms are those that characterize the domination of nature, whereas in art, forms are being controlled and regimented out of a sense of freedom. By repressing the agent of repression, art undoes some of the domination inflicted on nature. Control over artistic forms and over how they are related to materials exposes the arbitrariness of real domination which is otherwise hidden by an illusion of inevitability" (1984: 200).

What the artistic subject expresses in the technological forms borrowed from society, once having suppressed their language of instrumental domination, is "the latent language of things—a language that articulates itself through the radical use of technology" (1984: 89). This radical use of technology prefigures a reconciliation of humans and nature, in which human consciousness is a vehicle for realizing the needs of nature not merely outside of people, but inside them as well. But to prevent this promise of reconciliation from serving as a substitute for changing society, the artist must incorporate into the potential beauty of objective things some of the actual damage left on them by the antagonistic relations of a divided and repressive society. "That is, he embodies the social forces of production but does not necessarily feel bound to erase the bad marks given him by the relations of production" (65). The contradiction between the potentially beautiful use of technology to free the nature in things and humans and the existing ugliness of its use in an antagonistic society creates the critical consciousness to stimulate social change.

Let me offer an example of Adorno's proposed relation between art and technology drawn from my recent study of the art of architecture (Gartman 2009). The emergence of modern architecture in the early twentieth century was driven largely by new technologies of building, especially ferroconcrete—a mixture of Portland cement with sand and gravel, reinforced with steel bars embedded in the hardened mass. This technology was developed in the first decade of the twentieth century by American industrial architects, who used it to replace the brick-pier construction popular in factories of the day. Working under the instrumental imperatives of the market, these architects used the new material in ways that reflected a will to dominate, to render concrete a means of producing surplus value, not to develop its natural potentials. Even though concrete is inherently malleable because fluid before hardening, they poured it into rigidly rectilinear frames that were cheap to build because they required fewer skilled tradesmen. Reinforced-concrete factories, like Albert Kahn's famous Highland Park plant for Ford Motor Company, completed in 1910, also cut the costs of production within them. The greater strength of the new material allowed for longer spans between supports, which not only allowed more sunlight onto production floors, but also created large, unobstructed work spaces—a key requirement of mass production. This work process cuts labor costs by arranging work stations sequentially and closely together, thus reducing transportation and idle time between stations. Long-span ferroconcrete construction created the open, unobstructed interior space that allowed this free flow of work along assembly and production lines. Clearly, then, these industrial architects revealed in their concrete buildings the ugly marks imposed on the new technology by the capitalist relations of production, that is, the imperative to dominate humans and nature for the sake of profits. They did not, however, simultaneously reveal the inherent potentials of the new technology for meeting the needs of nature itself, both human and nonhuman, as Adorno's theory demands. This required autonomous artists, free of the demands of profit-making instrumental reason, like the architect Le Corbusier.

In his 1920s residential work in concrete, Le Corbusier used the rigid, rectilinear forms pioneered by American industrial architects. He clearly revealed in his writings that his intent was to express the domination of nature by the instrumental reason of humans. In 1925 Corbu wrote that rectilinear street grids were superior to curving lanes because the straight line represented the mastery of reason over nature and humankind. "Man governs his feelings by his reason; he keeps his feelings and his instincts in check, subordinating them to the aim he has in view. He rules the brute creation by his intelligence. . . . Man walks in a straight line because he has a goal and knows where he is going" (Le Corbusier 1987: 5). Corbu also used thin concrete columns, called pilotis, to elevate his buildings off the ground because, he argued, the "natural ground" harbored dirt and disease and was thus "the enemy of man" (Le Corbusier 1967: 55–56). He even sought to control and dominate the views of nature from his residences. At his Villa Savoye the roof terrace was surrounded by a concrete screen with precisely spaced slots that framed views of the countryside. Unwilling to let nature speak for itself, Corbu captured and controlled it within his architectural grid of rectilinear voids.

By the 1950s, however, Le Corbusier's work in concrete was tempering his one-sided rectilinearity symbolic of human domination of nature by exploring the inherently plastic qualities of this building technology. As Adorno might say, he was using concrete to reveal the natural potentials of this technique. In an apartment building of 1952, the Unité d'Habitation, the concrete frame was, as before, composed of a rational repetition of identically rectilinear elements. But this symbol of mechanical efficiency was countered by several organic elements. Corbu lifted his building off the ground with pilotis, but here they were no longer lithe, mechanical shafts but massive, ovoid legs, whose "muscles" seemed to strain under the weight of the building. And on the roof, where a gymnasium and playground were located, Corbu placed several monumental organic sculptures in concrete. Not just the shape but also the finish of his concrete here was more organic. Instead of finishing the concrete to a smooth, mechanical surface, he left it unfinished, crudely imprinted with the wooden forms into which it was poured. The architect thus exposed the imprint of the human hand on this modern material, giving it a woven texture. So in the concrete of this apartment building Le Corbusier certainly revealed, as Adorno demands, the ugly marks of the repressive relations of production on the technology. But he also exposed the potential beauty of concrete, its promise to speak the language of nature, both human and nonhuman, outside of domination.

Adorno's search for a source of cultural opposition in the forces of production is ingenious and innovative, but ultimately unconvincing. He is forced to resort to nature or the material world for critical content only because he arbitrarily closes off the social world, or the relations of production, as a site of conflict or contradiction. But Adorno's notion of the "*totally* administered society" is easily challenged on empirical grounds. It is one of the great ironies of intellectual history that Adorno lost faith in class conflict during his exile in America in the late 1930s and early 1940s, a place and a period that generated an explosion of class-based struggle and a critical popular culture. Adorno immigrated to New York in 1938 to work with the relocated Institute for Social Research, and was surely aware of the popular conflicts in the U.S. during the Great Depression. And he could not have avoided at least some awareness of the critical culture emerging from these conflicts. Thousands of artists were employed by the U.S. Government through New Deal programs like the Works Progress Administration, Federal Arts Project, and the Farm Security Administration. Many of them came from working-class backgrounds and were sympathetic to the radical movements that challenged the basic structures of capitalist America. The result was an explosion of critical art insulated from the demands of the market. Even the market-driven movies of Hollywood were influenced by these critical currents in the arts, with actor/directors like Orson Welles and Charlie Chaplin producing highly critical films innovative in both form and content (Denning 1996).

This Depression-era art may not meet Adorno's standards for truly progressive art. He does not care for realism, the style of much of the art of this period, in part because Georg Lukács simplistically asserted this to be the privileged style of progressive art (Adorno 1977). What is unforgivable, however, is Adorno's failure to acknowledge this art as a challenge to his portrait of a one-dimensional mass culture that suppresses social conflict by obscuring it under a facade of sameness. The struggles around some of the critical art of the Depression, such as Orson Welles's stage production of Marc Blitzen's *The Cradle Will Rock* and Diego Rivera's murals at the Detroit Institute of Arts and Rockefeller Center, testify to the multi-dimensionality of American culture during the period in which Adorno resided in the U.S.

I do not mean to say, however, that Adorno's notion of technology as a source of critical culture is without merit. Indeed, in certain historical conjunctures I believe that technology may contradict the existing social relations and provide a foundation for critical art and consciousness. But it can do so not because it stands *apart* from the nonconflictual social relations of production, but because it is an expression of continuing conflicts *within* society. Marx himself informs us that the ultimate contradiction of capitalism is that between the increasingly socialized forces of production and the necessarily privatized relations of production. Because humans are by nature social creatures, the productivity and power of their labor increases as it becomes less individual and more collective. Thus under capitalism the competitive pressure to increase productivity forces capitalists to socialize labor by inventing new forces of production that harness the cooperation of large numbers of workers. However, the coordination of workers' social labor is blocked by the chaos created by the privatization of capital, which prevents capitalists from consciously coordinating production between firms. Thus, for Marx the forces of production contradict the relations of production not because they express a nature apart from capitalist social relations, but because they embody the contradiction within capitalist society between the social character of production and the private character of distribution (Marx 1967b: 262–66). And this contradiction necessarily divides the classes, although it may not be expressed in overt conflict. It is the working class and its collective organization that represents the potential of consciously coordinated, socialized labor, while the divisions of capitalists represent the outmoded individualism of market allocation of resources. For Marx, unlike Adorno, this fundamental opposition between classes is the structural foundation of capitalism and cannot be overcome by the mere extension of greater consumption to workers, which he characterizes as "the better remuneration of slaves" (Marx 1964: 231). Thus, ultimately a critical culture must find its source in existing conflicts and contradictions within society, which is exactly what Bourdieu's late theory seeks to do.

BOURDIEU'S SOCIAL SOURCE OF CRITICAL CONTENT IN AUTOMONOUS CULTURE

For Bourdieu, as for Adorno, the autonomous cultural subfield of high art or restricted production is the privileged location within modern societies for the expression of social critique, for only it is insulated from the demand of the subfield of large-scale or mass production to make money by catering to the popular demand for superficially soothing works. Autonomous cultural producers are driven not to make money, but to freely follow the collectively made rules of the game, which brings them symbolic capital from other producers. In doing so, these cultural producers express what Bourdieu now acknowledges as the universal potential of all human beings for freedom and sociality, and thus provide an implicit critique of societies that are repressive and individualistic.

By Adorno's standards, however, there is something missing in Bourdieu's model of the autonomous cultural subfield prefiguring a free and collective society of individuals. His model certainly reveals how the world should and could be structured, but it does not oppose this ideal world of beauty to the real world of ugly conflicts and antagonisms. Without such an opposition, Adorno argues, culture degenerates into a comforting illusion that conspires with the existing society to sooth the discontent that could change it. Bourdieu does, however, provide a mechanism to introduce social conflicts and antagonisms into autonomous cultural fields—the habitus, a curious construct halfway between nature and society, a sort of second nature.

Bourdieu defines the habitus as a set of unconscious dispositions or propensities to act that is conditioned by childhood socialization in a specific class position. Depending upon the material conditions provided by class standing, an individual internalizes structures of perception and recognition that either take the necessities of life for granted, in the case of the dominant class, or take these necessities as a constant concern, in the case of the working class. Although the habitus is a product of social learning and not an inborn "nature," as the ideology of charisma mistakenly asserts, it does have some characteristics commonly associated with nature. First, it is durable and not easily changed. Once ingrained in early childhood, it tends to persist and shape the individual's actions for life. This is not to say that it is unchangeable—it can be affected and changed by later adult experiences, but only slowly and incompletely. Second, the habitus is implanted in not merely the mind but also the body, for it shapes and controls the physical contours, movements, and feelings of corporeal existence in ways not easily changed. The habitus, Bourdieu (1990b: 69) writes, creates "a practical sense, social necessity turned into nature." In it are inscribed "the most fundamental principles of the arbitrary content of a culture in seemingly innocuous details of bearing or physical and verbal manners, so putting them beyond the reach of consciousness and explicit statement."

Because the habitus of different classes shape different tastes for culture, the field of culture is a misrecognized and symbolic expression of conflict between the classes, especially between the dominant (bourgeois) class and the dominated (working) class. This conflict occurs not only among the consumers of culture, but also among its producers. Each class consumes culture from a different subfield, generally composed of producers of a similar class—the

dominant class, from the subfield of restricted or high culture; and the dominated class, from the subfield of large-scale or mass culture. Each subfield has
different goals and standards—the former is dominated by formality and distance from necessity; the latter, by practicality and functionality. But because
the dominant class monopolizes symbolic power in society, it has the ability
to define its own tastes as the standards of judgment for all, thus precluding
any *direct* confrontation between the classes over culture. The early Bourdieu
(1984: 318–19) paints a portrait of culture as a game in which the dominated
class concedes the contest from the outset, by letting its class opponent define
the rules. The dominated are forced to concede the superiority of the culture
of the dominant, while continuing to prefer their own "inferior" culture. And
within each separate subfield, which is composed of producers with similar
habitus, little fundamental conflict occurs, apart from competition for sales or
recognition among those who share the same values.

In his later works, however, Bourdieu provides for conditions under
which class conflict is introduced *within* the autonomous subfield of cultural production and becomes explicit, thus providing a consciousness of
social antagonisms that were heretofore misrecognized. This occurs, Bourdieu informs us in both *Homo Academicus* (1988) and *The Rules of Art*
(1996a), when homogenous rules of recruitment break down, and outsiders
from the dominated class slip into autonomous cultural fields bearing alien
habitus. The consequence of this breakdown in recruitment is a revolution
in the field under consideration—academics in the first of these books, and
literature in the second. And in both cases the breakdown is caused by an
increase in the educated populace that provides both the producers and
consumers of the field. Both of Bourdieu's cases of field revolution follow a
similar causal logic, but I will concentrate on his study of the French literary field because it more directly concerns art, which is my main focus.

The Rules of Art treats the emergence of an autonomous field in French
literature during the Second Empire period (1851–1871). Industrialization undermined the power and wealth of the aristocracy, leading to the
decline of the old patronage system for the arts. At the same time, however, industrialization created a new market for literature among the newly
empowered and enriched bourgeoisie. This class also contributed to the
field writers who produced work in the style of formal Romanticism, which
reflected the bourgeois habitus privileging form over function. This style
did not go unchallenged, however, for the expansion of education during
this period spread literacy to the working class, whose members began to
demand literature that reflected their habitus of practicality and function.
Soon writers from the working class, such as Émile Zola, entered the literary field and pioneered the style of social realism, focusing on the practical
interests and struggles of the oppressed. Finally, writers from the middling
position of the intellectual or liberal professions—what Bourdieu calls the
cultural bourgeoisie—entered the field as well, pioneering a new style that
sought to reconcile bourgeois formalism and social realism. Gustave Flaubert, the pioneer of this position, created a style of disinterested removal or

neutrality that reflected the habitus of this class. Flaubert's new style also found an audience in the growing ranks of cultural producers themselves, especially the underemployed bohemia in the emerging art fields. Consequently, the literary field found a source of support outside of the marketplace, and became increasingly autonomous.

The French literary field thus no longer reflected the rule or interests of any one authority or class, as did the society outside of it. There was only "a plurality of competing perspectives" (Bourdieu 1996a: 133). But through the habitus of the individual competitors, these perspectives represented the antagonistic structure of society as a whole—not directly, but indirectly through their aesthetic forms. In this way, the struggles over power in society, which are usually hidden through misrecognition, are remembered and revealed in autonomous cultural fields. "It is through this work on form that the work comes to contain those structures that the writer, like any social agent, carries within him in a practical way, without having really mastered them, and through which is achieved an anamnesis of all that ordinarily remains buried, in an implicit or unconscious state, underneath the automatisms of an emptily revolving language" (108). So, ironically, when art becomes autonomous and is no longer obligated to directly deliver an interested social message, it delivers a broader message about the structure of society as a whole. Artists with different class habitus are unconsciously attracted to particular positions in the field, where they *formally* contest the power and dominance of other positions. And this vision of artistic antagonism prevents any one aesthetic form from offering the illusion of a unified and whole beauty that might serve as soothing solace in an otherwise ugly world.

So unlike Adorno, Bourdieu finds a *social* source for the critical content of culture, a source that inevitably and unconsciously carries economic and political struggles into cultural fields and reflects them in form. This formal reflection of social struggles is only possible, however, in autonomous fields, where culture is freed from the practical necessity to make money by giving consumers what they want—beautiful illusions of freedom and individuality. And as we have seen, for Bourdieu this freedom of autonomous culture to reflect ugly antagonisms as well as beautiful wholeness rests on an independent source of economic support, which he argues in his later work must come from the institutional protector of universal interests, the state. But Bourdieu's last theory of culture has one more self-imposed obstacle to overcome before it can provide a satisfying explanation for critical culture. This obstacle is conceptualized in his early work but continues through his entire corpus—the scholastic fallacy.

THE PROBLEM OF AND SOLUTION FOR
BOURDIEU'S SCHOLASTIC FALLACY

As we have seen, Bourdieu holds that autonomous cultural fields insulate their participants from the distorting effects of economic interests. But he recognizes that this autonomy also introduces its own peculiar distortion. The privileged participants in these "scholastic" fields do not recognize that their ability to treat ideas as pure forms, removed from practical interests, rests on a base of independent economic resources that allows them to be unconcerned with practicalities. Consequently, they generalize their privileged position of autonomy, mistakenly seeing the entire world as a "school," and all actors in it as motivated, like themselves, by universal principles free of practical interest. This scholastic fallacy substitutes the scholar's relation to culture, a relation of disinterested contemplation, for the relation of the vast majority of social actors to ideas as interested means to practical ends. By thus attributing to all the freedom that intellectuals alone exercise due to their insulation from material necessity, the scholastic fallacy ideologically obscures not only the unfree conditions under which the majority of social agents operate, but also the privileged access to economic resources that permits the disinterested contemplation of intellectuals (Bourdieu 1990b: 30–41; 1998c: 127–40; 2000: 1–92). So autonomous cultural fields, upon which Bourdieu's theory relies for the universal knowledge to criticize social inequalities, have a structurally induced blindness to such inequalities, which facilitates the monopoly of universality by those with privileged access to economic capital.

In his last works, however, Bourdieu offers a convincing, if underdeveloped, solution to the scholastic fallacy. Combined with his concept of the state as the ultimate guarantor of universal access to autonomous culture, this solution comprises not merely a powerful theory of culture but also a practical program for ensuring a progressive and critical culture. Bourdieu attributes most dissent and conflict within society to hysteresis, the discrepancy between the subjective habitus embodied in agents and the objective structure of fields (Bourdieu 1990b: 62). Because the original habitus developed in childhood is durable and changes only slowly to accommodate changes in social fields, there is always the possibility of a mismatch between the dispositions of individuals and the structural requirements of the fields in which they participate. This is especially true of upwardly mobile individuals. When autonomous cultural fields expand, as did the French literary field in the mid-nineteenth century and the academic field in the mid-twentieth century, they often recruit new participants from the sons and daughters of the dominated classes previously denied admission due to deficits of both economic and cultural capital. This creates at least an initial discrepancy between the behavior motivated by the lower-class recruits' childhood habitus and that required by their current field positions. Bourdieu argues that it was just such a condition of hysteresis, or old habitus lagging behind new field requirements, that led to the explosion of protest among students and young instructors in the 1960s, as well as the revolution in literature in the 1850s and 1860s. In his last works, however, Bourdieu uses this situation to explain not merely conflict and dissent but also the reflexive knowledge of fields that allows some agents, like himself, to transcend the scholastic fallacy. As he writes in *Pascalian Meditations*:

> In particular because of the structural transformations which abolish or modify certain positions, and also because of their inter-or intragenerational mobility, the homology between the space of positions and the space of dispositions is never perfect and there are always some agents "out on a limb," displaced, out of place and ill at ease. The discordance . . . may be the source of a disposition towards lucidity and critique which leads them to refuse to accept as self-evident the expectations and demands of the post. . . . The *parvenus* and the *déclassés* . . . are more likely to bring to consciousness that which, for others, is taken for granted, because they are forced to keep watch on themselves and consciously correct the "first movements" of a habitus that generates inappropriate or misplaced behaviors. (Bourdieu 2000: 157, 163)

Thus, agents who are socialized in dominated-class positions but move up into the cultural bourgeoisie experience a mismatch between their childhood habitus and their structural positions. Their working-class habitus inclines them to practical action aimed at material necessities, while their position in an autonomous cultural field requires disinterested action that denies economic exigencies in the name of pure knowledge. The survival of the parvenus' practical dispositions and their sensitivity to material deprivation allows them to see that the cultural field's emphasis on pure, disinterested action actually rests on a privileged access to the very economic resources it disdains. In two of his last books, *Science of Science and Reflexivity* (2004) and *Sketch for a Self-Analysis* (2008), Bourdieu applies this insight to himself, accounting for his own ability to objectively penetrate the scholastic fallacy and its ideological misrecognition of the origins of social advantage.

Bourdieu argues that his childhood circumstances created in him a cleft or divided habitus. Both his parents came from poor peasant families, but his father became the clerk of the village post office at age thirty. This position carried the prestige of a white-collar job, but was poorly paid, and Bourdieu's father continued to vote for leftist parties and taught Pierre to respect working people. But the father's white-collar status deprived the son of solidarity with his working-class schoolmates, who rejected him as one "with white hands" (Bourdieu 2008: 85). Graduating to a boarding lycée, Bourdieu retained his status as an upwardly mobile outcast, rejected by both the rural, working-class boarders, with their loud-mouthed machismo and anti-intellectualism, and the urbane, bourgeois day students. Because he was himself a boarder from a rural, working-class background, he experienced the crudeness and cruelness of the nocturnal culture of the boarders, whose lives were dominated by the struggle for existence and all the pettiness that accompanies it. This underbelly of the school stood in stark contrast to the respectable face of its diurnal classroom culture ruled by the bourgeois day students, in which cool, universal standards were applied to all. The contrast between these two school cultures served for Bourdieu as a lesson in the material foundation of the academic world, the interested resources necessary for the disinterested pursuit of universal standards (90–100; see also Bourdieu 1993a: 269–70).

Bourdieu thus developed a contradictory relationship to the institution of academics, characterized by both rebellion and submission. His working-class habitus made him deeply skeptical of scholastic authority, but his success and upward mobility simultaneously made him grateful and submissive to its demands. He argues that this cleft habitus shaped his affinity to sociology as a field of research and study. Educated in philosophy at the École Normale Supérieure, he was disgusted by the arrogance and naivete of philosophers like Jean-Paul Sartre, who believe in the supreme power of disinterested ideas to shape the world. Bourdieu argues that such arrogant disregard for the practicalities of life is instilled by the scholastic institution in "overgrown bourgeois adolescents who have succeeded in everything"— that is to say, everything pertaining to abstract ideas (Bourdieu 2008: 24). He was attracted to sociology because it seemed practical and useful, and also because it repudiated the specious grandeurs of philosophy. "I had entered into sociology and ethnology in part through a deep refusal of the scholastic point of view which is the principle of loftiness, a social distance, in which I could never feel at home, and to which the relationship to the social world associated with certain social origins no doubt predisposes" (41).

Because Bourdieu is an outsider from a working-class background, he is imbued with a habitus that privileges practical knowledge and material necessities. Thus, he can see through the ideology that the scholastic world of autonomous cultural fields is totally free of economic interests. In reality, all the privileged agents in these fields have an interest in the independent economic resources that give them the ability to be unconcerned with practicalities. But because Bourdieu is also an insider in the scholastic field, he does not now merely reject these privileges as superfluous and inconsequential, as many working-class outsiders do. He is able to see the universal benefits of scholastic privileges—the freedom and sociality that all humans share as a potential, but can be realized only by those with access to resources.

THEORETICAL IMPERATIVES FOR A PRACTICAL PROGRAM OF CRITICAL CULTURE: AUTONOMY AND DIVERSITY

Neither Bourdieu nor Adorno offer practical prescriptions for creating the kind of critical culture that both believe modern society needs and deserves.

Both offer mainly critiques of existing culture, which supports the unequal and oppressive status quo of societies. But both theorists base their critiques on an ideal of what culture *should* be, and thus prefigure a culture that would facilitate the more egalitarian and free society that each prefers. In closing, I want to briefly explore the implications of these theories for the practical construction of a critical culture that could mobilize people to create a just and free society.

One requirement for a critical culture shared by both theorists is the autonomy of cultural producers from the economic imperatives of the marketplace. Only when artists and intellectuals are free from the demand of the market to make money by pleasing the masses of consumers are they able to expose the unpleasant truths about the existing society. For both Bourdieu and Adorno, such autonomy requires a source of economic livelihood for cultural producers that is independent of the market. But, as we have seen, the nature of this independent livelihood varies between theorists. Adorno sees no source of support apart from *private* wealth and philanthropy, thus ironically depending on capitalists to finance a culture that undermines capitalism. He cannot rely on the state as a support for autonomous culture, as does Bourdieu, because his theory of the totally administered society holds the state to be an integral part of monopoly capitalism. Following the theory of state capitalism pioneered by Friedrich Pollock (1978), the economist of the Frankfurt School, Adorno holds that the state is crucial to monopoly capitalism, for its rational planning of the economy is necessary to overcome the vicissitudes of the market and contain the capitalist contradictions detailed in Marx's *Capital*. Consequently, the state is thoroughly infected with the instrumental logic of the economy and cannot be relied upon to support critical cultural works that expose social contradictions in the name of human ends.

Bourdieu, by contrast, argues that the state is the privileged institution for the economic support of critical culture. While recognizing that it often serves the interests of the dominant class, he asserts that its ideology of universalism opens it to popular influence, which forces it to live up to its promise. State support of culture thus may provide artists and intellectuals with the autonomy from the market necessary to produce critical works, those that promise a more beautiful world but reveal how the ugly conflicts of the existing society prevent its realization. Thus, one policy recommendation for a critical culture that Bourdieu and Haacke (1995: 69–72) make explicit is increased state funding. Of course, this need not and should not mean that politicians make the decisions about the allocation of these funds. Surely what Bourdieu has in mind is the administration of state funds by intellectuals and artists recognized in their respective fields. This ensures the autonomy of cultural fields from the power of both the market and state.

Some propose a "third way" of funding culture between these stark alternatives of market and state. One such alternative is said to be provided by the non-profit sector, into which the majority of American art museums fall. Although this sector is usually funded by the private, tax-deductible donations of wealthy capitalists and corporations, independent boards are established to distribute the funds on the bases of artistic standards and the public good, rather than profitability. But Bourdieu and his artist coauthor, Hans Haacke, argue in *Free Exchange* (1995: 68–84) that the non-profit sector is really not much different from the market sector, because businessmen dominate the boards of trustees and are reluctant to fund art that offends or threatens their wealthy donors. Further, due to declining funds, these non-profit art institutions must increasingly rely on direct corporate sponsorship of exhibits that cater to mass tastes in order to attract the largest possible audience and create a favorable public image for the corporations (Wu 2002). So Bourdieu continues to see the state as the only supporter of culture that can guarantee artists and intellectuals autonomy.

Bourdieu's last theory of culture, unlike Adorno's, implies however that the autonomy of cultural fields is a necessary but not sufficient condition for a critical culture. For him, autonomy means merely that artists and intellectuals have the freedom to express in the forms of their works the aesthetic dispositions they import into the field through their habitus. But if all agents in an autonomous field are from the dominant class, their works will all express the distance from economic necessity characteristic of this class's habitus, and the scholastic fallacy will reign supreme—that is, the privileged will remain oblivious to the economic foundation for their autonomy provided by their privileged access to independent resources. Consequently, the real inequalities and antagonisms of society will be buried beneath a facade of unified beauty. Art, science, and other intellectual works may faithfully reflect the contradictions of society only when the participants in autonomous fields are drawn from diverse class backgrounds. Only when the dominated classes also have access to cultural fields will participants be forced to come to terms with the economic foundation of their works, the sensitivity to which the dominated carry in their habitus. The clash of different artistic forms in the cultural field, reflecting these different dispositions, may then provide a metaphor for the clash of classes in the social field as a whole. So the ugliness of social antagonisms disrupts the beautiful promise of art for reconciliation and happiness, protesting that the promise cannot be realized in *this* world, not yet, not until the odious inequalities of power and wealth have been eliminated and all have the privilege of free, sociable activity.

Thus Bourdieu's theory, with some support from Adorno's, implies two imperatives for the construction of a critical culture with the potential to transform society. The producers of culture must be both autonomous and diverse. Bourdieu's against-the-grain call for more, not less, public funding for cultural fields addresses both imperatives. Without state funding for works outside the market, artists and intellectuals will be chained to the demand to make money by pleasing consumers. And without public funding for the education of cultural producers, only members of those classes controlling private funds will be able to enter autonomous fields to begin with. But the recognition of these imperatives for a critical culture leaves one problem unsolved. How can one argue successfully for more public funds to create a critical culture in a society dominated by neoliberal ideas and policies? We cannot change culture without first changing society, that is, increasing public funding for culture. But changing society in this way requires a changed culture that recognizes the need for social changes. Caught in this dilemma, we can only hope that an increasingly obscure German philosopher and amateur economist was right in asserting that humankind always sets itself only such tasks as it can solve.

References

Adorno, T. 1973. *Negative dialectics*. New York: Continuum.

———. 1974. *Minima moralia*. London: Verso.

———. 1976. *Introduction to the sociology of music*. New York: Continuum.

———. 1977. Reconciliation under duress. In T. Adorno et al., *Aesthetics and politics*, 151–76. London: Verso.

———. 1978. On the fetish character in music and the regression of listening. In *The essential Frankfurt School reader*, ed. A. Arato and E. Gebhardt, 270–99. New York: Urizen.

———. 1981a. Arnold Schoenberg, 1874–1951. In *Prisms*, 147–72. Cambridge, MA: MIT Press.

———. 1981b. Veblen's attack on culture. In *Prisms*, 73–94. Cambridge, MA: MIT Press.

———. 1984. *Aesthetic theory*. London: Routledge and Kegan Paul.

———. 1989–90. On jazz. *Discourse* 12 (1): 45–69.

———. 1991a. Culture and administration. In *The culture industry: Selected essays on mass culture*, ed. J. M. Bernstein, 93–113. London: Routledge.

———. 1991b. The schema of mass culture. In *The culture industry: Selected essays on mass culture*, ed. J. M. Bernstein, 53–84. London: Routledge.

———. 1993. Theory of pseudo-culture. *Telos* 95: 15–38.

———. 1994. *Philosophy of modern music*. New York: Continuum.

———. 1997. Functionalism today. In *Rethinking architecture*, ed. N. Leach, 6–19. London: Routledge.

Aglietta, M. 1979. *A theory of capitalist regulation*. London: New Left Books.

Amin, A., ed. 1994. *Post-Fordism: A reader*. Oxford: Blackwell.

Balibar, E. 1970. The basic concepts of historical materialism. In L. Althusser and E. Balibar, *Reading capital*, 201–308. London: New Left Books.

Baran, P. A., and P. M. Sweezy. 1966. *Monopoly capital*. New York: Monthly Review Press.

Barthes, R. 1967. *Elements of semiology*. New York: Hill and Wang.

———. 1972. *Mythologies*. New York: Hill and Wang.

Baudrillard, J. 1975. *The mirror of production*. St. Louis: Telos Press.

———. 1981. *For a critique of the political economy of the sign*. St. Louis: Telos Press.

Bayley, S. 1983. *Harley Earl and the dream machine*. New York: Knopf.

Bellah, R., R. Madsen, W. M. Sullivan, A. Swidler, and S. M. Tipton. 1996. *Habits of the heart: Individualism and commitment in American life*, updated ed. Berkeley: University of California Press.

Bennett, T., M. Savage, E. Silva, A. Warde, M. Gayo-Cal, and D. Wright. 2009. *Culture, class, distinction*. London: Routledge.

Blake, P. 1964. *God's own junkyard: The planned deterioration of America's land-scape.* New York: Holt, Rinehart, and Winston.

———. 1976. *The master builders.* New York: Norton.

———.1977. *Form follows fiasco: Why modern architecture hasn't worked.* New York: Little, Brown.

Blau, J. R. 1984. *Architects and firms.* Cambridge: Cambridge University Press.

———. 1986. The elite arts, more or less *de riguer*: A comparative analysis of metropolitan culture. *Social Forces* 64: 875–905.

Boudon, P. 1972. *Lived-in architecture.* Cambridge, MA: MIT Press.

Bourdieu, P. 1977. *Outline of a theory of practice.* Cambridge: Cambridge University Press.

———. 1984. *Distinction: A social critique of the judgment of taste.* Cambridge, MA: Harvard University Press.

———. 1985. The social space and the genesis of groups. *Theory and Society* 14: 723–44.

———. 1988. *Homo academicus.* Stanford, CA: Stanford University Press.

———. 1988–89. Vive la crise! For heterodoxy in social science. *Theory and Society* 17: 773–87.

———. 1990a. *In other words.* Stanford: Stanford University Press.

———. 1990b. *The logic of practice.* Stanford: Stanford University Press.

———. 1993a. Concluding remarks: For a sociogenetic understanding of intellectual works. In *Bourdieu: Critical perspectives,* ed. C. Calhoun, E. LiPuma, and M. Postone, 263–75. Chicago: University of Chicago Press.

———. 1993b. The field of cultural production. In *The field of cultural production,* 29–73. New York: Columbia University Press.

———. 1993c. The market of symbolic goods. In *The field of cultural production,* 112–41. New York: Columbia University Press.

———. 1993d. The production of belief. In *The field of cultural production,* 74–111. New York: Columbia University Press.

———.1996a. *The rules of art.* Stanford, CA: Stanford University Press.

———. 1996b. *The state nobility.* Stanford, CA: Stanford University Press.

———. 1998a. *Acts of resistance.* New York: New Press.

———. 1998b. *On television.* New York: New Press.

———. 1998c. *Practical reason.* Stanford, CA: Stanford University Press.

———. 1998d. A reasoned utopia and economic fatalism. *New Left Review* 227: 125–30.

———. 2000. *Pascalian meditations.* Stanford, CA: Stanford University Press.

———. 2003. *Firing back.* New York: New Press.

———. 2004. *Science of science and reflexivity.* Chicago: University of Chicago Press.

———. 2008. *Sketch for a self-analysis.* Chicago: University of Chicago Press.

Bourdieu, P., and H. Haacke. 1995. *Free exchange.* Stanford: Stanford University Press.

Bourdieu, P., and J.-C. Passeron. 1977. *Reproduction in education, society and culture.* London: Sage.

Bourdieu, P. and L. J. D. Wacquant. 1992. *An invitation to reflexive sociology.* Chicago: University of Chicago Press.

Bourdieu, P., et al. 1999. *The weight of the world.* Stanford: Stanford University Press.

Bowles, S., D. M. Gordon, and T. E. Weisskopf. 1984. *Beyond the wasteland.* London: Verso.

Brain, D. 1989. Discipline and style: The École des Beaux-Arts and the social production of an American architecture. *Theory and Society* 18: 807–68.

Braverman, H. 1974. *Labor and monopoly capital.* New York: Monthly Review Press.

Business Week. 1959. Detroit makes an about-face on design. Feb. 28.

Clawson, D. 1980. *Bureaucracy and the labor process.* New York: Monthly Review Press.

Cohen, L. 1982. Embellishing a life of labor: An interpretation of the material culture of American working-class homes, 1885–1915. In *Material culture studies in America,* ed. T. J. Schlereth, 289–305. Nashville: American Association for State and Local History.

Coleman, R. P., and L. Rainwater. 1978. *Social standing in America.* New York: Basic Books.

Collins, R. 1975. *Conflict theory.* New York: Academic Press.

———. 1988. *Theoretical sociology.* San Diego: Harcourt, Brace, Jovanovich.

———. 1998. *The sociology of philosophies.* Cambridge, MA: Harvard University Press.

———. 2000. Situational stratification: A micro-macro theory of inequality. *Sociological Theory* 18: 17–43.

Crane, D. 1987. *Transformation of the avant-garde: The New York art world, 1940–1985.* Chicago: University of Chicago Press.

Crawford, D. 1974. *Kant's aesthetic theory.* Madison: University of Wisconsin Press.

Crawford, M. 1991. Can architects be socially responsible? In *Out of site: A social criticism of architecture,* ed. D. Ghirardo, 28–43. Seattle: Bay Press.

Cray, E. 1980. *Chrome colossus: General Motors and its times.* New York: McGraw-Hill.

Davidoff, P. 1993. Democratic planning. In *Architecture culture, 1943–1968,* ed. J. Ockman, 443–45. New York: Rizzoli.

Denning, M. 1996. *The cultural front.* London: Verso.

Diamonstein, B. 1980. *American architecture now.* New York: Rizzoli.

DiMagggio, P. 1977. Market structure, the creative process, and popular culture. *Journal of Popular Culture* 11: 436–52.

———. 1979. Review essay: On Pierre Bourdieu. *American Journal of Sociology* 84: 1460–74.

———. 1982a. Cultural capital and school success: The impact of status-culture participation on the grades of U.S. high school students. *American Sociological Review* 47: 189–201.

———. 1982b. Cultural entrepreneurship in nineteenth-century Boston. I: The creation of an organizational base for high culture in America. *Media, Culture and Society* 4: 33–50.

———. 1982c. Cultural entrepreneurship in nineteenth-century Boston, II: The classification and framing of American art. *Media, Culture and Society* 4: 303–22.

———. 1987. Classification in art. *American Sociological Review* 52: 440–55.

DiMaggio, P., and J. Mohr. 1985. Cultural capital, education attainment and marital selection. *American Journal of Sociology* 90: 1231–61.

DiMaggio, P., and M. Useem. 1978a. Social class and art consumption: Origins and consequences of class differences in exposure to the arts in America. *Theory and Society* 5: 109–32.

———. 1978b. Cultural democracy in a period of cultural expansion. *Social Problems* 26: 179–97.

———. 1982. The arts in class reproduction. In *Cultural and economic reproduction in education,* ed. M. Apple, 181–201. London: Routledge & Kegan Paul.

Donatelli, C. 2001. Driving the suburbs: Minivans, gender, and family values. *Material History Review* 54: 84–95.

Earl, H. 1954. I dream automobiles. *Saturday Evening Post* 227 (August 7): 17–19, 82.

Eaton, L. K. *Two Chicago architects and their clients: Frank Lloyd Wright and Howard Van Doren Shaw.* Cambridge, MA: MIT Press.

Ehrenreich, B. 1989. *Fear of falling: The inner life of the middle class.* New York: HarperCollins.

Elster, J. 1983. *Sour grapes: Studies in the subversion of rationality.* Cambridge: Cambridge University Press.

Ewen, S. 1976. *Captains of consciousness.* New York: McGraw-Hill.

———. 1988. *All consuming images.* New York: Basic Books.

Ewen, S., and E. Ewen. 1982. *Channels of desire.* New York: McGraw-Hill.

Featherstone, M. 1991. *Consumer culture and postmodernism.* London: Sage.

Flink, J. J. 1970. *America adopts the automobile, 1895–1910.* Cambridge, MA: MIT Press.

Fortune. 1947. Jukeboxes, F.O.B. Detroit. September.

Forty, A. 1986. *Objects of desire.* New York: Pantheon.

Frampton, K. 1992. *Modern architecture: A critical history.* New York: Thames and Hudson.

———. 1996. *Studies in tectonic culture.* Cambridge, MA: MIT Press.

Fromm, E. 1984. *The working class in Weimar Germany.* Cambridge, MA: Harvard University Press.

Galbraith, J. K. 1972. *The new industrial state.* New York: Mentor.

Gans, H. 1962. *The urban villagers.* New York: Free Press.

———.1999. *Popular culture and high culture,* rev. ed. New York: Basic Books.

Gartman, D. 1986. *Auto slavery: The labor process in the American automobile industry, 1897–1950.* New Brunswick, NJ: Rutgers University Press.

———. 1994. *Auto opium: A social history of American automobile design.* London: Routledge.

———. 2009. *From autos to architecture: Fordism and architectural aesthetics in the twentieth century.* New York: Princeton Architectural Press.

Garvey, P. 2001. Driving, drinking, and daring in Norway. In *Car cultures,* ed. D. Miller, 133–52. Oxford: Berg.

Giedion, S. 1967. *Space, time and architecture,* 5th rev. ed. Cambridge, MA: MIT Press.

———. 1969. *Mechanization takes command.* New York: Norton.

Gilroy, P. 2001. Driving while Black. In *Car cultures,* ed. D. Miller, 81–104. Oxford: Berg.

Goldthorpe, J., D. Lockwood, F. Bechhofer, and J. Platt. 1969. *The affluent worker in the class structure.* Cambridge: Cambridge University Press.

Gouldner, A. 1979. *The future of intellectuals and the rise of the new class.* New York: Seabury.

Green, P. H., and R. H. Cheney. 1968. Urban planning and urban revolt. *Progressive Architecture* 49 (Jan.): 134–56.

Gropius, W. 1938a. First proclamation of the Weimar Bauhaus. In *Bauhaus: 1919–1928,* ed. H. Bayer, W. Gropius, and I. Gropius, 18. New York: Museum of Modern Art.

———. 1938b. The theory of organization of the Bauhaus. In *Bauhaus: 1919–1928,* ed. H. Bayer, W. Gropius, and I. Gropius, 22–31. New York: Museum of Modern Art.

Gruenberg, B. 1983. The social location of leisure styles. *American Behavioral Scientist* 26: 493–508.

Hall, S., and M. Jacques. 1989. Introduction. In *New times: The changing face of politics in the 1990s,* ed. S. Hall and M. Jacques, 11–19. London: Lawrence and Wishart.

Halle, D. 1984. *America's working man*. Chicago: University of Chicago Press.

Harrison, B., and B. Bluestone. 1988. *The great u-turn*. New York: Basic Books.

Hebdige, D. 1979. *Subculture: The meaning of style*. London: Routledge.

———. 1988. *Hiding in the light: On images and things*. London: Routledge.

———. 1989. After the masses. In *New times: The changing face of politics in the 1990s*, ed. S. Hall and M. Jacques, 76–93. London: Lawrence and Wishart.

Heskett, J. 1980. *Industrial design*. New York: Oxford University Press.

Horkheimer, M. 1974. *The eclipse of reason*. New York: Seabury.

Horkheimer, M., and T. Adorno. 1972. *Dialectic of enlightenment*. New York: Herder and Herder.

———. 2002. *Dialectic of enlightenment*. Stanford: Stanford University Press.

Hughes, M. and R. A. Peterson. 1983. Isolating cultural choice patterns in a U.S. population. *American Behavioral Scientist* 26: 459–78.

Jackson, A. 1995. *Reconstructing architecture for the twenty-first century*. Toronto: University of Toronto Press.

Jackson, K. T. 1985. *Crabgrass frontier: The suburbanization of the United States*. New York: Oxford University Press.

Jameson, F. 1971. *Marxism and form*. Princeton, NJ: Princeton University Press.

———. 1981. *The political unconscious*. Ithaca, NY: Cornell University Press.

———. 1991. *Postmodernism, or, the cultural logic of late capitalism*. London: Verso.

———. 1997. Is space political? In *Rethinking architecture*, ed. N. Leach, 255–69. London: Routledge.

Jay, M. 1973. *The dialectical imagination*. Boston: Little, Brown.

Jencks, C. 1986. *What is post-modernism?* New York: St. Martin's.

Johnson, P. 1979. The seven shibboleths of our profession. In *Writings*, 143–47. New York: Oxford University Press.

Keats, J. 1958. *The insolent chariots*. Philadelphia: J. B. Lippincott.

Kellner, D. 1984. *Herbert Marcuse and the crisis of Marxism*. Berkeley: University of California Press.

———. 1984–85. Critical theory and the culture industries: A reassessment. *Telos* 62: 196–206.

Klein, N. 1999. *No logo: Taking aim at the brand bullies*. New York: Picador.

Koolhaas, R. 1994. *Delirious New York*. New York: Monacelli.

Lamont, Michèle. 1992. *Money, morals and manners: The culture of the French and the American upper-middle class*. Chicago: University of Chicago Press.

———. 2000. *The dignity of working men: Morality and the boundaries of race, class, and immigration*. New York: Russell Sage Foundation.

Lane, B. M. 1985. *Architecture and politics in Germany, 1918–1945*. Cambridge, MA: Harvard University Press.

Larson, M. S. 1993. *Behind the postmodern façade*. Berkeley: University of California Press.

Lears, T. J. J. 1983. From salvation to self-realization: Advertising and the therapeutic roots of the consumer culture. In *The culture of consumption*, ed. R. W. Fox and T. J. J. Lears, 1–38. New York: Pantheon.

Le Corbusier. (Charles-Edouard Jeanneret). 1967. *The radiant city*. New York: Orion.

———. 1986. *Towards a new architecture*. New York: Dover.

———. 1987. *The city of tomorrow and its planning*. New York: Dover.

Lieberson, S. 2000. *A matter of taste*. New Haven, CT: Yale University Press.

Lukács, G. 1962. *The historical novel*. London: Merlin.

———. 1971a. *History and class consciousness*. Cambridge, MA: MIT Press.

———. 1971b. *Theory of the novel*. Cambridge, MA: MIT Press.

———. 1973a. Idea and form in literature. In *Marxism and Human Liberation*, ed. E. San Juan, Jr., 109–31. New York: Delta Books

———. 1973b. The ideology of modernism. In *Marxism and Human Liberation*, ed. E. San Juan, Jr., 277–307. New York: Delta Books.

———. 1973c. The old culture and the new culture. In *Marxism and human liberation*, ed. E. San Juan , Jr., 3–19. New York: Delta Books.

———. 1980a. The novels of Willi Bredel. In *Essays on Realism,* ed. R. Livingstone, 23–32. Cambridge, MA: MIT Press.

———. 1980b. Reportage or portrayal? In *Essays on realism*, ed. R. Livingstone, 45–75. Cambridge, MA: MIT Press.

Lynd, R. S., and H. M. Lynd. 1929. *Middletown: A study in contemporary American culture.* New York: Harcourt, Brace.

MacMinn, S. 1984. American automobile design. In *Automobile and culture*, ed. G. Silk, 209–47. New York: Abrams.

Maier, C. S. 1970. Between Taylorism and technocracy: European ideologies and the vision of industrial productivity in the 1920s. *Journal of contemporary history 5* (2): 27–61.

Marcuse, H. 1960. *Reason and revolution*. Boston: Beacon Press.

———. 1964. *One-dimensional man*. Boston: Beacon Press.

———. 1966. *Eros and civilization*. Boston: Beacon Press.

———. 1968. The affirmative character of culture. In *Negations*, 88–133. Boston: Beacon Press.

———. 1969. *An essay on liberation*. Boston: Beacon Press.

———. 1972. The foundation of historical materialism. In *Studies in critical philosophy*, 1–48. London: Verso.

———. 1978. *The aesthetic dimension*. Boston: Beacon Press.

Marx, K. 1964. Economic and philosophical manuscripts. In *Karl Marx: Early writings*, ed. T. Bottomore, 63–219. New York: McGraw-Hill.

Marx, K. 1967a. *Capital*. Vol. 1. New York: International Publishers.

Marx, K. 1967b. *Capital*. Vol. 3. New York: International Publishers.

Marx, K. 1975. Contribution to the critique of Hegel's philosophy of law. Introduction. In *Karl Marx and Frederick Engels collected works*. Vol. 3, 175–87. New York: International Publishers.

Marx, K. and F. Engels. 1976a. *The German ideology*. In *Karl Marx and Frederick Engels collected works*. Vol. 5, 19–539. New York: International Publishers.

Marx, K. and F. Engels. 1976b. *Manifesto of the communist party*. In *Karl Marx and Frederick Engels collected works*. Vol. 6, 477–519. New York: International Publishers.

Mayer, A. J. 1981. *The persistence of the Old Regime*. New York: Pantheon.

Meikle, J. L. 1979. *Twentieth century limited: Industrial design in America, 1925–1939*. Philadelphia: Temple University Press.

Meyer, S., III. 1981. *The five dollar day*. Albany: State University of New York Press.

Michael, M. 2001. The invisible car: The cultural purification of road rage. In *Car cultures*, ed. D. Miller, 59–80. Oxford: Berg.

Mies van der Rohe, L. 1970. Working theses. In *Programs and manifestoes on twentieth-century architecture*, ed. U. Conrads, 74–75. Cambridge, MA: MIT Press.

Miller, D. 1987. *Material culture and mass consumption*. Oxford: Basil Blackwell.

———. 2001. Driven societies. In *Car Cultures*, ed. D. Miller, 1–33. Oxford: Berg.

Milkman, R. 1997. *Farewell to the factory: Auto workers in the late twentieth century*. Berkeley: University of California Press.

Montgomery, D. 1979. *Workers' control in America*. New York: Cambridge University Press.

Moorhouse, H. F. 1991. *Driving ambitions: An analysis of the American hot rod enthusiasm.* Manchester: Manchester University Press.

Mort, F. 1989. The politics of consumption. In *New times: The changing face of politics in the 1990s,* ed. S. Hall and M. Jacques, 160–72. London: Lawrence and Wishart.

Murray, R. 1989. Fordism and post-Fordism. In *New times: The changing face of politics in the 1990s,* ed. S. Hall and M. Jacques, 38–53. London: Lawrence and Wishart.

New York Times. 1906. Motorists don't make socialists, they say. March 4.

Noble, D. F. 1977. *America by design: Science, technology, and the rise of corporate capitalism.* New York: Knopf.

Nolan, M. 1994. *Visions of modernity: American business and the modernization of Germany.* Oxford: Oxford University Press.

O'Connell, S. 1998. *The car and British society: Class, gender, and motoring, 1896–1939.* Manchester: Manchester University Press.

O'Connor, J. 1984. *Accumulation crisis.* New York: Basil Blackwell.

O'Dell, T. 2001. *Raggare* and the panic of mobility. In *Car Cultures,* ed. D. Miller, 105–32. Oxford: Berg.

Packard, V. 1980. *The hidden persuaders,* rev. ed. New York: Pocket Books.

Paul, S. 1962. *Louis Sullivan.* Englewood Cliffs, NJ: Prentice-Hall.

Peterson, R. A., ed. 1976. *The production of culture.* Beverly Hills, CA: Sage.

———. 1994. Cultural studies through the production perspective. In *The sociology of culture,* ed. D. Crane, 163–89. Oxford: Blackwell.

Peterson, R. A., and D. G. Berger. 1975. Cycles of symbol production. *American Sociological Review* 40: 158–73.

Peterson, R. A. and R. M. Kern. 1996. Changing highbrow taste: From snob to omnivore. *American Sociological Review* 61: 900–07.

Peterson, R. A., and A. Simkus. 1992. How musical tastes mark occupational status groups. In *Cultivating differences: Symbolic boundaries and the making of inequality,* ed. M. Lamont and M. Fournier, 152–86. Chicago: University of Chicago Press.

Pollock, F. 1978. State capitalism: Its possibilities and limits. In *The essential Frankfurt School reader,* eds. A. Arato and E. Gebhardt, 71–94. Oxford: Blackwell.

Pulos, A. J. 1983. *American design ethic.* Cambridge, MA: MIT Press.

Rosenzweig, R. 1983. *Eighth hours for what we will: Workers and leisure in an industrial city, 1870–1920.* Cambridge: Cambridge University Press.

Rothschild, E. 1974. *Paradise lost: The decline of the auto-industrial age.* New York: Vintage.

Rubenstein, J. M. 2001. *Making and selling cars: Innovation and change in the U.S. automotive industry.* Baltimore, MD: Johns Hopkins University Press.

Scharff, V. 1991. *Taking the wheel: Women and the coming of the motor age.* New York: Free Press.

Scully, V. 1988. *American architecture and urbanism,* rev. ed. New York: Henry Holt.

Simmel, G. 1957. Fashion. *American Journal of Sociology* 62: 541–58.

Sloan, A. J., Jr. 1972. *My years with General Motors.* Garden City, NY: Anchor Books.

Smelser, N. 1959. *Social change in the industrial revolution.* Chicago: University of Chicago Press.

———. 1962. *Theory of collective behavior.* New York: Free Press.

Sparke, P. 2002. *A century of car design.* Hauppauge, NY: Barron's Educational series.

Stern, J., and M. Stern. 1978. *Auto ads.* New York: Random House.

Sullivan, L. 1947. *Kindergarten chats and other writings.* New York: George Wittenhborn.
Swartz, D. 1997. *Culture and power: The sociology of Pierre Bourdieu.* Chicago: University of Chicago Press.
———. 2003. From critical sociology to public intellectual: Pierre Bourdieu and politics. *Theory and Society* 32: 791–823.
Tafuri, M. 1990. *The sphere and the labyrinth.* Cambridge, MA: MIT Press.
Teige, K. 2002. *The minimum dwelling.* Cambridge, MA: MIT Press.
U.S. Bureau of the Census. 1975. *Historical statistics of the United States. Part I: Colonial time to 1970.* Washington DC: U.S. Government Printing Office.
Veblen, T. 1934. *Theory of the leisure class.* New York: Modern Library.
Venturi, R. 1977. *Complexity and contradiction in architecture.* New York: Museum of Modern Art.
Venturi, R., D. Scott Brown, and S. Izenour. 1977. *Learning from Las Vegas,* rev. ed.: Cambridge, MA: MIT Press.
Von Saldern, A. 1990. The workers' movement and cultural patterns on urban housing estates and in rural settlements in Germany and Austria during the 1920s. *Social History* 15: 33–54.
Weber, M. 1946a. Class, status, party. In *From Max Weber,* ed. H. H.Gerth and C. W. Mills, 180–95. New York: Oxford University Press.
———. 1946b. The social psychology of the world religions. In *From Max Weber,* ed. H. H. Gerth and C. W. Mills, 267–301. New York: Oxford University Press.
———. 1968. *Economy and society.* New York: Bedminster Press
Weinstein, J. 1968. *The corporate ideal in the liberal state, 1900–1918.* Boston: Beacon Press.
Wheatland, T. 2009. *The Frankfurt School in exile.* Minneapolis: University of Minnesota Press.
Whyte, W. H. 1956. *The organization man.* New York: Simon and Schuster.
Wiebe, R. 1967. *The search for order, 1877–1920.* New York: Hill and Wang.
Wiggershaus, R. 1994. *The Frankfurt School.* Cambridge, MA: MIT Press.
Wilensky, H. 1964. Mass society and mass culture. *American Sociological Review* 29: 173–97.
Willis, S. 1991. *A primer for daily life.* London: Routledge.
Wilson, R. G., D. H. Pilgrim, and D. Tashjian. 1986. *The machine age in America, 1918–1941.* New York: Harry Abrams.
Witkin, R. 2003. *Adorno on popular culture.* London: Routledge.
Womack, J. P., D. T. Jones, and D. Roos. 1991. *The machine that changed the world.* New York: Harper Perennial.
Wright, F. L. 1932. *The disappearing city.* New York: William Farquhar Payson.
Wu, Chin-tao. 2002. *Privatising culture.* London: Verso

Index

education: Bourdieu on, 8, 37, 49; and class differences, 43; as factor in cultural change, 109, 121, 125–27, 158–59; Veblen on, 37
environmental movement, 70, 119
existence minimum, 97–98

F

field of cultural production, 9, 105. *See also* subfield of mass (large-scale) cultural production; subfield of restricted (small-scale) cultural production
Flaubert, Gustave, 158
food, 41–42
Ford, Henry, 22
Ford Motor Company, 22–23, 25, 28, 58–59, 62, 68–69, 112, 154
Fordism, 62, 68–69, 88, 93
Frankfurt School: and the administered society, 65, 152; and Bourdieu, 1–2, 9, 39, 131–65; criticisms of, 17, 52, 155–56; on history, 45, 139–40; and Marx, 4; and reified culture, 4–5, 15–17. *See also* Adorno, Theodor; Horkheimer, Max; Marcuse, Herbert
functionalism, 85–87
furnishings, 42, 89

G

Gans, Herbert, 123, 126
Garvey, Pauline, 75
Geddes, Norman Bel, 28
gender, 58–60, 67, 68, 75
General Motors Corporation, 28, 59–60, 67, 112–13, 115
Gilroy, Paul, 75–76
Gouldner, Alvin, 82
Gropius, Walter, 93

H

Haacke, Hans, *Free Exchange*, 164
habitus: and artistic production, 81–82; and automobile design; 64; and class, 35–36, 47–48; and conflict in autonomous culture, 157–58; defined, 8, 157; as a factor in cultural change, 125–26; and mass media, 150,
Hall, Stuart, 72
Halle, David, 42
Hebdige, Dick, 72–73
homology, 43, 49, 64, 109, 124–25

Hood, Raymond, 91
Horkheimer, Max, 140; "The Culture Industry," 65; *Dialectic of Enlightenment*, 15–16, 151
hot rodders, 74
hysteresis, 160–62

I

individuality: Adorno on, 138–39, 141; and automobile design: 61–69, 112–13; Bourdieu on, 141; and postmodernism, 76
industrial design, 19, 27, 29, 90. *See also* automobile design
instrumental (or technological) rationality: and art 151–52; defined, 15–16; and modern architecture, 94–96, 101

J

Jameson, Fredric, 81–83, 95
Johnson, Philip, 122

K

Kahn, Albert, 154
Kant, Immanuel, 14, 132–33, 143
Keats, John, 69

L

Lamont, Michele, 117
Larson, Magali Sarfatti, 83
Lazarsfeld, Paul, 38
lean production, 71; and optimum lean production, 76–77
Le Corbusier [Jeanneret, Charles-Edouard], 26–27, 94–96, 98–99, 154–55
Liberson, Stanley, 103–4
lifestyle enclaves, 77
literary field, 109, 142–43, 158–59
Lukács, Georg: definition of culture by, 12; culture as symbolic politics, 52–53; and the Frankfurt School, 4; *History and Class Consciousness*, 14; and modern literature, 14; theory of cultural reification, 3–4, 13–15, 52–53
luxury, 65–66
Lynd, Robert and Helen, *Middletown*, 25

M

machine (functionalist) aesthetic, 26–27, 85; and instrumental rationality, 95–96; as rejected